EXPERIMENTAL COLLABORATIONS

EASA Series

Published in Association with the European Association of Social Anthropologists (EASA)

Series Editor: Aleksandar Bošković, University of Belgrade

Social anthropology in Europe is growing, and the variety of work being done is expanding. This series is intended to present the best of the work produced by members of the EASA, both in monographs and in edited collections. The studies in this series describe societies, processes, and institutions around the world and are intended for both scholarly and student readership.

For a full volume listing, please see back matter.

EXPERIMENTAL COLLABORATIONS

Ethnography through Fieldwork Devices

Edited by
Adolfo Estalella and Tomás Sánchez Criado

berghahn
NEW YORK • OXFORD
www.berghahnbooks.com

First published in 2018 by
Berghahn Books
www.berghahnbooks.com

Library of Congress Cataloging-in-Publication Data
Names: Estalella, Adolfo, editor. | Criado, Tomás Sánchez, editor.
Title: Experimental collaborations : ethnography through fieldwork devices /
edited by Adolfo Estalella and Tomás Sánchez Criado.
Description: New York : Berghahn Books, [2018] | Series: Easa series |
Includes bibliographical references and index.
Identifiers: LCCN 2017052604 (print) | LCCN 2018006166 (ebook) | ISBN
9781785338540 (ebook) | ISBN 9781785338533 (hardback : alk. paper)
Subjects: LCSH: Ethnology--Fieldwork.
Classification: LCC GN346 (ebook) | LCC GN346 .E96 2018 (print) | DDC
305.80072/3--dc23
LC record available at https://lccn.loc.gov/2017052604

British Library Cataloguing in Publication Data
A catalogue record for this book is available from the British Library

ISBN 978-1-78533-853-3 hardback
ISBN 978-1-80073-015-1 paperback
ISBN 978-1-78533-854-0 ebook

Contents

Illustrations

Acknowledgements

The editors wish to thank Eeva Berglund (former EASA Series Editor) for her support and encouragement in the production of this book. Special thanks also go to the authors, without whose ethnographic projects the argument of the book would have been no more than an intuition.

Our warmest appreciation goes to 'Intermediae' for their funding support to organize a special workshop in Madrid in July 2015, which allowed us to discuss the book's contents in full with the authors. Thanks also to George E. Marcus and Sarah Pink for their kindness in reviewing, commenting on and endorsing the proposal.

The introduction has been upgraded many times after the kind comments of the book's contributors and two anonymous reviewers, and after the insights provided in different presentations and many conversations with Alberto Corsín Jiménez, Isaac Marrero Guillamón, Ignacio Farías, Israel Rodríguez-Giralt, Marisol de la Cadena and Debora Lanzeni.

This book is specially dedicated to the people with whom we have learnt to make and think experimental collaborations: Basurama, En torno a la silla, and Zuloark.

Adolfo Estalella and Tomás Sánchez Criado, Madrid and Munich, July 2017

Foreword

Collaboration Mode 3

A Found Condition of Anthropological Field Research Today ... and What Might Be Made of It

George E. Marcus

Since the turn of the century, 'collaboration' has become a keyword evoking desirable sociality in projects of all kinds. Despite its problematic past associations (e.g. during the Second World War), it is an indispensable term, tinted with virtue and hope, to refer to collective, voluntary (and thus negotiated) effort to conduct inquiry, to solve problems, to create and apply knowledge, also to pursue political, ethical, and aesthetic ends in the technologically transformed public spheres present today. Collaboration is a 'grass-roots' imaginary that people of means and purpose can undertake to interrupt older practices and habits of relating to, and being effective in, the world at a level of personal relations that the idea of collaboration evokes. Its popularity, in a lower key, is undoubtedly associated with the much more hyped drive for 'innovation' (and improvement) in every sphere of contemporary human experience.

As a current practice within the past methodologies of the social/human sciences – especially anthropology – collaboration has ambiguous, alternative meanings and implications. In very specific ways, the positive value placed on collaboration almost everywhere has the potential of altering older habits and practices of achieving considerable mutual surprise and learning (representing the contemporary innovation 'bug' in many academic disciplines), sometimes smoothly, often not. As brilliantly performed in the conception and execution of this volume, edited by Adolfo Estalella and Tomás Sánchez Criado from their EASA workshop, collaboration has a very particular and potential value for thinking about the way that the signature ethnographic method of anthropology can adapt to its times. With modesty, this volume's framework morphs potentials in anthropology's deeply committed and signature method as a field science towards remaking its relationships with its subjects, as well as its forms of communicating knowledge.

'Writing Culture' of the 1980s was about narrative and representation in ethnographic texts, with unresolved implication for the doctrines of fieldwork that significantly define professional identity. With a lineage from that period rich in experiment and critique that Estalella and Sánchez Criado recognize, this volume now brings that same spirit, reinforced by anthropology's subsequent immersion in the issues of the Science and Technology Studies (STS) movement, many of which have examined the methods of science such as experiment, to anthropology's entanglement of its identity with signature research practices. These require new imaginaries for bringing them into existence today, project by project, inspiring inquiries that are driven by events, emergent trends and the future (that is, 'the state of being in the contemporary', as theorized by Paul Rabinow). Encountering and needing partners, as much as classically developing informants, anthropology enters the general trend that favours collaborative engagement, and it has the opportunity to redefine its mythos of method in those terms. This volume makes considerable strides in defining concepts and practices for how this trend is occurring instrumentally and perceptually as anthropologists move recursively through sites, spaces, and across scales that define 'the field' today.

With modesty and courage, Estalella and Sánchez Criado have designed a volume that takes on the core trope of traditional method – participant observation – without disposing of it. They create an idea of collaboration that qualifies the power of solitary reflection, based on observation. Rather than replacing the latter, they provide an attractive and incremental encouragement to experiment within the process of fieldwork – and to create forms whereby such experiment can be witnessed and discussed by granular receptions, all the way up and down, and alongside, the course of research.

In the original spirit of ethnographic inquiry, what Estalella and Sánchez Criado have proposed to their contributors encourages the latter to take advantage of what they can find – to look again at or within projects that they have undertaken or are still undertaking, eventually in one or another accepted genre of publication. To do this requires a more ingenious, open-ended play with method, one that becomes thought about as acts of collaboration. In their introductory chapter, they create certain terms to pursue this re-entry into processes of research undertaken in the signature mythos of fieldwork. Under the strong influence of anthropology's experience in STS and its major exponents, they evoke experiment and they encourage the creation of devices, which seem often to be acts of making something together. They offer a relatively simple frame in which anthropologists can rethink their specific projects in terms of the repressed in much contemporary anthropological research – namely, more developed notions of what is involved in the collective intellectual labour of collaboration among subjects and facilitators. These develop stakes in the concept work and demonstrations of fieldwork, and accordingly, of the emergence of designed second-order observations and interventions within fieldwork devices of various kinds that have been a controversial, if not virtually forbidden, topic in the professional culture of anthropological method.

Finally, then, with this volume, we have a practice-oriented idea about how collaboration dynamically works as invention within contemporary research. To accomplish this, Sánchez Criado and Estalella distinguish three modes of collaboration, two of which (perhaps the most common contemporary usages) are defined to clarify the third, which is exactly where they want to define the substance of their thinking. Collaboration Mode 1 is about how collaboration is already embedded in long-standing fieldwork practices, but which, as Sánchez Criado and Estalella indicate, is extractive and hierarchical, and privileges detachment as well. Collaboration Mode 2 is about the attraction of public anthropology as its primary rationale for research, and the pull towards politics' explicit alliance with activist groups that are indeed both subjects and partners in research, but with a deference to, and a fitting of fieldwork into, the situations that they might predefine. Collaboration Mode 3, where Sánchez Criado and Estalella come to focus, defines the conceptual and practical space for conceiving of collaboration as innovation in method. And here, they provide the terms ('experiment', 'device') and the counsel to contributors to attempt to perceive and elaborate a perhaps uncharted imaginary of practice, and to capture emergent aspects of collaboration in their work. Sánchez Criado and Estalella give them an eye for Collaboration Mode 3, and encourage the impetus to act on this alternative kind of observation.

The resulting range of treatments in the papers of this volume is instructive, and indeed makes the volume itself a pedagogical tool. It burrows within the rather minimalist framework in which method is taught and then pursued as research careers in anthropology.

There is an element of pride in this aspect of professional culture, with which Sánchez Criado and Estalella effectively align themselves. The minimalism is retained. They are not arguing for new rules of method but, in a sense, for an opportunism through devices that require relations of Mode 3 collaboration after being well into field research through the powerful starter of participant observation.

Yet, in launching their discussion and orienting it to a reigning culture of fieldwork method, participant observation serves as their foil. Of course, this makes sense. It is the main trope of professional culture in which the foundational norms of otherwise underarticulated fieldwork practice (except for the very important informal tellings of 'tales of fieldwork') are condensed: detachment, being meditatively alone among others, the intimacy of fieldnotes when they are recorded, Malinowski in his tent ... Collaboration Mode 1 qualifies this principle of being in the field without arguing against it. Collaboration Mode 2 places participant observation at the service of a cause, which creates its own contradictions. Collaboration Mode 3 further socializes participant observation and productively puts it at risk.

On my own account, I might have evoked 'dialogue' or the 'dialogic' as the alternative foundational principle of fieldwork, instead of participant observation, with which to orient and launch a discussion of Collaboration Mode 3. While it is perhaps not quite as iconic as participant observation in the Anglo-American tradition, dialogue stands for the traditional principle of engaged fieldwork; it was the primary modality by which fieldwork was evoked in the discussions of ethnographic representation of the 1980s (for example, through the theoretical influence, at the time, of the writings of Mikhail Bakhtin, among others). And it has constituted a not quite as well instantiated historic, but nonetheless key generic alternative to the symbolic centrality of participant observation as the trope of method (such as, for example, the dialogic co-production of emergent histories by anthropologist and informant in the fieldwork of Franz Boas, brilliantly revived as alternative by Matti Bunzl in 2004 at a time by happenstance of the increasing interest in collaboration as a condition of fieldwork).

For me, there are two enduring legacies of the 1980s critique of ethnographic representation that have created the present conditions favourable to the encouragement of experimental collaboration granularly in the evolution of contemporary fieldwork projects. First is the thoroughgoing reflexive licence that the 'Writing Culture' discussions (which were as much a product of the other major critique, practice-oriented intellectual movements of the time, mainly feminist theory) bequeathed not only to ethnographic genre writing, but to the frames in which research problems were conceived, followed into the field, and challenged. Collaboration Mode 3, by way of STS scholarship, would not be imaginable without the strong institutionalization of the at least double critical review of conceptual thinking in research that reflexive thinking licensed as its constant shadow and context.

Second is the ideal of polyphony or polyphonic expression in writing, and by implication in field research practices. It was a much more qualified success in ethnographic writing than the reflexive strategies of framing accounts. There were a very few exemplars of co-authorship in conventional genres, experiments in the representation of voice in texts, and most importantly the opening of at least the conceptual space in imaginaries of being in fieldwork that now respond to contemporary calls for the development of collaborative sociality as a key form and condition of organizing inquiry. But the connection between polyphony as a problem of representation and its close connection to the existing and potential conditions of collaboration in fieldwork long remained undeveloped.

Experimental collaboration, as evoked by Sánchez Criado and Estalella, is in a sense a current methodological response to the polyphonic implication of all dialogues. They become in fieldwork projects, 'going concerns' – social relationships needing reflexive conceptualization in the scenes of research. Here, collaborations grow contextually about matters of mutual practice, back to issues of representation, but inside fieldwork. The emphasis, however, is now not textual, at least in terms of traditional genres, but on intermediate forms that may begin in performance and intervention (thus the currency of design disciplines and conceptual art movements in influencing the impulse towards Collaboration Mode 3 in inquiry), but will also develop textual expressions, conventional and innovative, as they move towards a range of granular receptions, and responses from micro-publics, to receptions by professional academic constituencies as a final docking point, or more likely, as an influential waymark of a project.

How, or whether, experimental collaboration ends, out of fieldwork, what its continuing forms of expression are, and what the range of access and receptions are along the way, are the most crucial open-ended questions that the enterprise of Collaboration Mode 3 poses to anthropology. Of the papers included in this volume, the one that most thoroughly aligns with my own current interest in these issues and develops their implications within the probing for Collaboration Mode 3 in his research is that of Isaac Marrero-Guillamón. His thinking about this mode in his work is greatly influenced, as in my own recent projects, by close partnerships with artists whose ideas for intermediate forms or media along the way – online platforms as well as local publications – shape issues of fieldwork in the professional sphere of anthropology. How artists constitute publics for their work locally, and how these publics are reproduced for subsequent and progressive performances of evolving forms of learning and understanding, importantly open fieldwork projects that run alongside and in collaboration with them to the means of experiment through assemblages of devices to which Sánchez Criado and Estalella refer. In their own case of working together, as they describe it, it is sustained collaborations with architectural designers in the urbanscape that initially provide this resource to fieldwork.

Far from the terms in which anthropological authority was posed by James Clifford, to launch the 'Writing Culture' discussions in the 1980s, the question of such authority nonetheless returns, but now in the not yet defined conditions of Collaboration Mode 3 and the vastly transformed worlds of mutually constructed relationships by which fieldwork projects are defined and carried out. So, the refunctioning of anthropological method is ongoing. Its accompanying restatement is something that this work bridges and archives. I have encountered no better 'workbook' as guide than this volume for pursuing collaboration as potential perceived in the course of a range of contemporary projects of fieldwork in progress.

George E. Marcus (UC Irvine) is chancellor's professor of anthropology at the University of California, Irvine. He co-authored *Anthropology as Cultural Critique* (1986), and co-edited *Writing Culture* (1986). He was the founding editor of the journal *Cultural Anthropology*. In recent years, after founding the Center for Ethnography at UC Irvine (2005), he has been interested in various mergings of anthropology's emblematic ethnographic method with design thinking, and more generally, in how calls for, and experiments with, collaboration have both changed and preserved long-standing ideas that have shaped anthropology.

Introduction
Experimental Collaborations

Tomás Sánchez Criado and Adolfo Estalella

Anthropologists conducting fieldwork in distinctive sites populated by 'epistemic communities', such as public institutions, activist collectives, artistic spaces and laboratories, have recently engaged in intense reflexive examination of their research practices and methodological engagements. This book presents a series of ethnographic accounts in which authors share their methodological anxieties and reveal the creative inventiveness emanating from fieldwork practices that challenge what they had assumed to be the norm and form of ethnography. Populated by activists, artists, designers, public servants and scientists, these ethnographic sites appear to compel us – or provide the opportunity – to reconsider not only the epistemic practices, types of relationships and forms of engagement in our fieldwork, but also our accounts of the field. Taking on this challenge, contributors explore a descriptive approach to their projects, narrating the intimate relationships established with their counterparts – now turned into epistemic partners – and the interventions devised as forms of epistemic collaboration in the field that open venues for experimental interventions in ethnography.

Our discussion resonates with recent reflections contending the need to readdress fieldwork and reformulate its practice (Faubion and Marcus 2009; Fabian 2014). We echo debates on the place of ethnography in the production of anthropological knowledge (Ingold 2008) and the transformation of the norm and form of fieldwork in a series of projects that have injected an experimental drive (Rabinow et al. 2008). The reflections of Douglas Holmes and George Marcus (2005,

2008) are particularly relevant: their ethnographic projects led them to argue that if anthropology was to enter into domains populated by subjects that shared anthropologists ethnographic-like practices, or in their idiom, 'para-ethnographic' practices, it was essential to 're-function ethnography' (Holmes and Marcus 2005). In these ethnographic sites, collaboration would be the cornerstone from which to undertake fieldwork.

In the accounts compiled in this book, ethnography occurs through processes of material and social interventions that turn the field into a site for epistemic collaboration. Through creative interventions that unfold what we term 'fieldwork devices' – such as co-produced books, the circulation of repurposed data, co-organized events, authorization protocols, relational frictions, and social rhythms – anthropologists engage with their counterparts in the field in the construction of joint anthropological problematizations. In these situations, the traditional tropes of the fieldwork encounter (i.e. immersion and distance) give way to a narrative register of experimentation, where the aesthetics of collaboration in the production of knowledge substitutes or intermingles with the traditional trope of participant observation. Building on this, we propose the concept of 'experimental collaborations' to describe and conceptualize this distinctive ethnographic modality.

Para-siting Ethnography

Our discussion stems from a methodological quandary experienced in our most recent ethnographies, which intensified when contrasted with the projects of our doctoral dissertations. Our presence in the field shifted from the previously experienced modality of 'participating in order to write' (Emerson et al. 1995: 26) to a more engaged and interventionist practice. We note similar experiences in the contributions to this book. The tension that arises in these situations, which sparked both our original discussion and a desire to bring the issue to the fore, is perhaps best exemplified in Isaac Marrero-Guillamón's account. Working with activists and artists protesting against the 2012 Olympics in London, Marrero-Guillamón vividly describes his methodological anxiety: 'I had wanted to *follow* some artists' work, but I was invited to become a *collaborator*; I had imagined a fieldwork based on some kind of *distance* with the objects and subjects of study, but I had instead *participated* in the production of the very things I was studying' (this volume, Chapter 8). His 'original sin' (the term is his) reverberates with Andrea Gaspar's remark that her frictional presence amongst Milanese interaction designers was 'not as detached as it should be' (this volume, Chapter 4). These reflexive experiences are significant, for the transgressing of such conventions may lead ethnographers to view their own projects as failures.

Ethnography is generally considered a flexible method, and field-work usually requires substantial improvisation. Indeed, undertaking an ethnographic project is far removed from applying a recipe. Nevertheless, despite an openness in the forms of engagements allowed within the ethnographic method, our contributors mark the pervasive presence of a compelling canon restricting the way anthropologists should conduct themselves in the field (as illustrated in the quotes above). Yet these accounts do exhibit transgressions of this canon and outline a different modality for ethnographic fieldwork, one renouncing the supposed distance required in field-work and overturning certain conventions learned in introductory anthropological training.

Tomás faced such a dilemma in late 2012, when he proposed under-taking participant observation in a nascent Barcelona-based project for the open design of technical aids entitled En torno a la silla (ETS), as part of his postdoctoral ethnographic project on self-care tech-nology design. Despite the initial 'we are really looking forward to working with you' (Tomás's fieldnotes, 22/11/2012), they also stated: 'You can't be a mere observer here' (ibid., 29/11/2012). This condi-tion was aligned with the independent-living movement's motto and philosophy, which permeated the group: 'Nothing about us without us' – a slogan that would shape his subsequent ethnographic project. He was not the only researcher in the group, since other participants were also involved in their own design and political investigations, and reflecting on their experiences in depth.[1]

Alida Díaz, Antonio Centeno and Rai Vilatovà, the three initial members of ETS, had met in the 2011 occupation of the city's central square, Plaça de Catalunya, around the time the 'Indignados' move-ment (the outraged, the Spanish precursor of the Occupy movement) emerged: Alida was an architect with substantial experience in the city's activist collectives; Antonio was a mathematician, a powered wheelchair user and one of the most renowned independent-living activists in the country; and Rai, who was also an experienced activ-ist, was an anthropology graduate who worked as a craftsman. Having been restricted by the lack of accessible spaces during their early friendship, they developed the idea for a project to proto-type an open-source wheelchair kit, which could 'habilitate other

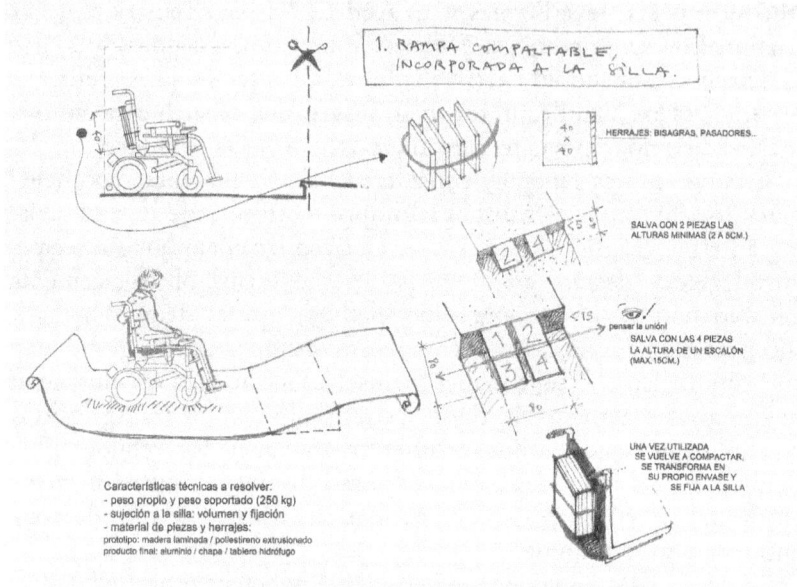

Figure 0.1 First draft of an open-source portable wheelchair ramp. Picture by En torno a la silla (July 2012).

possibilities' for wheelchair users and their potential allies. Without previous experience in the construction of technical aids, they started by reconceptualizing the very idea of a wheelchair: it was to be 'a little agora that brings together not only its user but other people with whom the wheelchair user interacts, be it at home, in the streets, bars, classrooms, wherever the people are'.[2] The kit comprised three elements: a portable wheelchair ramp (see Figure 0.1), a foldable table, and an armrest-briefcase, developed with a small amount of funding from the cultural centre Medialab-Prado (Madrid).[3]

Tomás's ethnographic site may be aptly characterized as a para-site, as can the venues populated by urban guerrillas where Adolfo, in collaboration with his colleague Alberto Corsín, conducted his urban fieldwork in Madrid (Corsín Jiménez and Estalella 2016). Both sites resemble the ones that contributors to this book have investigated: a wide gamut of spaces populated by professionals, natural scientists, artists, activists, designers and civil servants. These ethnographers were faced with subjects engaged in highly reflexive, creative and investigative practices, whether in their professional contexts or everyday activities. These are contexts populated by 'epistemic communities' in which '"research", broadly conceived, is integral to the function of these communities', the lab serving as the paradigmatic example, but also realizing that 'an experimental ethos is now … manifest in countless settings' (Holmes and Marcus 2008: 82).

Indeed, laboratories are not the only spaces we would like to mention, given their modernist and lettered or expert connotations. We believe we should also expand our attention towards other spaces of 'the contemporary', such as the different activist spaces of the former 'colonized Others' of the discipline (black, indigenous, people of colour, women, people with disabilities, etc.). Due to their particular dialogic structure and argumentation-oriented modes of sociality, these epistemic communities explicitly counter and render impossible any form of 'allochronic' relegation (Fabian 2014) of our ethnographic counterparts – that is, their treatment as primitive, illiterate, or ancient, forcing anthropologists to consider them as 'coeval'.

Certain recent ethnographic accounts of these sites have avoided the conventional aesthetics of the field encounter, drawing instead on an idiom of intervention, underlining the ways in which anthropologists go beyond both the distant and engaged modalities of participant observation. An example of this is a series of ethnographic projects based on the construction of digital platforms for scholarly interdisciplinary work, which have become the very ethnographic sites of the anthropologists who established them (Kelty et al. 2009; Fortun et al. 2014; Riles 2015). The field of these ethnographies displaces naturalistic conventions and traditional tropes of immersion. It is not merely that these ethnographers assume their site is not a geographically bounded location (Gupta and Ferguson 1997) or that they bluntly acknowledge the laborious construction, both theoretical and practical, involved in the process of establishing relationships (Amit 2000). There is something beyond this: the field appears literally to be an object of careful design that gathers together those who would be part of the project. A different articulation of digital technologies in ethnographic practice is described in Karen Waltorp's chapter, where she introduces us to her fellow Danish Muslim second-generation immigrants' shared use of digital technologies. Mobile phones, email and message applications unfold a series of interfaces in the field that prompt Waltorp to conceptualize 'an ethnography where the field takes the form of an interface: a field of ambiguous condition because it links together those things that it at the same time separates' (this volume, Chapter 5).

Another para-sitical situation is instigated when anthropologists assume institutional positions among their prospective informants. This was the case in Paul Rabinow's ethnography of a large research project on synthetic biology, where he assumed the leading role within an ELSI programme (Ethics, Law, and Social Impact), with responsibility for the social dimensions of the project. Rabinow has suggested he had to resort to re-equilibrating the traditional balance between participation and observation in the quest for a different relationship in the field: '[T]he need for a new form of collaboration was instigated by the desire to redesign a form of anthropology to be more adequate to the contemporary' (Rabinow 2011: 143).

Holmes and Marcus (2005, 2008) have similarly hinted at collaboration as the best epistemic strategy for developing fieldwork in these sites. Drawing on their experience, they have argued that anthropologists working in para-sitical contexts cannot maintain the conventional dichotomy between informant and observer when the proximity of the epistemic practices of the former provides anthropologists with the opportunity to turn them into epistemic partners. Therefore, the challenge Holmes and Marcus present anthropologists with is 'to construct models of fieldwork as collaboration for themselves, models that let them operate with their own research agendas inside the pervasive collaboratories that define social spaces today' (Holmes and Marcus 2008: 130). However, collaboration in parasitical contexts may not always be the best option, or even possible. This is the argument Maria Schiller makes in recounting a project carried out in the municipal institutions of three different European cities, intended to study how diversity was produced and managed in practice. She describes the very different roles and positions she was able to establish, 'sometimes defining our relationship in more collaborative terms, and on other occasions confining my research to a more conventional participant observation' (this volume, Chapter 2). This fluctuating relationship underlines the need to consider the nuances of fieldwork, such as the relevance of the anthropologist's features and the convenience of further developing and differentiating forms of 'para-sites'. In these ethnographies, moving away from the vocabularies of observation and participation, collaboration takes central stage.

Epistemic Collaborations

Collaboration has a long tradition in anthropology, and ethnographers have historically drawn on different forms of partnership in their professional activity (Riles 2015). From the early anthropological accounts based on key informants through the work of armchair anthropologists grounded in third-party narratives to the more modern fieldwork practices, anthropologists have always depended on others for the production of knowledge (Stull and Schensul 1987; Ruby 1992; Choy et al. 2009). Native American anthropology is an example of the critical role that key informants have played in the discipline. Luke Eric Lassiter (2008) has described how from Lewis Henry Morgan to Franz Boas, the work of these key informants was not reduced to providing anthropologists with information. On the contrary, these counterparts in the field were often engaged in practices of translation and even the co-authoring of texts, as has been explicitly recognized in a number of classic studies. Nevertheless, explicit acknowledgment of these forms of collaboration has tended to be the exception rather than the norm, and field relationships have been dominated by an asymmetric balance between the informant Other and the informed anthropologist. Describing this kind of relationship as collaboration requires clarification of the extractive act and the asymmetric roles embodied in these situations. In a heuristic attempt, we suggest referring to this as 'Collaboration Mode 1'.

In the 1980s, during attempts to renew and reinvigorate the discipline, collaboration was hailed as either a means of creating more engaged public forms of anthropology (Lassiter 2005) or as a methodological strategy that would enable anthropologists to articulate their ethical responsibility (Hymes 1974) and political commitments (Juris 2007) towards more 'dialogic' forms of research (Fabian 2014). We would like to highlight two different routes in these pleas for collaboration. One locates collaboration in the time and space of fieldwork, invoking it as a strategy for establishing more symmetrical and horizontal relationships (Rappaport 2008). For Nancy Scheper-Hughes (1995) this form of collaboration was an attempt to engage with and empower marginalized communities. In contrast, Eric Lassiter (2005, 2008) locates the paradigmatic locus of collaboration in the space of representation, advocating coproduction of written ethnographic output. The argument for this is that collaboration lays the foundations for the incorporation of voices and interpretations of our counterparts in the field, enriching the final account with more nuanced, dialogic and polyphonic writing (Field 2008). We call this mode of infusing fieldwork with a political or ethical commitment 'Collaboration Mode 2'.

We may thus distinguish these two established modes of collaboration in anthropology: whereas Mode 1 pays attention to the constitutive flows of fieldwork information, Mode 2 highlights the capitalization of information by anthropologists and proposes a symmetrical and ethics-laden form of relationship. We do not intend to criticize these ethnographic endeavours, but merely emphasize the differing idioms that inform these conceptualizations of collaboration. Each denotes specific loci for collaboration (translating and providing data or taking part in and representing marginalized or political communities) and motives (production of information or ethical commitment). These collaborative modes are thus not historical stages but distinctive ways of understanding the locus, meaning and practice of collaboration.

In recent years the idiom of collaboration has pervaded anthropology and many other social domains, capturing the imagination of a wide range of professional domains. We often witness calls for collaboration in the arts (Bishop 2012), sciences (Olson, Zimmerman and Bos 2008) and technological design (Benkler 2009). In all these contexts, collaboration has been invested with a series of virtues that Monica Konrad (2012: 9) has synthesized as follows: 'the expectation of mutual advantages', 'an increased awareness of the other parties' work', and in the case of her institutional studies, 'more effective work styles and an enhanced organizational capacity' resulting from different actors with diverse knowledge backgrounds and from multiple disciplines working together. Collaboration is praised as an ideal mode of either social organization or knowledge production: 'a new overarching motif for research and practice' (Riles 2015: 147). A different take might be Marisol de la Cadena's (2015: 12–34) conceptualization and praise of 'co-labouring': a series of practices aimed at elucidating and controlling 'equivocations' in conceptual translations and dialogues with our epistemic partners.

The contributors to this book describe their field engagement in collaborative terms, although here collaboration is usually neither a constitutive condition of fieldwork nor a deliberate strategy informed by political and ethical commitments. Instead, collaboration is an epistemic figure that describes how anthropologists creatively venture into the production of venues of knowledge creation in partnership with their counterparts in the field. Tomás's fieldwork is exemplary in this sense. Due to the ethnographic documentary practices he displayed in the first encounters, he was rapidly brought in to the shared exploratory material fabrication activities of ETS, and placed in charge of the project's documentation. At times this involved taking pictures of measuring, sketching and manufacturing, and producing notes of meetings and events; on other occasions, gathering and scanning the many different ideas or sketches being produced, whether in notepads or on table napkins (see Figure 0.2). The aim was not only

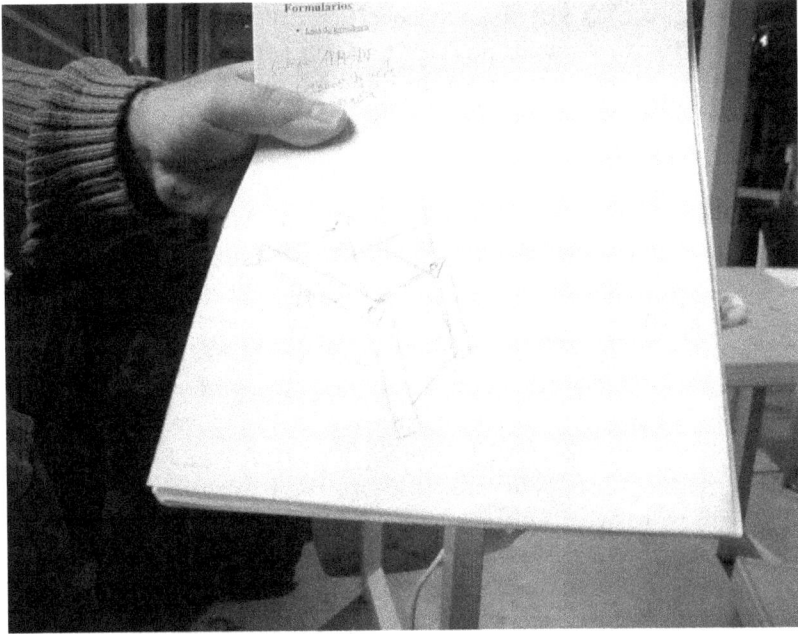

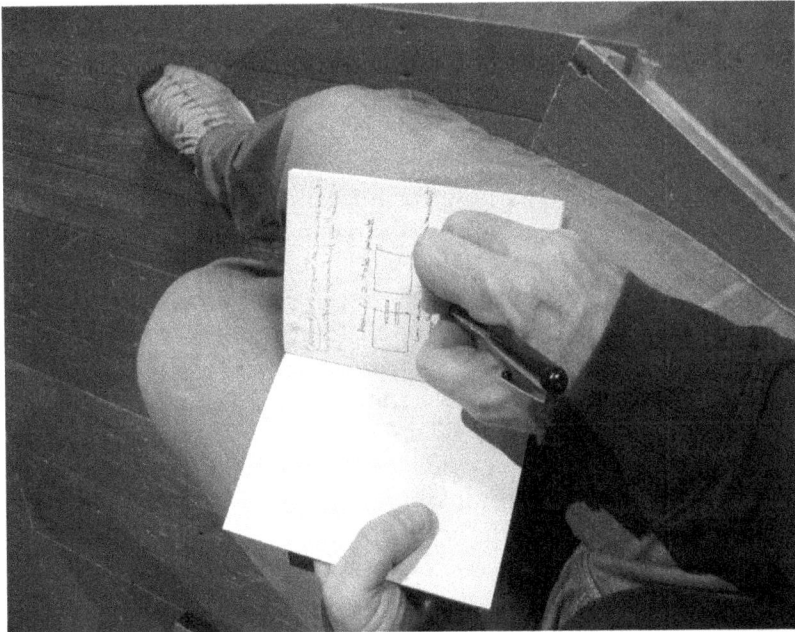

Figures 0.2 and 0.3 Pictures of the sketches being produced in discussions about folding methods for the portable wheelchair ramp. Pictures taken by Tomás Sánchez Criado (January 2013).

to compile records but also to generate an account through textual and audiovisual materials such as tutorials. To this end, Tomás set up a digital infrastructure for the archiving, publication and circulation of these materials. Sharing all this was essential to ETS: not only would the process and all results be made public, it was hoped this would inspire others to start their own explorations.

Tomás's experience resonates with that of Alexandra Kasatkina, Zinaida Vasilyeva and Roman Khandozhko, who describe for us a large project based on interviews conducted with Soviet nuclear scientists and engineers. These authors relate the cumbersome process of obtaining authorization from their interviewees to publish the transcripts. What was assumed to be a straightforward process embroiled them in an unexpected arena of toing and froing over these texts, which were substantially modified, transforming the transcripts into something else. While the authorization process presented an opportunity to work with interviewees and produce new empirical data, elicit interpretations, and establish new relationships, the authors hesitate to qualify these instances as collaboration, describing them rather as 'forms of partnerships shaped around knowledge production' (this volume, Chapter 6).

We have used the concept of collaboration to refer to these situations in the field: a para-sitical collaboration taking place in contexts where anthropologists meet para-ethnographic others. However, rather than notions of solidarity and equity, for us collaboration takes the form of tentative situations in which anthropologists appear to be prompted to repurpose their traditional techniques (taking notes and interviewing) or are drawn into intense interventions in the field, at times working smoothly with counterparts, at other times clashing with them. In these situations, the ethnographic method is re-equipped with new infrastructures, spaces of knowledge production, relationship forms and modes of representation. Taken this way, collaboration would not be the traditional constitutive condition of any fieldwork characterized by an asymmetric relationship (Mode 1), nor a deliberate strategy infused by political and ethical commitments (Mode 2). Rather, it would be a form of engaging in joint epistemic explorations with those formerly described as informants, now reconfigured as epistemic partners. We have come to think of this process as one that unsettles the observational convention of ethnography and reveals other epistemic practices in fieldwork. We call this 'Collaboration Mode 3'.

Without a definitive idea of what such a mode might entail, we have realized that Mode 3 tends to involve experimentation with the vocabularies in use. An interesting example of this is Anna Lisa Ramella's chapter on her fieldwork with a band. Instead of a vocabulary of place-making and even relationships, she uses the rhythmic analogies of touring and musical performance to describe her experimental engagement with participant observation in terms of 'rhyming together'. Whilst touring she was required 'to navigate within and become a rower in a boat where people, objects and practices were constantly being negotiated' (this volume, Chapter 3).

The para-sitical collaborations described by the contributors to this book delineate different empirical contours of such a Mode 3. In many cases this is a type of field situation that neither takes the shape of horizontal relations nor implies the erasure of (disciplinary) differences. On the contrary, the para-sitical collaboration of Mode 3 is often brought into existence against a background of disciplinary frictions, differing knowledges, epistemic diversity and social misunderstandings. Take, for instance, Tomasz Rakowski's account of his project in a rural area of Poland. Working with artists and a segment of the rural population extremely skilled in their DIY practices, Rakowski states: 'The collaboration is made possible, as there is an acknowledgment of a certain clash of different forms of knowledge and different energies' (this volume, Chapter 7). This clash takes place between the vernacular knowledges of the amateur craftspeople, the artists seeking to give them visibility, and the anthropologist. In all these cases, collaboration is an epistemic figure resulting from the careful craft of articulating inventive, shared modes of doing together with our counterparts in the field. The contributions in this book strive to find the appropriate vocabularies to narrate this. It is precisely in this para-sitical collaboration where the experimental impulse takes central stage within ethnography.

Experimentation and Observation

Working side by side with scientists, activists, public servants and artists has led anthropologists to intertwine with different forms of expertise, problematizing their conventional practices of knowledge production in fieldwork. The observational stance is then replaced with an experimental approach deeply rooted in these para-sitical collaborations. One of the broadest explorations of experimentation in ethnography in recent years was undertaken by Paul Rabinow and his collaborators (Rabinow 2011; Rabinow and Bennett 2012; Rabinow and Stavrianakis 2013; Korsby and Stavrianakis 2016), as part of his wider reflection on what he refers to as the anthropology of the contemporary. His most recent project on synthetic biology has been described as an experiment unfolding a twofold collaboration: between anthropology and biology; and between Rabinow and his co-researchers (PhD students and postdoctoral researchers). This project is driven by the desire to redesign, 'to experiment with the invention and refinement of practices of venue construction and modes of presentation, as well as concept formation and clustering' (Rabinow 2011: 114).

The increasing incorporation of digital platforms in anthropology – at times as spaces for collaboration, at others as repositories for exploring the formats of empirical data – has often been accompanied by appeals for experimentation. Kim and Michael Fortun's Asthma Files project is paradigmatic in this sense: a set of digital platforms, private and public databases with interviews and various ethnographic findings, intended to record the different and fragmentary sources of knowledge and expertise available on this multiple disease. In the researchers' own description, theirs are 'digital tools aimed to animate the comparative perspective of anthropology' (Fortun et al. 2014: 633). Digital platforms in the form of archives and coordinating tools have also been the locus for experiments with ethnographic writing genres (Fabian 2008). Digital platforms certainly serve a different purpose from that of publicizing projects or the presentation of results; they are essential pieces of equipment in the production of records, concepts and interpretations during fieldwork. Nevertheless, the key point is their status as infrastructures for inquiry, an integral part of ethnographic forms of engagement. This is fundamental for arguments advocating experimentation in ethnography: it allows anthropologists to put in practice forms of inquiry that make the forging of new anthropological problematizations possible.

Although appeals for experimentation are sometimes vague and attribute diverse meanings to the process, the use of this figure is not a mere metaphorical flourish. Descriptive accounts of experimentation bring to life new ethnographic imaginations that either transform field informants into epistemic partners (Holmes and Marcus 2005), remediate the form of ethnography in the company of others (Rabinow 2011), or even trade the traditional comparative project of anthropology for one of collaboration (Riles 2015). The experimental becomes a distinctive articulation of the empirical work of anthropologists shaping their relationships in the field collaboratively. We take this invocation of the figure of experimentation in fieldwork seriously because we believe it constitutes attempts to describe distinctive forms of knowledge production, and with this book we seek to further delineate the contours of this form of practice. As Emma Garnett suggests in her contribution when describing her work in an interdisciplinary team of epidemiologists and chemists: 'The concept of experiment is useful for an anthropological approach to interdisciplinary knowledge making because it offers a material means of ethnographic engagement' (this volume, Chapter 1).

Despite the innovative formulation of experimentation in various contemporary projects, the trope of participant observation as the epistemic figure through which fieldwork is described often remains. Experimentation, hence, is conceived here as a kind of deviation from participant observation, where the experiment sets the stage for the expansion of limits and possibilities (Rabinow and Stavrianakis 2013). While these considerations provide fruitful insights to experimental practices during fieldwork, we contend that the ethnographic experiment should not be seen merely as a deviation but as a distinctive ethnographic modality for the production of anthropological knowledge. Put differently, the specific object of the ethnographic experimentation is not participant observation but the social worlds in which anthropologists are involved. The chapters in this collection delve into descriptions of their experimental interventions, and provide hints of the specific venues, infrastructures and forms of relationality that are mobilized in experiments in the field. In so doing, they outline an ethnographic figure that surfaces in their fieldwork and stands apart from participant observation. We do not intend to set this ethnographic modality against participant observation. On the contrary, the ethnographic accounts gathered here bear witness to the multiple and entangled relations between both ethnographic modalities: at times they alternate, at others experimentation replaces participant observation, and very often they coexist in intricate alliances. An analogous relationship has been demonstrated in the history of science concerning the historical distinctiveness and relationships between observation and experimentation as epistemic practices. This literature is, indeed, a source of inspiration for our discussion.

Work within the history of science has demonstrated that, until very recently, observation and experimentation have been interrelated scientific practices: only since the second half of the nineteenth century have they been interpreted as two detached and differentiated epistemic categories (Daston and Lunbeck 2011). This was part of a process of attributions that characterized the experiment as an active process demanding ideas and ingenuity, while reducing

observation to a passive instance restricted to the mere recollection
of data (Daston 2011). Each practice was then located in a specific
space: the laboratory for experimentation, the field for observation.
Historians of science have demonstrated the sheer diversity of 'styles
of experimentation' (Klein 2003) that have characterized this form of
knowledge production and, importantly for our argument, have disputed the confining of experimentation to the laboratory, by revealing the existence of many forms that took place in the field (Schaffer
1994). Robert Kohler (2002), for instance, has described biologists
practising experiments in the wild during the last decades of the
nineteenth century. The laboratory may be the paradigmatic spatial
organization of experimentation, but it is not the only one.

A historical detour into the origins of anthropology demonstrates
that this intricate entanglement between experimentation and observation can be witnessed at the very moment the discipline's modern
methodological canon was articulated. The historical record provides
authoritative evidence of how early anthropological expeditions
modelled the discipline's fieldwork methods after the field practices
of biology, zoology and oceanography (Stocking 1983; Kuklick
1997). Less established is the claim that these experiences received
the influx of forms of self-experimentation by medical and psychological practitioners (Schaffer 1994). In their historical account
of the 1908 expedition by A.M. Hocart and W.H.R. Rivers to the
Solomon Islands, Edvard Hviding and Cato Berg describe details of
how forms of prolonged fieldwork, which laid the foundations of the
contemporary canon of participant observation, were the result of an
exercise of ethnographic experimentation with the Solomon villagers:
'[T]he fieldwork was to be a mutual experiment in which initiative
was simultaneously ethnographic and indigenous' (Hviding and Berg
2014: 4).

Our intention in highlighting this is neither to bestow contemporary projects with a halo of radical methodological novelty nor
to posit an absolute rupture with the conventions of ethnography.
On the contrary, we suggest that the experimental nature of these
ethnographies connects with and continues a prolonged history of
creative exploration within the discipline. In particular, we would
like to expound on the idea that this experimentation draws from
the creative exploration of writing genres inaugurated in anthropology during the 1980s in what became known as 'the reflexive turn'
(Marcus and Fischer 1986; Clifford and Marcus 1986), a time when
many explorations in textual and audiovisual genres brought to the
fore a 'crisis of representation' (Russell 1999). As George E. Marcus

and Michael J. Fischer phrased it at the time: 'What is happening seems to us to be a pregnant moment in which every individual project of ethnographic research and writing is potentially an experiment' (1986: ix). Yet, while this epistemic reorientation in the discipline focused on the space of representation (particularly the written form) as the locus for creative reinvention of the ethnographic norm and form, we are now witnessing a shift that identifies the empirical site of fieldwork as the locus for devising modalities of ethnographic experimentation (Marcus 2014).

'Devicing' Fieldwork

We now return to Tomás's ethnographic experience, to sketch out the distinctive modality of the experimental drive within his fieldwork. One of the most important projects of the early En torno a la silla (ETS) involved the design and fabrication of a portable wheelchair ramp. Produced after trial mock-ups in an intensive collective work environment (see Figure 0.3), the final incarnation consisted of

Figure 0.4 Collaborative testing of one of the first metal ramp prototypes in Medialab Prado. Picture taken by Tomás Sánchez Criado, published by En torno a la silla (January 2013).

two foldable aluminium sheets, each capable of taking 250 kg and enabling a powered wheelchair to deal with 20 cm high steps.[4] ETS described their do-it-yourself (DIY) exploratory fabrications with the pejorative term *cacharrear*, to tinker, characterized by playful learning processes – a mundane exploratory practice of sketching and fabricating in which inspiration was often sought from online tutorials and conversations. An integral part of the tinkering process was the production of appropriate documentation to make their prototypes public, inspiring others to start their own processes. This led to significant exploration of formats, genres and styles of recording, as well as aesthetic languages of publication.

In his role as documenter, Tomás had to establish a shared digital environment for his own *cacharreo* (tinkering). Since he was required to take pictures and make quick notes using one device, the customary notepad was superseded by a smartphone application; on other occasions he jotted down exhaustive minutes of meetings in draft emails, which he would later send to ETS members. He collected material from various sources, archiving these in the cloud, and learnt to use a blog platform to manage the different aspects of documentation. Working within the project, Tomás equipped his field with a digital infrastructure for documentation, and as a consequence, remediated his ethnographic practice of note taking. Tomás's intense engagement led him to take a crucial role in constructing the basic infrastructure of the collective he was investigating. This turned his ethnographic project into one concerned with designing and maintaining a space of which he was also a part. Yet this was not the only way he intervened: on other occasions he promoted the organization of public events (talks, presentations, etc.) in order to produce situations of knowledge elicitation and further documentation, therefore acting as a kind of curator for the group.

A similar form of engagement is described by Isaac Marrero-Guillamón. As part of his ethnographic project among artists he had intended to produce an edited volume, but when undertaking fieldwork he met an artist and curator with matching ambitions. The two combined their efforts on a book that though initially a collaborative project later became something else. Marrero-Guillamón notes the collaborative dimension of this book produced in close partnership with the curator and a designer, yet he focuses attention on the later process of public circulation, when a series of events provided contributors with the opportunity to raise and discuss issues. Unexpectedly, in this situation the book became a platform for the enactment of public encounters: 'a hosting device which allowed contributors and others to raise issues of concern, present ideas, and make new connections'. These events became highly significant for Marrero-Guillamón's fieldwork, the hospitable conditions transforming his ethnography into 'a collaborative device for the production of public forums or platforms' (this volume, Chapter 8).

These two accounts illustrate a form of field intervention materializing and/or spatializing the ethnographic method: in the first it takes the form of a digital infrastructure that sustains a complex process of DIY design, in the second a book that in its public circulation generates new spaces for ethnographic encounters. Both articulate fieldwork with specific material and social forms. In an attempt to convey these instantiations of fieldwork, we draw on John Law and Evelyn Ruppert's conceptualization of such methods as 'devices'. In their own words, these are patterned arrangements that 'assemble and arrange the world in specific social and material patterns' (Law and Ruppert 2013: 230). In contrast to formulations that reduce methods to instruments or simple recipes, this conceptualization emphasizes the precarious, processual and creative nature of methods, its situated condition – the boundary of what counts as a method always depends on one's questions and agendas – and its performative character: 'methods are shaped by the social, and in turn they act as social operators to do the social' (ibid.: 233).

We think that the contributions gathered in this volume provide sharp insights into the potential of the device idiom for the description of our ethnographic modalities of engagement. Describing the role of anthropologists organizing events, introducing interfaces in the field, utilizing friction as a relational mode, and managing rhythms, these accounts present a vocabulary to illuminate the presence of fieldwork interventions that 'device' ethnographic venues for epistemic collaboration. These accounts narrate the minutiae of assembling the material and social conditions needed for the joint construction of knowledge: 'devicing the field' for the elaboration of anthropological problematizations. In Tomás's case, these problematizations emerged and interweaved with the ones produced by ETS in its tinkering practices. One instance of such problematizations can be seen in the blog post 'The ramp is not the solution',[5] summarizing collective reflections on what the portable ramp was for:

> With it we do not claim to be solving the problem of universal accessibility. Neither do we search for a definitive solution. We seek instead to activate some possible relations with the environment. The ramp displaces the problem to the person responsible for a given urban setting. The problem is transferred to this place, this shop, that space ... and

from here we might create a possible link, with all the difficulties to solve thereon. The ramp doesn't solve anything. On the contrary, it displays the problem, making it evident, tangible and attainable. (Blog post excerpt, translated and published in full in Sánchez Criado, Rodríguez-Giralt and Mencaroni 2016: 34)

The ramp had been put to use in the previous months in collective actions jokingly called '*a-saltos*' by ETS members, a play on the double meaning of *asaltos* (assaults), and *ir a saltos* (jumpy walking) (see Figure 0.4). But deploying the ramp would have been a mere series of events ending with the retracting and folding of the ramp were it not for the durability afforded by documentation and the dialogic digital infrastructures set up by ETS (a blog and social media) to accompany their actions. Documentation of the design process was crucial for ETS, since their central exploratory concerns had always been to understand not only whether the results of their tinkering were working in design terms but also potential uses and problems prior to and after production. Although the documentation produced and compiled by Tomás was relatively basic (pictures, minutes or notes), it was never used without careful selection and appropriate elaboration. Indeed, everything had to be collectively discussed and agreed upon (remember, 'nothing about us without us'). ETS members gathered around Tomás's computer to debate and select the impressions, memories of the moments recorded and pictures to be made public in their reports.[6] The documentation facilitated many fine-tuning discussions within ETS and, once public, prompted debates with other accessibility advocates.

The reflexivity afforded by revising and publishing the open documentation gradually turned ETS into a space of discussions and joint research, enabling the construction of shared problems in and around their tinkering processes. Using Rabinow's anthropological reinterpretation of Foucauldian problematizations, the tinkering practice of ETS emerged as 'the situation of the process of a specific type of problem making, as simultaneously the object, the site, and ultimately the substance of thinking' (Rabinow 2003: 19). Each participant (be they designer, wheelchair user, craftsperson or documenter) was tinkering with something, since he or she 'invents technologies, and then shares these technologies with the people with whom he also shares problems or situations'.[7] Indeed, for ETS the explorations of collaborative design undertaken in their tinkering practices became central, so much so that their reflexive version of design practice could be narrated as an interrogative form of 'joint problem-making' around the conditions of open-source technical aid

Figure 0.5 En torno a la silla's members testing the portable wheelchair ramp by 'assaulting' public spaces. Picture by En torno a la silla (July 2013).

production rather than as a form of problem-solving through design (Sánchez Criado and Rodríguez-Giralt 2016).

Tomás's tinkering with documentation proved crucial in generating many of these reflexive situations. However, the production of this documentation was not straightforward. It involved various forms of *mise en documentation*, from the publication of mere technical specifications to tutorials and how-to manuals, as well as more poetic experience-based texts and political essays. It included an exploratory process with tentative and uncertain roles and aims. Tinkering with format, genres and styles, Tomás's documenting practice not only inscribed the social world for his personal use as an ethnographer,[8] it also contributed to the emergence of a shared research space. In such a space, Tomás's problematizations merged into a wider and shared process of problem-making in and around the open design of technical aids. Indeed, Tomas's tinkering with documentation – and the reflexive and performative practices it afforded – produced a context that redistributed ethnographic practice, expanding the how and who of knowledge production in the field, with all members of ETS contributing to the documentation, elaboration and conceptualization efforts surrounding their practices. Therefore, while ETS was a space of 'joint problem-making' around design, Tomás's tinkering practice proved vital to ETS becoming a space of 'ethnographic joint problem-making' – or, to phrase this differently, a space of ethnographic experimentation.[9]

Experimental Collaboration

Drawing on our own empirical experience, we have outlined an ethnographic modality that is conducted in close relationship with our counterparts. Developed in certain para-sitical locations – such as design companies, scientific laboratories, activist/artistic/cultural contexts, and public institutions populated by diverse advocates, technicians and experts – it is a form of engagement that entails field interventions through material and spatial arrangements that enable the articulation of inventive ways of working together. At times these interventions take the form of events, while on other occasions the anthropologist is responsible for setting up digital infrastructures, or making the articulation of rhythms an instrument of ethnographic work. The contributors to this book address all these instances – in our jargon, 'fieldwork devices' – to underline what we have conceptualized as 'devicing the field': the production of unforeseen and unexpected matters of shared concern in close complicity with the anthropologist's counterparts in the field. The experimental condition we appreciate in the ethnographies described here has particular effects on the nature of the field site. This is not just a location for the production of empirical data, or a space for learning, but a site where the construction of problematizations is central both to the anthropologist and their field counterparts, now transformed into epistemic partners – companions sharing the endeavour of problematizing the world. We use 'experimental collaboration' to denote this distinctive mode of devicing fieldwork through 'joint problem-making'.

The ethnographic accounts gathered here provide significant insights into the diversity and variability of ethnographic experimentation. Despite the limited geographical and empirical scope of these projects (broadly speaking, expert sites in Europe and the United States), we believe they help to advance the traditional anthropological endeavour of narrating the diversity of cultures by resourcing the ethnographic imagination with different modes of engaging social worlds. Indeed, we wish to consider that these modes of ethnographic fieldwork could take place beyond these geographical and empirical locales. These contributions portray the kind of epistemic relationships that shape their experimental take on ethnography, detailing the venues devised – or perhaps 'deviced' – to produce knowledge with their companions. This set of accounts, thus, presents us with descriptive vocabularies and conceptual idioms that renew our tales of the field, opening up venues for reimagining (and practising) other forms of being in the field with others.

We cannot avoid mentioning that almost all the contributors' projects (as well as those of the editors) took place in their early careers, whether as doctoral dissertations or postdoctoral research. Although unintentional, we think this reveals a significant factor: a preoccupation among scholars in the early stages of their careers with the methodological contours of their ethnographies when they appear to deviate from a certain taken-for-granted canon. Ethnographic endeavours always place anthropologists in uncertain situations, yet the anxieties and preoccupations described by these contributors have a different source, originating in the contrast between their ethnographic engagement and what they learned in training. Their vulnerability comes from the acute experience that their fieldwork appears to transgress what is understood to be the canonical norm and form of the ethnographic method. These contributions, thus, demonstrate the need for an initial training that explores the nuances and diversity of fieldwork modalities, and acknowledges not only the tensions in these early stages but also the opportunities that arise. This would compel us to suggest the need for a renewed pedagogic programme in and around the multiple possible modalities of ethnography.

We are even tempted to say that our evocation of experimentation does not signal a new form of engagement in the field but a common practice, an ethnographic modality that despite its presence has rarely been noted or recounted in our tales of the field. This is why it is so important to explore the descriptive vocabularies that can account for these ethnographic modalities. Ethnographic exploration of the specific sites we have portrayed is certainly not new: the anthropology of organizations, for instance, has a long tradition of studying these kinds of corporative and institutional environments populated by technicians and experts. Therefore, the reflections on epistemic practices and forms of engagement provoked when studying these sites are not simply a result of their nature. We believe they bear witness to an emerging sensibility that takes shape in these encounters and seeks to device other forms of field engagement.

In close partnership with their counterparts, our contributors narrate the convoluted, heterogeneous and unpredictable forms of collaboration that are unfolded during fieldwork. In contrast to more naturalistic or purely observational forms of engagement, these authors avoid the tropes of distance or participation, and highlight the tensions and frictions of collaboration, its particular rhythms and the material infrastructures or spaces required for its production and maintenance. Thus they explore the descriptive vocabularies and conceptual idioms that could renew descriptions of forms of engagement, open a new register, different even from what are sometimes conceived as experiments within participant observation. Here, experimentation is an ethnographic modality independent from observational stances. However, as stated earlier, we do not intend to place experimental collaboration and participant observation in opposition, but only highlight their specificities. Indeed, our contributors skilfully illustrate the diverse forms of entanglement, juxtaposition and intermittent connections between observational practices and experimental stances that occur in fieldwork. Our introductive account has followed the same path: we have attempted a description that, by applying an ethnographic sensibility to the anthropological method, has sought to faithfully describe our epistemic practices, with the hope that these could open up new forms of engagements with the worlds we study.

Overview of Chapters

In *Experimenting with Data: 'Collaboration' as Method and Practice in an Interdisciplinary Public Health Project*, Emma Garnett explores multiple data practices concerning air pollution. Having subtly characterized how the various scientists in the project deal with data, producing versions and coordinations of air ontologies, she reflects on the recursive implications for her participant observation work. In this tale, 'data' appears as a fieldwork device for the anthropologist, implicated in the production of data in such a context, in an experimental practice of tracing the material and conceptual processes in the ongoing generation of new articulations of air pollution.

Maria Schiller, in *The 'Research Traineeship': The Ups and Downs of Para-siting Ethnography*, describes her ethnographic experimentation with fieldwork roles in her participant observation study of multiculturalism as practised and conceived in diversity offices across Europe. Drawing on the literature of organizational ethnography, she presents the experimental 'devicing' of the ambiguous role of 'research trainee' as enabling her not only to access everyday para-ethnographic practices, but also to provide a complex account of the para-site in her comparison of three offices. In *Finding One's Rhythm: A 'Tour de Force' of Fieldwork on the Road with a Band*, Anna Lisa Ramella plunges us into the rhythmic ebbs and flows of being on tour. In her participant observation of musicians' touring practices, an experimental impulse can be found in her attempt to find her own rhythm. In her narration, Ramella utilizes the vocabulary of rhythm for a narration of fieldwork practices that differs greatly from those that usually employ categories of place; rhythm is also a refreshing way of describing collaboration as ongoing attunements in the field.

This expansion of vocabularies to narrate experimental forms of epistemic collaboration also features in Andrea Gaspar's *Idiotic Encounters: Experimenting with Collaborations between Ethnography and Design*. Gaspar recounts the many frictional events in her participant observation study of a Milanese interaction design studio. Describing the relationships between anthropology and design (usually, to use our terms, between a Mode 1 extractivist use of ethnographic data by designers, and a Mode 2 critical engagement with design practice), she seeks an interventionist take on the interdisciplinary field of design anthropology. Friction becomes not only a category accounting for tense epistemic relations between designers in their search for 'the new', but also a device of fieldwork engagement that could pave the way for more speculative ethnographic practices in design settings, transforming not only design but also anthropology.

The exploration of forms of 'in-between-ness' in the field takes centre stage in Karen Waltorp's chapter, *Fieldwork as Interface: Digital Technologies, Moral Worlds and Zones of Encounter*. Focusing on the use of digital technologies (smartphone apps and a digital camera) in her relations with the Danish Muslim women with whom she carried out participant observation, she produces a vernacular account of her fieldwork as an 'interface': an experimental space that devices connections between moral worlds, an encountering zone, not only to prolong relations but also to clarify interpretations of events in their connected yet separated cultural worlds. It is perhaps in the final three projects described here – all ventures into forms of fieldwork conducted solely in and through particular devices, events and platforms – that we see most clearly the difference between the mode of experimental collaborations and experimental forms of participant observation.

A collaborative piece by Alexandra Kasatkina, Zinaida Vasilyeva and Roman Khandozhko, *Thrown into Collaboration:*

An Ethnography of Transcript Authorization, describes in detail the effects produced in an interview-based research project – seeking to document the lives and careers of scientists involved in the Soviet nuclear project at Obninsk – by a platform for transcript authorization. Emerging in a context of state secrets and rising concerns over personal privacy, access was restricted to the time spent interviewing. However, their ethnography of authorization shows how epistemic forms of collaboration emerged through the authorization process, which in turn authorized the authors to undertake a particular form of ethnography.

In *A Cultural Cyclotron: Ethnography, Art Experiments, and a Challenge of Moving towards the Collaborative in Rural Poland*, Tomasz Rakowski narrates the 'experimental encounters' of various artists, ethnographers and Polish villagers in nuanced detail. His chapter has a twofold aim: on the one hand, by showing the forms of research made available by collaborative exhibitions of the creative gadgets and devices produced by the villagers, Rakowski demonstrates how art-related practices could transform what we mean by ethnography and the ethnographic site; on the other, this is carried out within a wider discussion of the challenges posed by the many asymmetries and symbolic inequalities traversing these endeavours.

Lastly, in *Making Fieldwork Public: Repurposing Ethnography as a Hosting Platform in Hackney Wick, London*, Isaac Marrero-Guillamón undertakes an analytical reconstruction of the 'unexpected trajectories' that led him to repurpose his project. What was to have been a participant observation study of the artists and activists opposing the transformation of East London's Hackney Wick following the 2012 Olympics, took on the shape of various 'hosting platforms': collaboration in an art installation, and production of a book and zine that, recursively, produced gatherings for the public generation of knowledges and practices he had initially intended to study.

Acknowledgements

The conversation that created the conditions for this book was initiated at the 2014 EASA conference, in a panel we convened with the title 'Ethnography as collaboration/experiment'. These introductory arguments have been redeveloped many times thanks to the ongoing dialogue, both amongst the authors of the book and the colleagues of the new Collaboratory for Ethnographic Experimentation (#colleex),

an EASA network to whose initial debates we would like this book to contribute.

The English in this introduction has been fine-tuned by Joanna Baines.

Tomás Sánchez Criado (Humboldt-University of Berlin) is Senior Researcher and Director of the Stadtlabor for Multimodal Anthropology at the Chair of Urban Anthropology of the Department of European Ethnology. Working at the crossroads of anthropology and Science and Technology Studies (STS), he has developed a particular concern around how bodily diversity comes to matter in the knowledge, material and care politics of city-making. In his work he has been experimenting with different forms of public engagement, ethnography and pedagogy.

Adolfo Estalella is Assistant Professor at the Department of Social Anthropology of the Complutense University of Madrid. He is interested in grassroots urbanism and digital cultures and he has investigated the knowledge practices of activist movements in urban contexts in Madrid (Spain). His second research line explores and intervenes in the epistemic transformations of anthropological modes of inquiry, an endeavour that takes expression in the xcol platform (http://www.xcol.org).

Notes

1. This stems from the debate around 'emancipatory research' and research as a joint endeavour, which is a much-debated topic in disability studies and in the independent-living movement as a whole. In one of the most classic works articulating that debate, Michael Oliver stated that 'the major issue on the research agenda ... should be: do researchers wish to join with disabled people and user their expertise and skills in their struggles against oppression, or do they wish to continue to use these skills and expertise in ways that the disabled people find oppressive?' (Oliver 1992: 102). Of

course, this debate resonates widely with indigenous peoples' attempts at 'decolonising' research practices and methodologies (Smith 1999).

2. Excerpt translated from https://entornoalasilla.wordpress.com/el-proy ecto-original/ (accessed 9 May 2016).

3. Medialab-Prado Madrid is a cultural hub of Madrid City Hall's Area of Arts and Culture that has specialized in the production of open-source projects. ETS took part in Medialab-Prado Madrid's 'Funcionamientos' (Functionings) workshops between Winter 2012 and Spring 2013, which sought to host group and individual projects coproducing or experimenting with the 'open design' of objects, and infused with the philosophy of 'functional diversity'.

4. See Sánchez Criado, Rodríguez-Giralt and Mencaroni (2016) for a more detailed description of the ramp's open design and construction process, as well as its open documentation.

5. 'The ramp is not the solution' post was published after slightly rewriting collectively a draft proposed by Alida, the architect of the group, who took the lead after having re-read Rabinow's 'Space, Knowledge, Power' interview with Foucault (1984), and their conversations concerning law, the freeing capabilities of architectural projects, and the practice of freedom being the only warrant of freedom (clearly resonating with the politicizing practice of displaying inaccessibility issues with the portable ramp as something different from the legal activism of regular accessibility politics). The original post in Spanish can be accessed here: https:// entornoalasilla.wordpress.com/2013/11/10/la-rampa-no-es-la-solucion-noviembre-2013/ (last accessed 6 May 2016).

6. This practice resonates with participatory strategies in visual and digital anthropology (Gubrium and Harper 2013).

7. Excerpt translated from a choral presentation by ETS members in Barcelona's BAU Design School (May 2014): https://entornoalasilla. wordpress.com/2014/07/01/cuidar-a-traves-del-diseno-presentacion-en-objetologias-junio-2014/ (last accessed 6 May 2016).

8. Geertz appositely described ethnography as an act of 'inscribing social discourse', writing it down with the intention of transforming it 'from a passing event, which exists only in its own moment of occurrence, into an account, which exists in its inscriptions and can be reconsulted' (Geertz 1973: 19).

9. Indeed, STS researchers have characterized experimentation as an epistemic practice of 'tinkering' (Knorr-Cetina 1981: 34), an apt metaphor for narrating Tomás's forms of devicing fieldwork, since it not only emphasizes experimentation as an 'opportunistic' and open-ended reasoning practice, but also the importance of tweaking experimental devices and the spaces of representation in situations that, if successful, may enable experimenters to pose new questions they did not have in advance (Rheinberger 1997).

References

Amit, V. (ed.). 2000. *Constructing the Field: Ethnographic Fieldwork in the Contemporary World*. London: Routledge.

Benkler, Y. 2009. *Next Generation Connectivity: A Review of Broadband Internet Transitions and Policy from around the World*. Cambridge, MA: The Berkman Klein Center for Internet & Society.

Bishop, C. 2012. *Artificial Hells: Participatory Art and the Politics of Spectatorship*. London: Verso.

Choy, T.K., et al. 2009. 'A New Form of Collaboration in Cultural Anthropology: Matsutake Worlds'. *American Ethnologist* 36(2): 380–403.

Clifford, J., and G.E. Marcus (eds). 1986. *Writing Culture: The Poetics and Politics of Ethnography*. Berkeley, CA: California University Press.

Corsín Jiménez, A., and A. Estalella. 2016. 'Ethnography: A Prototype'. *Ethnos* 82(5): 846–866.

Daston, L. 2011. 'The Empire of Observation: 1600–1800', in L. Daston and E. Lunbeck (eds), *Histories of Scientific Observation*. Chicago, IL: Chicago University Press, pp. 81–113.

Daston, L., and E. Lunbeck (eds). 2010. *Histories of Scientific Observation*. Chicago, IL: Chicago University Press.

de la Cadena, M. 2015. *Earth Beings: Ecologies of Practice across Andean Worlds*. Durham, NC: Duke University Press.

Emerson, R.M., R.I. Fretz and L.L. Shaw. 1995. *Writing Ethnographic Fieldnotes*. Chicago, IL: Chicago University Press.

Fabian, J. 2008. *Ethnography as Commentary: Writing from the Virtual Archive*. Durham, NC: Duke University Press.

———. 2014. *Time and The Other: How Anthropology Makes its Object*. New York: Columbia University Press.

Faubion, J.D., and G.E. Marcus (eds). 2009. *Fieldwork Is Not What It Used to Be: Learning Anthropology's Method in a Time of Transition*. Ithaca, NY: Cornell University Press.

Field, L.W. 2008. '"Side by Side or Facing One Another": Writing and Collaborative Ethnography in Comparative Perspective'. *Collaborative Anthropologies* 1(1): 32–50.

Fortun, K., et al. 2014. 'Experimental Ethnography Online: The Asthma Files'. *Cultural Studies* 28(4): 632–42.

Foucault, M. 1984. 'Space, Knowledge, Power', in P. Rabinow (ed.), *The Foucault Reader*. New York: Pantheon Books, pp. 239–56.

Geertz, C. 1973. *The Interpretation of Cultures*. New York: Basic Books.

Gubrium, A., and K. Harper (eds). 2013. *Participatory Visual and Digital Methods*. Walnut Creek, CA: Left Coast Press.

Gupta, A., and J. Ferguson. 1997. 'Discipline and Practice: "The Field" as Site, Method and Location in Anthropology', in A. Gupta and J. Ferguson (eds), *Anthropological Locations: Boundaries and Grounds of a Field Science*. Berkeley, CA: University of California Press, pp. 1–46.

Holmes, D.R., and G.E. Marcus. 2005. 'Cultures of Expertise and the Management of Globalization: Toward the Re-Functioning of Ethnography', in A. Ong and S.J. Collier (eds), *Global Assemblages: Technology, Politics, and Ethics as Anthropological Problems*. Oxford: Blackwell, pp. 235–52.

———. 2008. 'Collaboration Today and the Re-Imagination of the Classic Scene of Fieldwork Encounter'. *Collaborative Anthropologies* 1(1): 81–101.

Hviding, E., and C. Berg (eds). 2014. *The Ethnographic Experiment: A.M. Hocart and W.H.R. Rivers in Island Melanesia, 1908*. New York: Berghahn Books.

Hymes, D. (ed.). 1974. *Reinventing Anthropology*. New York: Vintage.

Ingold, T. 2008. 'Anthropology is Not Ethnography'. *Proceedings of the British Academy* 154: 69–92.

Juris, J.S. 2007. 'Practicing Militant Ethnography with the Movement for Global Resistance in Barcelona', in S. Shukaitis and D. Graeber (eds), *Constituent Imagination: Militant Investigations, Collective Theorization*. Edinburgh: AK Press, pp. 164–76.

Kelty, C., et al. 2009. 'Collaboration, Coordination, and Composition: Fieldwork after the Internet', in J.D. Faubion and G.E. Marcus (eds), *Fieldwork Is Not What It Used to Be: Learning Anthropology's Method in A Time of Transition*. Ithaca, NY: Cornell University Press, pp. 184–206.

Klein, U. 2003. 'Styles of Experimentation', in M.C. Galavotti (ed.), *Observation and Experiment in the Natural and Social Sciences*. Dordrecht: Kluwer, pp. 159–85.

Knorr-Cetina, K.D. 1981. *The Manufacture of Knowledge: An Essay on the Constructivist and Contextual Nature of Science*. Oxford: Pergamon.

Kohler, R. 2002. *Landscapes and Labscapes: Exploring the Lab-Field Border in Biology*. Chicago, IL: Chicago University Press.

Konrad, M. 2012. 'A Feel for Detail: New Directions in Collaborative Anthropology', in M. Konrad (ed.), *Collaborators Collaborating: Counterparts in Anthropological Knowledge and International Research Relations*. New York: Berghahn Books, pp. 3–39.

Korsby, T.M., and A. Stavrianakis. 2016. 'Moments of Collaboration: Experiments in Concept Work'. *Ethnos*. DOI: 10.1080/00141844.2015.1137606

Kuklick, H. 1997. 'After Ishmael: The Fieldwork Tradition and its Future', in A. Gupta and J. Ferguson (eds), *Anthropological Locations: Boundaries and Grounds of a Field Science*. Berkeley: University of California Press, pp. 47–65.

Lassiter, L.E. 2005. *The Chicago Guide to Collaborative Ethnography*. Chicago, IL: University of Chicago Press.

———. 2008. 'Moving Past Public Anthropology and Doing Collaborative Research'. *NAPA Bulletin* 29(1): 70–86.

Law, J., and E. Ruppert. 2013. 'The Social Life of Methods: Devices'. *Journal of Cultural Economy* 6(3): 229–40.

Marcus, G. 2014. 'Prototyping and Contemporary Anthropological Experiments with Ethnographic Method'. *Journal of Cultural Economy* 7(4): 399–410.

Marcus, G.E., and M.J. Fischer. 1986. *Anthropology as Cultural Critique: An Experimental Moment in the Human Sciences*. Chicago: University of Chicago Press.

Oliver, M. 1992. 'Changing the Social Relations of Research Production?' *Disability, Handicap & Society* 7(2): 101–14.

Olson, G.M., A. Zimmerman and N. Bos. 2008. *Scientific Collaboration on the Internet*. Cambridge, MA: MIT Press.

Rabinow, P. 2003. *Anthropos Today: Reflections on Modern Equipment*. Princeton, NJ: Princeton University Press.

———. 2011. *The Accompaniment: Assembling the Contemporary*. Chicago, IL: University of Chicago Press.

Rabinow, P., and G. Bennett. 2012. *Designing Human Practices: An Experiment with Synthetic Biology*. Chicago, IL: University of Chicago Press.

Rabinow, P., and A. Stavrianakis. 2013. *Demands of the Day: On the Logic of Anthropological Inquiry*. Chicago, IL: University of Chicago Press.

Rabinow, P., G.E. Marcus, J.D. Faubion and T. Rees. 2008. *Designs for an Anthropology of the Contemporary*. Durham, NC: Duke University Press.

Rappaport, J. 2008. 'Beyond Participant Observation: Collaborative Ethnography as Theoretical Innovation'. *Collaborative Anthropologies* 1(1): 1–31.

Rheinberger, H.-J. 1997. *Toward a History of Epistemic Things: Synthesizing Proteins in the Test Tube*. Stanford, CA: Stanford University Press.

Riles, A. 2015. 'From Comparison to Collaboration: Experiments with a New Scholarly and Political Form'. *Law and Contemporary Problems* 78(1–2): 147–83.

Ruby, J. 1992. 'Speaking For, Speaking About, Speaking With, or Speaking Alongside: An Anthropological And Documentary Dilemma'. *Journal of Film and Video* 44(1–2): 42–66.

Russell, C. 1999. *Experimental Ethnography: The Work of Film in the Age of Video*. Durham, NC: Duke University Press.

Sánchez Criado, T., and I. Rodríguez-Giralt. 2016. 'Caring through Design?: En torno a la silla and the "Joint Problem-Making" of Technical Aids', in C. Bates, R. Imrie and K. Kullman (eds), *Care and Design: Bodies, Buildings, Cities*. Oxford: Wiley, pp. 200–20.

Sánchez Criado, T., I. Rodríguez-Giralt and A. Mencaroni. 2016. 'Care in the (Critical) Making: Open Prototyping, or the Radicalisation of Independent-Living Politics'. *ALTER – European Journal of Disability Research* 10(2016): 24–39.

Schaffer, S. 1994. *From Physics to Anthropology – and Back Again*. Cambridge: Prickly Pear Press.

Scheper-Hughes, N. 1995. 'The Primacy of the Ethical: Propositions for a Militant Anthropology'. *Current Anthropology* 36(3): 409–40.

Smith, L.T. 1999. *Decolonizing Methodologies: Research and Indigenous Peoples*. New York: Zed Books.

Stocking, G. 1983. 'The Ethnographer's Magic: Fieldwork in British Anthropology from Tylor to Malinowski', in G. Stocking (ed.), *Observers Observed: Essays on Ethnographic Fieldwork*. Madison, WI: University of Winsconsin Press, pp. 70–120.

Stull, D.D., and J.J. Schensul (eds). 1987. *Collaborative Research and Social Change: Applied Anthropology in Action*. Boulder, CO: Westview Press.

1

Experimenting with Data

'Collaboration' as Method and Practice in an Interdisciplinary Public Health Project

Emma Garnett

Interdisciplinary Data Practices of Air Pollution

Air is something we are embedded in and entangled with, whilst, at the same time, it is problematic to visualize and sense, always eluding any boundaries we attempt to build or fix around it. Air's lapsing of spatial, temporal and analytical scales is interesting ethnographically, particularly in scientific knowledge making, because of the difficulty of materializing and measuring air in any authoritative way (Shapin and Schaffer 1985; Choy 2012). During my fieldwork with an interdisciplinary scientific project called Weather Health and Air Pollution (WHAP), different disciplinary approaches did not simply provide 'another perspective'; rather than negotiating different epistemologies of air pollution as uncertain and ambiguous, I found researchers were engaged in what I have come to refer to as 'modes of experimenting'. In this chapter, I explore the different scientific practices that construct air pollution as a research object, tracing the ways in which these contingent 'versions of air' were negotiated and reconfigured in the process of stabilizing a shared air pollution.

> What is air pollution? That is a great question. What is a weed? A plant in the wrong place. What is dirt? Matter in the wrong place. Pollution is, gases and particles in the wrong place. (Peter, Interview 6 November 2011)[1]

Experimenting was both a sensibility and a series of practices, carried out through the making, sharing and reuse of 'data'. The concept of experiment has been subject to examination in the history of science (Shapin and Schaffer 1985), social and cultural studies of science (Knorr-Cetina 1981, 1999; Rheinberger 1994, 1997) and more recently as a way of re-thinking interdisciplinary research endeavours more broadly (Fitzgerald and Callard 2014). In many sociological accounts of science, the concept has been used to empirically explore and theorize about the uncertain nature of socio-technical relations in the making. As Stengers (2005) and Rheinberger (1994) have described, experimenting allows us to pose new kinds of questions, and can enable us to speak and think otherwise about non-human entities. I found that it was these modes of experimenting that enabled researchers to engage explicitly with difference and multiplicity, and to think about others' ways of knowing and doing in creative and productive ways.

Anthropological approaches to ontology (de la Cadena et al. 2015) have shown that when one focuses on practices and takes material agency seriously, other kinds of access points to the worlds of informants are made possible (Gad, Jensen and Winthereik 2015: 74). I found that data were informational and material forms that all researchers were involved in making, as well as the means by which scientists communicated, contested and conceptualized the research process.

> The problem is that the modelled and monitored data aren't measuring quite the same thing; we are not going to have the gold standard and we are not comparing like for like – and it's a struggle to try and address this (Principal Investigator, liaison meeting, 2 April 2012)

As this quote highlights, data are embedded in heterogeneous relations, involving, for example, particular kinds of devices to sense and materialize air pollution. To study air pollution collaboratively, as an interdisciplinary matter of concern, was problematic because different data practices (what scientists made, used and shared) enacted different versions of air pollution. Because of the relational nature of data, the articulation of data's material formation also shapes collaborative research relations. This shifts cross-disciplinary scientific practices into what can be characterized as an experimental mode. As Knorr-Cetina describes, the structure of knowledge making is entangled with the social relations of research:

> The experiment becomes constituted as a distinctive and powerful structure in its own right ... it is the work of rearranging the social order, of breaking components out of other ontologies and of configuring, with them, a new structural form. The repackaging of efforts accomplished during the birth of a new experiment is also the repackaging of social composition and the creation of a new form of life. (Knorr-Cetina 1999: 214)

That data were ontologically distinct things in WHAP meant that working with and through multiple data were moments where new constructions, social compositions and forms of life could potentially emerge.

This is also the case for the ethnographer, where difference and uncertainty are not only intriguing, but may also be fruitful in their ability to generate more creative ways of thinking about field sites. Ultimately, multiplicity was an ethnographic tool that enabled me to configure a sense of 'otherness' in the field, so that differences between and within data practices became my ethnographic focus. Taking data practices seriously, and as interesting anthropologically, also extended what counted as 'the field' during my research. Explicit attention to practices of making data offered an ethnographic vantage point from which to consider data 'from within', rather than as externally bounded forms. In this way, data practices emerged as both an analytical and empirical figure in my research.

As Fitzgerald and Callard (2014) have shown, experimenting is particularly applicable to interdisciplinary relations, or 'interdisciplinary assemblages', because it is in such arrangements that the boundaries between disciplines become fuzzy, and the affective and practical relations that hold them together become more pronounced. Indeed, it was the articulation and management of difference through the multiplicity of data practices that captured my attention: for how does this seemingly 'successful research team'[2] function in practice, when there are tensions between the ways of making data of air pollution and articulating air pollution through data?

From 'Translation' and 'Difference', to 'Equivocation'

Studies of epistemic difference in other fields of collaborative inquiry have proposed a number of ways in which tensions are managed and worked through in practice. Star's concept of 'boundary objects' has been the principal means of describing translation across very different kinds of fields of practice (Star and Griesemer 1989; Fujimura

1992; Star 2010). In such analyses, the metaphor of trade and exchange across borders has been dominant (see, for example, Galison 1996), where the role of boundary objects enables epistemological dialogue, and thereby the movement and mutual construction of knowledge. There has been less focus, however, on the role of boundary objects in the making and remaking of the boundaries between human and non-human relations in interdisciplinary research. These kinds of entanglements were fundamental in the coordination of different fields of practice in WHAP.

In WHAP, there were a number of boundary objects or 'shared values'. Health was used by researchers in their explanations of their roles and reasons for participating in an interdisciplinary project. Research about health was an unquestioned 'good', and therefore working on a public health project was a socially and politically imbued act. Air pollution was a means of linking up 'the environment' and 'human health' – a useful coupling to orientate and justify the interdisciplinary nature of the project. However, although air pollution and health as shared matters of concern worked rhetorically, they functioned less well in everyday practice. As I have highlighted, in data practices air pollution was conceptualized, articulated and materialized in multiple ways, which meant that researchers on WHAP were not only engaging with different epistemologies of air pollution but with different kinds of air pollution altogether (Mol 2002; Law 2004).

Another way of approaching difference has been through the concept of 'coordination', which foregrounds the ontological dimensions of managing multiplicity in practice. As Mol's (2002) ethnography of how the disease atherosclerosis multiplies in practice has detailed, different versions of objects can also be made to 'hang together'[3] in ways that do not imply fragmentation. Yet, our empirical problem remains rather different, because the aim of the interdisciplinary project was to produce shared knowledge on a singular air pollution, so that rather than seeking 'coordination' researchers confronted difference 'head on'.

Viveiros de Castro's concept of 'equivocation'[4] may be more appropriate for this 'studying of studying difference', for it enables the consideration of the material and ontological work of objects in the making, where what objects 'are' is also subject to boundary work. Thus, rather than epistemological impasse, where different perspectives represent a singular phenomenon in the world, equivocation suggests that the same epistemological term can be used to refer to different things (Viveiros de Castro 2004a). This shifting of the anthropologist's focus can be useful for thinking through the multiplicity of research worlds that make up WHAP. Rather than supposing a plurality of views of a single world, a single view of different worlds is made possible when differential disjunction is located in bodily or instrumental differences (Viveiros de Castro 2004b: 6). Indeed, on using the concept in her research on indigenous cosmopolitics, de la Cadena shows how equivocation can bring into conversation a view from different worlds, and as a result extend anthropological knowledge production:

> Thinking about Andean mountains as sites of equivocation that enable circuits between partially connected worlds without creating a unified system of activism, can build awareness of the also partially connected alliances between environmentalists and indigenous politicians in Andean countries, allowing for more than their definition as a movement for cultural or environmental rights. (de la Cadena 2010: 351)

In this way, approaching scientific research as configured by cosmo-politics rather than the politics of knowledge permits the anthropologist to extend rather than narrow the relations they follow, and thereby the partial connections they make through and with emergent research worlds.

'Data' as Fieldwork Device: Attuning to Practices of Experimenting

The WHAP project was based across several universities in the UK and their research coordinated as part of the 'Environmental Health' initiative of a leading UK research council. This was a joint research programme between several research councils and, as one senior researcher on the project explained, one of the first to combine 'human health' and 'the natural environment' in their call for bids. This required joining forces with several institutions and drawing upon different disciplinary expertise, including that of epidemiologists, atmospheric chemists, environmental chemists, building physicists, sociologists and an anthropologist. The interdisciplinary shape of the project was something researchers reflected on in my discussions with them, and was enthusiastically drawn upon to characterize the 'trail-blazing' nature of the WHAP project.

Nonetheless, my role as ethnographer on WHAP was rather ambiguous. My research was framed in the project protocol as an 'independent component' of the project. In this way I was not expected to contribute formally to the project outputs, nor participate in the production of knowledge on air pollution. My role was described in the project protocol as 'producing knowledge on the knowledge production process'. The contribution of this research was therefore assumed to be 'unscientific' because it focused on the relations of the team of scientists, rather than the technological and material relations of air pollution. However, as my discussions of the data entanglements making up the WHAP project will highlight, interdisciplinary engagements are also socio-material processes, and it was the division between 'administrative' and 'technical' work (in terms of emails, the organization of meetings, and 'who' gets counted in these communication practices), and the instigation of disciplinary or institutional boundaries at particular moments, that demonstrated the ways in which distinctions, and thereby partiality, also compose, comprise and sustain interdisciplinary research relations.

Fieldwork involved attending weekly meetings and bi-annual 'collaborators meetings' (where we physically met at alternate institutions); following email threads and the online sharing of documents; physically moving between institutional sites, both within and external to the project, and observing different data-making practices across these; and tracing the material work of sharing and reusing data in the project. As the 'social science' component of interdisciplinary relations, I was both a data producer and field site enabler. My very presence on the project was part of doing collaborative interdisciplinary research, and reflecting on this process was considered to be a legitimate and perhaps valuable process. It was this simultaneous difficulty of carving out a field site on the project of which I was officially a member that led me to consider the meaning and affect of 'collaboration' as a scientific relation. As such, following data was also a way for me to move between situated practices; data functioned as particularly good devices because they were not only the end point of research but the very 'stuff' of researching. Data became a fieldwork device, functioning as a legitimate object of concern – being both the everyday labour of science as well as the form of scientific output – and as a material form through which I could articulate and make active anthropological knowledge making.

An Interdisciplinary Tension

On 18 May 2012, at another weekly liaison meeting, everyone was gathered round the table in the basement meeting room at the university.

General chatter livens up the sparse, white room, and coffee is being poured and distributed. The usual technical issues of the web-conferencing software are being worked out before the meeting begins. The meeting agenda lists a major item for discussion, 'the modelled and monitored data issue', which is something that has been taking shape for the last six months or so and requires contributions from all the researchers on the project. Everyone quietens down as the PI speaks slowly and clearly into the microphone to check whether 'the modellers' are there: 'Can you see and hear us all from 400 miles away?' They can. The PI [an epidemiologist] begins by detailing the main discussion item for today's meeting, namely, how we are going to use modelled and monitored practices in the project. He explains that they, the epidemiologists need to use measures of air pollution to work out the relationship between levels of air pollution and negative health effects, and that they are unsure about using modelled data in their analysis, because, 'as epis,[5] what we trust is when we see measurements, because we see it and we know how it works; and that is a version of reality'. The modellers – a group of three today – start murmuring a response, and with a slightly exasperated sigh, Elizabeth [co-PI and atmospheric chemist] states: 'The measurements made by monitors do not take into account the different chemical processes that make up concentrations of pollutants'. There is a silence that seems resistant to further discussion. To break this sense of impasse, the PI suggests that the team creates a shared document, starting out with the epidemiologists' perspective, in order to conceptualize how we are thinking about air pollution on the project.

In this anecdote, claims to 'reality' and 'the truth' about air pollution are framed as relative, relating to different kinds of data. Indeed, the PI concludes that 'you [modellers] might say it [monitored data] doesn't represent all these different things, but epidemiologists don't trust models – and the modellers, you say, you don't trust the single point measurements'. However, this reduction of disciplinary difference to the epistemic contours of data occludes wider ontological dimensions of the tension between and within data, which was not about trusting either data more or less, but about what kinds of relations make up air in research practices.

Modelling and monitoring practices are different ways of making data of air pollution. Each involves an instrument making a numerical measurement of the amount (the concentration) of a particular air pollutant in an air sample under certain conditions. What is of interest for each practice is, in the first place, air rather than air pollution: how to 'capture' it (monitoring), and how to 'simulate' it (modelling). It is the measurement contexts – temperature, time of day, season, location, for example – that make the measurement meaningful and, as a result, 'data'. Working out the right relations of air was one of the key components of making data of air pollution, and these are different for modelling and monitoring. In comparing the ways in which numerical readings were made, I found that different enactments of air pollution emerged from the particular research practices that make up data.

Monitored Data and Modelled Data

Making monitoring data of air pollution involves placing monitors in strategic locations, often in areas considered as having high levels of urban pollution. The stations are small cabins containing a number of different monitors, each of which measures specific pollutants. These monitors draw in samples of the surrounding air through tubes that connect the inside of the station to the world outside. Once in the tubes, the air sample goes through a process of purification, where the 'wrong' parts of air are taken away with a scrubbing device, so that the relations of interest – a particular pollutant – are separated and measured by the sensor inside the monitor (Garnett 2016). The sensor functions by passing a UV light beam through the tube, and the reaction that results from this process is a measure of the pollutant. A series of fluctuating numbers – unstable measurements – are shown on the screen on the front of the monitor, and in order to turn these numbers into data the numerical readings are checked to ensure they have not been unduly influenced by the instrument used.

Making modelled data is a different kind of practice and has a different kind of material situatedness to monitoring. Yet there were also resonances with monitoring, in terms of the processes and transformations through which the numerical measurements became data. Both practices attend to the construction and control of the setting from which a measurement can be made. For modelling, the measurement setting was built with computer code, so the complexities that make up a controlled environment, such as temperature, weather conditions and time, were also preconceived and constructed within the model. This contrasts with monitoring, where the complexities in making a measurement influenced the setting in which the monitor was located. In monitoring, data other than air pollution are also collected and recorded, including the temperature in the monitoring station, the technician's tests and their results, and details of the kind of air being measured at the site (e.g. is it 'road side'?), which contextualizes the readings being taken so they can become meaningful data.

Rather than taking away other parts of air, modelling adds relations to air through the building and running of a computer simulation of the atmosphere, in which air pollution comprises physical and chemical interactions. Air pollution is abstracted in a different way here, and therefore requires different contextual information in order to make data meaningful and translatable beyond the research setting. Making modelled data was framed by a logic of knowing not just air pollution, but air pollution in the atmosphere, a three-dimensional form in flux and in process, and therefore something that articulates with a global scale of governance and regulation.

Different Data, Different Air Pollutions

I have shown that modelling and monitoring data practices, as particular engagements with the world, enact different versions of air pollution in practice. Specifically, I have delineated how modelling and monitoring configure air pollutions differently, by transforming numerical readings into data in ways that make them meaningful: the particular arranging and articulating of 'the measurement setting' sets the scale and mobilizes the right kinds of relations. In other words, as explained by Lisa Gitelman and Virginia Jackson, numbers became numerical data through 'framing', by materializing and making tangible a context of air pollution which can be translated into the measurement setting, even if this ultimately involves taking away that context in the process of stabilizing data:

> Data too need to be understood as framed and framing; understood, that is, according to the uses to which they are and can be put. Indeed, the seemingly indispensable misperception that data are never raw seems to be one way in which data are forever contextualised – that is, framed – according to the mythology of their own supposed decontextualisation. (Gitelman and Jackson 2013: 6)

I have exemplified these framing practices in detailing the making of modelled and monitored data, where the transformation of a numerical reading to data relies on a number of different kinds of relations and attachments – from assemblages of sensing, theories about reality, and disciplinary norms, to technologies of representing and communicating data. Data were epistemologically similar in the sense that they were something that could be understood by other researchers as the outputs of scientific work. Furthermore, their ability to act as 'other' meant they were also used to potentially shed light on the situated and contingent nature of data practices. Data also seemed to have currency in the project, with the capacity to extend research questions and the material and conceptual boundaries of the phenomena in question. Most significantly, however, data were framed by researchers as 'standing in' for phenomena (i.e. representations of air pollution). As such, there is something about data that shapes the ways in which the empirical and conceptual problem of studying a shared air pollution plays out. By thinking about data as a mode of doing interdisciplinary research – as a methodological device for all researchers on WHAP – data's material expression becomes paramount.

That there was no shared articulation of air pollution in the WHAP project meant a space was left open within which air pollution could be (re)configured. Indeed, as a result of the multiplicity of data on air pollution, just how data were materialized and expressed became a shared concern, both for myself and other researchers, so that the very practices, processes and materiality of making data were of empirical interest. That there were multiple ways in which air pollution was enacted through data practices meant that data were also a way to materially engage with different air pollutions. Data, then, overflow the observational conventions of scientific practice and also the observational and participatory conventions of ethnography. It was not that I was participating in data practices, but that my own data practices were being questioned, mobilized and reconfigured, primarily because other researchers also were not taking data as a 'natural given', and this was therefore becoming ethnographically challenging.

Experimenting with Data

Data were not only an everyday concern, but the material form through which the team communicated both with myself and other researchers. For example, the visualization of data, as maps of air pollutant concentrations across the UK, or time series graphs of observational and modelled results, produced a shared work space, where different articulations of air pollution through data could be considered together. Graphs also imply a singular world, and thereby making, contesting and revising maps a very explicit process of configuring a shared research world for studying air pollution. In a similar way, the boundaries of space took the form of the '5x5 km grid square' across different data practices, which functioned as the empirical, spatial contours within which air was to be studied and data of air pollution made.

Primarily, the way in which air pollution was experimented with was by making additional new data. This was done in two ways: first, by using small sensors, referred to as DIY instruments, which could be manually placed in particular locations to measure air pollution at particular points in time (on a smaller scale than monitoring stations); and, second, by comparing modelled and monitored data of air pollution in a statistical model. Both these new kinds of data practices experimented with air pollution in explicitly collaborative and interdisciplinary ways.

DIY Data and the Spatial Heterogeneity of Air Pollution

> Another area is variation of exposure within grid square, and that's only something our additional measurements could get some sort of handle on, and to examine ways in which variations of days with high Ozone vary within a grid square ... But still it is possible to get an idea of the magnitude of variability and whether anything in particular drives this so that we could do something more systematic about what's going on within a grid square.
>
> —PI, liaison meeting, 2 April 2012

The collection of 'DIY measurements' by the environmental chemists (in close liaison with the modellers and epidemiologists) was a way to generate multiple and more sensitive measurements of air pollution than those made by the model and the monitor. These additional measurements were used as a way to understand air pollution and its heterogeneity within the spatial remits materialized by the modelled and monitored data. DIY instruments were manually placed at particular spatial and temporal points within a specific geographical area, with the purpose of providing information on the air pollution that monitors and models were not measuring – its spatial heterogeneity.

The DIY instruments function in a similar way to the monitors, by measuring the absorption of a pollutant on a gauze soaked in a special chemical mixture, placed at the top of the tube. In a monitoring station this is measured by UV light, in DIY data practices it is measured in the laboratory.

This experiment took place in one city in the UK, and involved taking lots of measurements of air pollution at different points in time and space. This was aided by a process called 'conditioning', which involved the use of an open source software tool (analysing air) to 'characterize the data further'. The tool enabled the modelled data, monitored data and DIY data to be compared together as a way to produce a multiple-data graphic of air pollution.

The new data enabled the comparison of modelled and monitored data by expanding the empirical detail and material form of air pollution as a research object. The process highlights the different informational value that data offer, but also their material intervention in the process of working out what air pollution is. The DIY data were a way to get a sense of air pollution beyond the spatial and temporal remits of the modelled and monitored data. In this way, experimenting offered purchase on data practices as well as expanding the material contours of air pollution research.

Statistical Data on Modelled and Monitored Data

A second way that modelled and monitored data were experimented with was through the making of statistical data from other data by the epidemiologists on WHAP. By running a statistical model on Excel, using old modelled and monitored data sets, new data on air pollution were made. There are about ninety monitoring sites in the UK, which means there are only a few locations where you can directly compare monitored data with modelled data.

Comparing these old sets of modelled and monitored data was a way to work out whether the model or monitor produces better data according to statistical values of confidence and error. By measuring the error in modelled and monitored data, a new data set was made with error statistically removed. These statistically 'true data' were used as a reference to judge modelled and monitored data's ability to measure air pollution in spaces where humans breathe, as error affects how the health effects of air pollution are measured (Garnett 2016).

The new 'data of data' were the material means by which the epidemiologists came to anticipate and evidence error on their own terms. In this way, experimenting with data in the statistical model enabled the extension of what data can do and mean beyond that of the on-site production of modelled and monitored data. Error was re-represented in Excel, only to become a particular component of a formula through which it can subsequently be statistically removed. These statistical practices shifted the focus from what was talked about as a problem of representation, to the material means by which a statistical solution could then be generated in order to frame data in a way that would enable health claims to be made. In this way, the statistical data of data were able to intervene in the modelled and monitored data tension, articulating air pollution in a new, locally contingent way.

Multiple Data and the Making of a Singular Air Pollution

> The epidemiologists suggest using both modelled and monitored data according to the results of the simulation study and DIY data. This would mean using modelled data for some pollutants and monitored data for others. ... Modelled and monitored data are juxtaposed in a table showing the simulation study results as a visual comparison and a means to distinguish which data should be used for which pollutants.
>
> —Team meeting, 13 June 2013

It was suggested that the epidemiological data practices would become the hybrid space where different data could be used for different pollutants in separate analyses. This would be a way to produce data on air pollution and health whilst avoiding ontological anxiety. The DIY data and the statistical data were both situated as part of an emergent interdisciplinary space. These were characterized by collaborative attempts of interdisciplinary coherence, explicitly responding to non-local values and recognizing the practical, material demands of data's reuse within the wider project. This work of experimenting brought modelled and monitored data into new fields of practice, where their informational and relational capacities could be balanced in relation to a collaborative affective sensibility.

Subsequent to these productive practices of experimentation, a physical team meeting was organized involving all the scientists and the types of data made and used by WHAP. The meeting made an interdisciplinary response and materially articulated a shared air pollution. Primarily, the tension was reduced to one kind of pollutant: very fine particulate matter ($PM_{2.5}$):

> Recent epidemiological studies have indicated that smaller particles and their components derived from combustion sources (i.e. $PM_{2.5}$) are principally responsible for cardiovascular hospitalisations, and this is methodologically relevant because $PM_{2.5}$ is internally heterogeneous, and 'there are lots of processes we don't know until they are simulated', which means monitored data becomes redundant. (PI, Team Meeting, 13 June 2013)

What worked about $PM_{2.5}$ was its internal heterogeneity, and therefore intrinsic multiplicity. Particulate matter is a pollutant defined by its size: a non-ambiguous material characteristic that does not rely on a situated understanding of atmospheric relations in order to determine its toxicity. Second, particulate matter is lots of kinds of particles, therefore giving scope and potential for both modelled and monitored data to contribute to its representation. Third, there is scientific consensus around its related negative health effects. Most significant, however, is that the computer model is the only method of measuring $PM_{2.5}$ because the monitor data does not distinguish between particles over 10 micrometres (PM_{10}) in diameter and those 0.25 micrometres in diameter ($PM_{2.5}$). $PM_{2.5}$, then, carried wider meaning in terms of the configuring of new relations between air pollution and health as an epidemiological object of concern, whilst also appealing to the particular research interests of the atmospheric chemists, and the technical and theoretical potential of their model.

The role $PM_{2.5}$ played in the material negotiations between the modellers and the epidemiologists demonstrates a shift from a discourse of representation to the making of air pollution with data. The particulars of data as 'kinds of air pollution' became the object around which the different interests of the epidemiologists and the modellers could be accommodated. The DIY data and the statistical data of data did not directly contribute to this new articulation of air pollution, because neither data practice produces comparative data on $PM_{2.5}$. Yet, these experimental data forms did facilitate the process of coordination because they enabled researchers to do more than simply share data. Extending beyond epistemic relations, the 'DIY data' and 'statistical data' intervened in the tension around what data to use, and therefore the kind of air pollution to study. Through these experimental negotiations the tension altered in form and focus, so that researchers were engaged in working out what kind of air pollution to study rather than what data to use. By foregrounding the multiplicity of air pollution, and taking seriously different data practices, air pollution was enacted in new ways. The intervening data enlivened and materialized data in ways that engaged with difference, so that difference was not just made to 'hang together' – and a new configuration of the research object emerged as a result.

Composing a 'Common Air'

As Fortun's study of environmental information systems suggests, information is playing an increasingly performative role:

> Setting up comparison or connecting bits of information previously unrelated performs cultural work. So do click throughs. Zooming in and out, learning to consider the implications of scale involves what Antonio Gramsci termed 'elaboration', the labour of working out common sense. This kind of labour can't be reproductive. It involves a play of signs and systems that is always unsettling. (Fortun 2012: 322)

The on-going and heterogeneous process of generating information about the environment also points to the possibilities for its reordering and revisualization. In light of the non-humanist materialities emphasized in recent science studies research, however, I argue that Fortun's focus on information technologies also highlights the performance of natures-cultures which make up interfaces between phenomena of research, science and politics. Indeed, new technologies and ways of collecting and using information means considering the ways in which the material qualities (Barad 2003; Ingold 2007) of phenomena play out in different actions and interactions.

During the WHAP team meeting the experimental data took centre stage, and their visualization in graphs and tables configured a collaborative research space. Both these practices of experimenting with data – the DIY data and the statistical data of data – meant the research object, air pollution, could be set in motion and reconfigured. Data were an effect of certain forms of socio-material relationships that we could call collaboration. Air pollution was always in emergence rather than a singular, stable or tangible thing, and data were thereby a means to move with and through these relational practices and processes. As a result, different versions of air pollution were mobilized by the WHAP scientists – in the form of material traces, numbers and graphics – and their transformation into different data were the moments when multiplicity was also articulated.

By producing ethnographic data on making and intervening with multiple data I was able to trace how difference emerges, and thereby make symmetrical the multiplicity of air pollution in practice. The work of experimenting with data was a way to trace the unfolding of the interdisciplinary tension, and also 'slow down' (Stengers 2011) my own research practices. As a result, rather than focus only on the network of relations that materialize a stable research object, I have foregrounded the experienced, playful and affective dimension of these. I have also developed my own analysis of science in action, alongside the researchers on WHAP. Making data of air pollution were situated practices, but during modes of experimentation these entanglements became collaborative processes that extended along the multiplicity of data practices comprising WHAP.

De la Cadena claims that it is the visibility of hybridity that leads to potential awareness of our analytical categories as equivocations. Researchers were actively working with different articulations of air pollution, and these were made explicit during experimental practices and the unfolding of the interdisciplinary tension. The multiplicity of air pollution in data practices was a finding that led researchers to explicitly bring difference to the fore, as an active component of interdisciplinary knowledge making. The process of translation through data for the researchers on WHAP is productive along similar lines to those described by de la Cadena. By acknowledging the difference between particular enactments of air pollution, a view of these different research worlds materialized that changed the definition of the tension analytically: from one about epistemology to one with ontological dimensions. Moreover, experimenting extended the empirical and conceptual remit of air pollution as a research object, so that studying it became more than a process of stabilizing a relationship between an instrument and an air sample, and ultimately involved reflecting on, acting with, and reconfiguring that very relationship. This was a process that involved reconstituting modes of making data and therefore enabled new articulations of air pollution.

Experimenting with Data as an Anthropologist

Experimenting with data was, then, a material and conceptual process of testing the capacities of data to generate new articulations of air pollution. If air pollution is 'equivocation', experimenting with data was the means by which different air pollutions were brought together and partially aligned. Following data and experimental practices was not only a way to study the material work of interdisciplinary knowledge production, but an empirical process of coming to sense and appreciate the reflexive work and care[6] that 'sharing data' and interdisciplinarity entail. This is perhaps something anthropologists can learn from, where the affective labour and sensibilities that underpin collaborative ways of doing and knowing are managed and coordinated rather successfully through material, practical work.

Part of this tentative process of configuring a shared air pollution meant that my own fieldwork practices shifted and adapted too. As I have already suggested, my research intervened in the research process. I contributed to the multiplicity of data practices on WHAP, making lateral relations between different data in my own data practices. The material work of studying air pollution through data also destabilized my role as an anthropologist. In many ways, my role as anthropologist was made obsolete, as other researchers on WHAP did their own ethnographic fieldwork and reflexively sought to understand and work with epistemological and ontological differences in analytical and empirical ways. This has been referred to as para-ethnography (Marcus 2013) – situations where the anthropologist and informant are difficult to distinguish in any epistemic sense. By thinking with this notion of experiment, I suggest that para-ethnography can also be understood as the mutual study of world-makings.

I have re-narrated this shift from epistemology and ontology through tracing my ethnographic encounter with data. For example, when data's form and meaning were contested in their movement to other practices I came to appreciate data as air pollutions, rather than, say, representations of the phenomena in question. Following data required me to take data seriously as forms that have the capacity to overflow their own material and conceptual contours. As such, data had a multiplying effect, as emergent articulations of air pollution (as both material and conceptual processes) they were not necessarily the outcome of scientific working but constitutive of it. Such an experimental mode of ethnographic engagement can be understood as more fluid, as an emergent set of relations between scientists, non-human forms, the material arrangement of research settings and ethnographer. Becoming a part of these experimental moments meant that, for example, it was the very instruments and sensing practices that also became key informants (Traweek 1988). This enabled me to pose new kinds of questions – about the nature of interdisciplinary inquiry and the kind of anthropological knowledge I was making as a result.

I extend the notion of para-ethnography to incorporate the embodied and material dimensions of working across difference, and to take seriously others' ways of doing research and intervening in research worlds. As a result, I was not producing an account of a particular viewpoint, of the modellers or the epidemiologists, but was enfolded in the tension, as a component of doing interdisciplinarity. I was reliant on the capacity of data and experimenting with data to make visible the kinds of human and non-human relations that formed my ethnographic sites. In order to consider data as different kinds of 'things' required me to focus, for example, on the material and affective negotiations by which data is stabilized and made meaningful in practice. It was the careful work of moving and using data in particular ways that led me to appreciate the labour of balancing multiple interests and expectations in a large, multi-sited research collaboration.

Nonetheless, the data I produced was often less tangible than the moving of digital data sets from software to software and their visualized form in graphs and tables like those generated by my co-collaborators. I did, however, often re-represent these and make them visible in my own data, as ethnographic subjects in their own right. Researchers also engaged with my narrative accounts of the research process. Indeed, on sharing an ethnographic account of the emergence of the modelled and monitored data tension with the team, several researchers argued that it was not 'a tension' but 'a debate', an ongoing dialogue between different fields of practice rather than something fundamentally problematic. Another team member suggested that I had perhaps 'over-emphasized the tension'. Indeed, researchers were not interested in accentuating the tension but rather focused on ways of managing and resolving it, in very practical ways. This resonated with my experience of research meetings, where discussions were not often framed as epistemological but as processes of an ongoing practical achievement.

In this particular ethnographic case of interdisciplinary research in action, the ethnographer's view is no more 'other' than those of the different scientists. I have shown that the multiple ways of enacting air pollution were not treated in opposition to each other, but as an empirical reality of studying a fluid and indeterminate material formation. The concept of equivocation highlights the ways in which scientists on WHAP treated data of air pollution(s) as different things rather than different perspectives. As such, the anthropological knowledge I gained on air pollution as equivocation was part of this process, which mobilized the circuits (via data) between partially existing worlds (different fields of scientific practice), without placing one discipline (and its data practices) over and above another.

Conclusion

Although air pollution was framed as a complex problem that required multiple disciplines to study and respond to it, in practice I found air pollution was not revealed further through bringing different perspectives together. Rather, air pollution was configured in new ways through interdisciplinary working. I have focused specifically on the experimental questions that multiple kinds of data enable in interdisciplinary research, because it was the very stability of what counts as 'scientist', 'instrument', 'air pollution' that was under negotiation. 'Experimenting with data' was a mode of collaborating shaped by a set of institutional and disciplinary arrangements, but it was also the very shape that material work took. It was the arrangements of data, rather than individual scientists, for example, that enabled the posing of new questions. In accordance with Stengers, it was the work with data that allowed data to 'speak' in particular ways and thereby intervene in, and ultimately coordinate, the multiplicity of air pollution as a research object. Building on the Fitzgerald and Callard's notion of interdisciplinary assemblages, I offer an account that is more materially imbued. It was the multiple data-instrument relations, and how these effect and affect one another, that have come into play in my ethnographic narrative.

The concept of experiment is useful for an anthropological approach to interdisciplinary knowledge making, because it offers a material means of ethnographic engagement whilst bringing to the fore the practical ways in which frictions are managed and harnessed in productive and creative ways. Rather than taking data as the outcome of interdisciplinary working, practices with data were also moments when non-representational modes of knowledge making emerged. Thus, although I focused on the explicit material work of by-passing tensions, this was based on the careful management of maintaining research relations and by taking seriously others' ways of knowing, even if this meant working in more-than-disciplinary ways. These experimental data practices were where the materially informed sensibilities productive for interdisciplinary working played out, which often get silenced in normative, epistemological accounts of interdisciplinary knowledge production. Experimenting with data made multiplicity tangible, and therefore emergent forms that could be engaged with by different researchers. So, although different data and different air pollutions were the initial problem, they also formed the basis through which a (temporary) collaborative and compositional approach to air pollution was achieved.

Acknowledgments

Special thanks to researchers on the WHAP project, whose patience and support made this research possible. Thanks also to Judy Green, Catherine Montgomery and Simon Cohn for guidance during the course of the PhD on which this work is based, and to Tomás Sánchez Criado and Adolfo Estalella for their insightful comments on earlier versions of this chapter. Fieldwork for this research was supported by the Natural Environmental Research Council, UK. Financial support for the writing of this chapter was provided by the Foundation for the Sociology of Health and Illness. Ethical approval was granted by the London School of Hygiene & Tropical Medicine Ethics Committee.

Emma Garnett (King's College London) is a postdoctoral research associate at the School of Population Health and Environmental Sciences, King's College London. Her research sits between Social Anthropology and Science and Technology Studies, with interests in air pollution science, urban public health and body–environment relations. She recently held a postdoctoral fellowship at the London School of Hygiene & Tropical Medicine, and has published on the topics of interdisciplinary research, 'Big Data' practices and post-human approaches to global health.

Notes

1. All names are pseudonyms.
2. The senior researchers on WHAP had worked together previously on various research projects, and throughout the WHAP project they successfully received further collaborative grants.
3. Mol looks at the day-to-day diagnosis and treatment of atherosclerosis to examine the ways in which the disease is made to cohere through a range of tactics including transporting forms and files, making images, holding case conferences, and conducting doctor–patient conversations.
4. 'Equivocation' is a concept coined by anthropologist Viveiros de Castro to make the case for the contribution of 'Amerindian Perspectivism' to

anthropological theory. He argues that anthropology's defining problem consists less in determining which social relations constitute its object, and much more in asking what its object constitutes as a social relation: 'In this sense, perspectivism is not relativism as we know it – a subjective or cultural relativism – but an objective or natural relativism – a multinatural-ism' (Viveiros de Castro 2004b: 6).

5. The term 'epis' was the shorthand name used to refer to the epidemiologists on WHAP.
6. Maria Puig de la Bellacasa envisions care as an ethico-political issue for 'ways of knowing', where theories and concepts have ethico-political and affective effects on the perception and refiguration of matters of fact and socio-technical assemblages (Puig de la Bellacasa 2011: 87).

References

Barad, K. 2003. 'Posthumanist Performativity: Toward an Understanding of How Matter Comes to Matter'. *Signs* 28: 801–31.

Choy, T. 2012. 'Air's Substantiations', in S.K. Rajan (ed.), *Lively Capital: Biotechnologies, Ethics, and Governance in Global Markets*. Durham, NC and London: Duke University Press, pp. 121–55.

de la Cadena, M. 2010. 'Indigenous Cosmopolitics in the Andes: Conceptual Reflections beyond "Politics"'. *Cultural Anthropology* 25: 334–70.

de la Cadena, M., et al. 2015. 'Anthropology and STS: Generative Interfaces'. *Hau: Journal of Ethnographic Theory* 5: 437–75.

Fitzgerald, D., and F. Callard. 2014. 'Social Science and Neuroscience beyond Interdisciplinarity: Experimental Entanglements'. *Theory, Culture & Society* 32: 3–32.

Fortun, K. 2012. 'Biopolitics and the Informating of Environmentalism', in S.K. Rajan (ed.), *Lively Capital: Biotechnologies, Ethics, and Governance in Global Markets*. Durham, NC and London: Duke University Press, pp. 306–29.

Fujimura, J. 1992. 'Crafting Science: Standardized Packages, Boundary Objects, and "Translation"', in A. Pickering (ed.), *Science as Culture and Practice*. Chicago, IL: University of Chicago Press, pp. 168–211.

Gad, C., C. Bruun Jensen and B. Ross Winthereik. 2015. 'Practical Ontology: Worlds in STS and Anthropology'. *NatureCulture* 3: 67–86.

Galison, P. 1996. 'Computer Simulations and the Trading Zone', in P. Galison and J.D. Stump (eds), *The Disunity of Science: Boundaries, Contexts, and Power*. Stanford, CA: Stanford University Press, pp. 118–157.

Garnett, E. 2016. 'Developing a Feeling for Error: Practices of Monitoring and Modelling Air Pollution Data'. *Big Data & Society*. Available from https://doi.org/10.1177/2053951716658061.

Gitelman, L., and V. Jackson. 2013. *Raw Data is an Oxymoron*. Cambridge, MA: The MIT Press.

Ingold, T. 2007. 'Materials against Materiality'. *Archaeological Dialogues* 14: 1–16.

Knorr-Cetina, K. 1981. *The Manufacture of Knowledge: An Essay on the Constructivist and Contextual Nature of Science*. Oxford: Pergamon Press.

———. 1999. *Epistemic Cultures: How the Sciences Make Knowledge*. Cambridge, MA: Harvard University Press.

Law, J. 2004. *After Method: Mess in Social Science Research*. London: Routledge.

Marcus, G. 2013. 'Experimental Forms for the Expression of Norms in the Ethnography of the Contemporary'. *Hau: Journal of Ethnographic Theory* 3: 197–217.

Mol, A. 2002. *The Body Multiple: Ontology in Medical Practice*. Durham, NC and London: Duke University Press.

Puig de la Bellacasa, M. 2011. 'Matters of Care in Technoscience: Assembling Neglected Things'. *Social Studies of Science* 41(1): 85–106.

Rheinberger, H.J. 1994. 'Experimental Systems: Historiality, Narration, and Deconstruction'. *Science in Context* 7: 65–81.

———. 1997. *Toward a History of Epistemic Things: Synthesizing Proteins in the Test Tube*. Stanford, CA: Stanford University Press.

Shapin, S., and S. Schaffer. 1985. *Leviathan and the Air-Pump: Hobbes, Boyle, and the Experimental Life*. Princeton, NJ: Princeton University Press.

Star, S.L. 2010. 'This is Not a Boundary Object: Reflections on the Origin of a Concept'. *Science, Technology and Human Values* 35(5): 601–617.

Star, S., and J. Griesemer. 1989. 'Institutional Ecology, "Translations" and Boundary Objects: Amateurs and Professionals in Berkeley's Museum of Vertebrate Zoology 1907–39'. *Social Studies of Science* 19: 387–420.

Stengers, I. 2005. 'The Cosmopolitical Proposal', in B. Latour and P. Weibel (eds), *In Making Things Public: Atmospheres of Democracy*. Cambridge, MA: MIT Press, pp. 994–1003.

———. 2011. 'Another Science is Possible! A Plea for Slow Science'. Inaugural lecture. Faculté de Philosophie et Lettres, Universite Libre de Bruxelles.

Traweek, S. 1988. *Beamtimes and Lifetimes: The World of High Energy Physicists*. Cambridge, MA and London: Harvard University Press.

Viveiros de Castro, E. 2004a. 'Exchanging Perspectives: The Transformation of Objects into Subjects in Amerindian Ontologies'. *Common Knowledge* 10: 463–84.

———. 2004b. 'Perspectival Anthropology and the Method of Controlled Equivocation'. *Tipití: Journal of the Society for the Anthropology of Lowland South America* 2: 3–20.

2

The 'Research Traineeship'

The Ups and Downs of Para-siting Ethnography

Maria Schiller

Introduction

In my training as a social anthropologist, participant observation was taught as the core methodology of social anthropology. In seminars, I learned about fieldwork, where researchers assumed that their interlocutors have different intellectual capacities to abstract and reflect than the anthropologist. However, these assumptions about the less powerful and silent subject have become increasingly criticized over the past years, culminating in new ideas about the directionality and the character of fieldwork relations.

My fieldwork as a 'research trainee' in municipal organizations in Amsterdam, Antwerp and Leeds in 2009–10 was an experiment for conceiving my role and my relationship with local officials in a less closed-ended way and for being open to different possible roles of researcher and researched, as well as for engaging with some of the obstacles to collaboration. Local officials today increasingly have an academic background and thus often have similar analytical capabilities to the ethnographer. In addition, their tasks are no longer only technical but often knowledge-based and creative. The capacities of my interlocutors open new possibilities of reflexive conversations about the issues at stake in a particular field. However, I will also show that, despite the similar capacities of my interlocutors, their roles and our relationships were far from uniform across the field sites. I will argue that we need a differentiated understanding of the contemporary anthropological field, which takes into account the organizational culture, individual self-conceptions of interlocutors and their position of power.

Being open to different relationships that emerged, and addressing my pre-conceptions of fieldwork relations, provided some challenges. In some instances, I caught myself trying to keep some distance or being unsure how close I could get to my interlocutors. As I was developing some more personal connections and becoming friends with some local officials, I also gained information about their private lives. Spending some time together during lunch breaks or free time in the evening and at the weekend, I was not only learning about professional issues, but also about problems with children, about separations from one's partner, about physical and psychological ill-nesses and burn-out, about issues with neighbours and about being an expat in the city. In a few situations, I also was open with them about my personal life, exchanging on my own career plans, future dreams, and personal situation. However, combining fieldwork and friendship was an 'ambivalent experience' (Coffey 1999) for me:

> I really enjoyed telling a little bit about my partner and family over lunch. As I was talking, I realized how draining this somewhat alien status as a participant observer within the team was. However, I also worried to what degree it was legitimate to discuss my personal affairs with them. How far can I be 'a professional researcher', while at the same time having a more personal relation with my research subjects? To strike this balance to date seems very difficult to me. (Fieldwork journal extract, Antwerp)

In one research relationship with one officer, who was pursuing an MA degree in tandem with his job, I also felt too much closeness was hampering my agenda of doing research. Being interested in my expertise as someone who had just written a PhD thesis, he repeat-edly tried to entangle me in social science discussions, and asked me whether I would be willing to discuss his MA thesis ideas with me. I was somewhat surprised, as I had not expected to find myself dis-cussing sociological theories or methodological approaches with my research subjects. In this case, it was not me trying to become closer to them, but the other way round, and my feelings were ambigu-ous. Although I enjoyed the discussion, I felt this was at some point coming too close, and I realized that this activity, while pleasant, did not serve the purpose of my research. I needed some distance and I tried to limit this exchange to a few instances. It however also made me reflect on the capacities of my research subjects – and the col-laborative potential of ethnography in contemporary organizations.

The following chapter engages with the evolving relationships and moments of collaboration between researcher and researched as an important element of the epistemic knowledge production in research fields, where interlocutors share similar capacities as the researchers. Introducing the research traineeship, I will argue that this method allows experimentation with para-ethnography, and engagement with the specific conditions for 'studying up' and 'sideways'.

From Participant Observation to Para-ethnography

As an undergraduate student of social anthropology, I learned that the ethnographic method has much to offer. Much of the existing literature and many of the anthropological methods of teaching reverberate the iconic work of Bronislaw Malinowski on fieldwork and 'participant observation' (Malinowski 1922). Ethnography, so the general argument goes, allows access to the mundane everyday knowledge and provides a sense of the polyphony in, and a rich description of, the field (Bate 1997: 1166), and it is meant to offer 'a new sort of truth' (ibid.: 1168). It communicates an impression of truly having 'been there' and the intense familiarity with the subjects and their ways of knowing (ibid.: 1163). Ethnography implies being intensely involved in the field over a period of time (Watson 2011: 206–7). It is self-immersed, longitudinal and reflexive (Bate 1997: 1151). It includes doing fieldwork, in which one tries to 'penetrate another form of life' and 'grasp the native's point of view', involving a variety of methods, such as participant observation, interviews, attending meetings, and document research (ibid.: 1152). The advantage of not only conducting interviews but also participant observation is evident, as Watson (2011: 211) argued. Participant observation is a research practice in which the investigator joins the group, community or organization being studied, as either a full or partial member, and participates in or observes activities, asks questions, takes part in conversations, and reads relevant documents (ibid.: 206). It is about getting close to human actions and social interactions in order to allow the making of more general statements about organizations and identities (ibid.: 205). Overall, this delineation very much reflects mainstream definitions of the method, which was also part of my own socialization as an anthropologist.

Since the 1980s, however, we also witness the re-evaluation of some of these traditional conceptions of participant observation and 'the anthropological subject'. Anthropologists often elect to study not only exotic others of faraway lands, but oddly familiar domestic others who might be cohorts at work or neighbours (Hirsch and Gellner 2002: 3). As some have argued, the context of a globalized and interconnected world, and of professionalized, expertise-based groups, provides a different context that calls for new ethnographic practices. Laura Nader (1974) for instance suggested 'studying up' in order to engage with people in power, with resources and privileges. Nader's approach aimed to understand social stratification and the linkages between different layers of society. The method of 'studying sideways', developed by Ulf Hannerz (1992), seeks to bring into view the peers of anthropologists, who work in related areas of expertise, and to discuss their professional networks. 'Shadowing' can then be a useful anthropological technique, as it allows one to closely follow individuals as they move within and outside of their organizations (Czarniawska-Joerges 1992). Moreover, Shore and Wright's (1997) proposition to 'study through' and to follow policy processes allows an analysis of the definition of problems and the decision making of policies. In the course of the chapter, I will show how these different dynamics of studying up, through and sideways have become relevant in the different field sites.

Interlocutors who have similar capacities to researchers provide different challenges as well as opportunities for relationships of the researcher and the researched, as Holmes and Marcus (2008) as well as Hannerz (1992) have argued. In the words of Holmes and Marcus, we are dealing with counterparts rather than 'others' – who differ from us in many ways but share broadly the same world of representations with us, and the same curiosity and predicament about constituting the social in our affinities (Holmes and Marcus 2005: 250). This differs decisively from conceptions of an anthropologist's research subjects as being less powerful and formally silent (Holmes and Marcus 2008: 85), and it diverges from the anthropologist's aim of getting as close as possible to the 'native's point of view' (ibid.: 92).

Observing these changed characteristics of the anthropologist's interlocutors, Holmes and Marcus posit the opportunity of collaboration between researcher and researched. Collaboration, according to Marcus, means 'to integrate the analytical capacities of our subjects to define the issues at stake in our projects and the means by which we explore them' (Holmes and Marcus 2008: 86). In order to capture this new reality, they developed the concept of 'para-site' or 'para-ethnography'. According to Holmes and Marcus, 'the para-ethnographic experiment is both to ask for and perform a kind of shared conceptual labour with our collaborator-subjects at key moments in ongoing projects of ethnographic research' (ibid.: 97). However, Holmes and Marcus have not provided much qualification when and how para-ethnography is possible, or with what results. By demonstrating the variety of responses to my presence as a research trainee in the three local state organizations, I argue that we need a differentiated conception of the 'para-site', as not all research sites provide the same opportunities for collaboration. I delineate the specificities of different research sites and the conditions that allow more or less collaboration.

The Research Traineeship

In my study, I investigated whether local administrative practices[1] in European cities reflect the purported shift of multiculturalism, a discourse that was quite dominant in the European political and public sphere in the first decade of the millennium. I was interested in how local state administrations and diversity officers in their everyday work appropriated and interpreted this new policy concept of diversity. To carry out participant observation in local administrations I made some particular choices in the ways in which I conceived my role and my relationship with my interlocutors, which I discuss below.

When preparing for my possible research stay in diversity departments of municipal authorities, one of my informants referred to it as 'a sort of traineeship, but for doing research'. This is how the notion of research traineeship emerged. Framing my stay as a 'kind of' traineeship made it intelligible to the officials who needed to approve my stay. It allowed them to translate my presence into something they were familiar with. Giving my stay a label that made sense to the officials was important. Adding the word 'research' made it clear that my purpose was primarily that of conducting research.

Given the rather closed character of bureaucratic organizations, my first challenge was to get access as a researcher. I established a first contact by way of approaching officials at international city network[2] events and through interviews. In these interactions, I enquired about the possibility of a research stay within the unit, and offered to carry out a small project in return. After I had discussed the general possibility of a research stay, I submitted a written research proposal to the head of unit, including the proposed length of stay (4–8 weeks in each city; the research took place in 2010–11), a short outline of my broad research interests and the purpose of the stay. The proposal announced my intended participation in the everyday work of the diversity unit, the carrying out of interviews with different team members, the idea of accompanying them to meetings and other activities, and the project in return. We also agreed on the allocation of one of the team members as a central intermediary with whom I could have a scheduled meeting once a week (even though in practice these meetings took on a more informal character in all cities). In two of the cities, this was the officer I had initially interviewed, and with whom I had already established rapport.

Once in the field, I spent 36–40 hours a week with the officers and participated in their everyday rituals and routines, such as making tea in the Leeds office, walking to the coffee machine in Amsterdam, and having collective canteen lunches in Antwerp. Just as outlined in the various handbooks on the ethnographic method (see, for example, Hauser-Schäublin 2003), I took part in meetings, all kinds of interactions in the open plan office, the representational activities of officers at public events, and the coordination activities with political representatives in my role as a participant observer. I also followed some of the officers whenever they invited me to come along or agreed that I could come along. I was 'shadowing' (Czarniawska 2007) them not in the sense of following each of their steps, but I tried to be present and take all opportunities that came up for accompanying individual officers. Given that my desk, in all three cities, was in the open office space, it was easy to be around and 'hang out'. It also allowed access to relevant documents through the computer system and shared folders, which I collected and analysed. I furthermore conducted problem-centred, semi-standardized interviews (Mayring 2002; Flick 2009) with nearly all team members. They provided the space and time for more in-depth initial conversations and allowed me to get to know each of them more individually. Canteen lunches and staff outings provided the space to interact outside of 'working hours' in a more casual atmosphere. As I became acquainted with the individual team members, some of them invited me to birthday parties, to after-work dinners and to weekend outings.

The weekly regular meetings with my main intermediaries turned out to be important moments of reflection on my observations. In Antwerp, these meetings would often happen over lunch, for example. In Amsterdam, my main intermediary and I usually met in the room of the coffee machine or by way of having walks along the canals around the block of the office. Moreover, in Leeds these regular 'intervisions' took place over lunches and during a weekend hike to which my intermediary had invited me. These meetings allowed me to collect additional explanations for things I had observed but not quite understood, and also to ask for additional contacts within the organization.

The project in return also became an important element of my research traineeships. I had defined them in collaboration with the head of unit and my main intermediary in the unit. The objective was to make my outsider perspective fruitful for them also, and to tailor a project that addressed a need or interest of the unit at the time. What I had not anticipated was that these projects would become crucial for gaining further insights into the position of the diversity unit within the municipal departmental structure, their relationships with local NGOs, and the atmosphere and internal cleavages within the teams. In the case of Antwerp, I carried out research on how other administrative departments perceived the diversity unit, which informed the reorientation of the unit's work focus. This meant that I could interview managers at different levels of the organization. In Amsterdam, I assessed the perception of the merger of two units into the diversity unit among unit members, and discussed my reflections in a general team meeting at the end of the research traineeship. Furthermore, I was involved in setting up forms of cooperation between the diversity units in Amsterdam and Rotterdam. In Leeds, I evaluated the perception of the municipality's reporting requirements by municipal NGOs and service providers. My report informed the future definition of relationships and requirements between municipality and local organizations.

This insider position and my conduct of projects 'in return', raise numerous questions about my position vis-à-vis my interlocutors and the ways in which we can characterize the emerging roles and relationships in fieldwork in contemporary Western organizations. As I will argue, my research traineeships turned out to be fundamentally different to classic participant observations, due to the specific conditions of contemporary local state organizations, and the capacities of the more strategic officials in these organizations. I can identify two crucial issues, which I wish to spend some time reflecting upon in the following section: the first is the way in which local officials positioned themselves vis-à-vis the researcher; the second is the interpretation of my role as a 'research trainee' in practice, and the possibilities for epistemic knowledge production in such a position. Analysing some of the unexpected situations and my often ad hoc responses to them, allows me to critically re-evaluate widely shared assumptions about participant observations and to think about the potential of collaboration in such 'para-sites'.

Local Officials as Para-ethnographers

In my research, many of the local officials interviewed pointed out that they had a social science degree and/or had worked in research before. They therefore said that they had a good idea of what ethnography was about, or what to expect in an interview. At the same time, these officials were also conscious and outspoken about their role as implementers of diversity policies and state power. Their role differed from mine, as one interlocutor emphasized. In his view, researchers can analyse the state and critically assess the ways in which the state develops its power through discourses and institutions, and by entertaining strategic relationships with some societal actors.

When interviewing public officers, some of them actively intervened in my research. For instance, one interviewee from the very outset reacted to each of my interview questions by querying the question and why I had asked it. This officer then made suggestions on how I could rephrase my question in order for her to give me what she thought would be a more interesting answer. Later in the interview, she told me about her own initial career as a sociologist, and I realized that her interventions were meant to signal to me her own expertise. In the case of another official, he asked me at the outset of our interview how my own research would improve the situation of ethnic minorities. He was strongly committed to challenging ethnic discrimination and was involved in many immigrant networks. When I answered by emphasizing possible indirect yet positive policy effects of social science research, but also conceding some of its limits, he challenged whether I had set the aim of my research high enough. He was convinced that research should have direct effects on the life chances of ethnic minorities.

My interlocutors clearly had the disposition and the motivation to inform my research. By aligning their own role (from official to researcher) in making suggestions for my potential engagement, the officials tried to 'participate sideways', emphasizing what we had in common rather than what differentiated us. This negotiation of our respective roles allowed for potential collaboration.

As we can see from some of these examples, local state organizations have an increasingly educated, internationally connected and mobile workforce, whose work is often strategic and evidence-based. This also means the interlocutors themselves have the capacity to reflect and analyse their situation in modern organizations, which facilitates challenging the old, highly problematic assumption in much anthropology about anthropologists' view of their own superiority. Their interlocutors in such a conception lack the capacity to abstract from their role and position.

Ethnographic research in state organizations and with bureaucrats provides an interesting case for discussing the conception of the relationship between ethnographer and interlocutor. If state officials and ethnographers have similar capacities, then we can expect a more direct influence from our interlocutors on the knowledge production, but we can also expect some ethical issues, as co-optation with government agendas.

Opportunities for Collaboration as a Research Trainee

Defining my fieldwork in terms of a 'research traineeship' facilitated my access to the field, but it also informed the knowledge production when I was in the field. My self-representation as a research trainee incorporated the idea of presenting me as an acceptable incompetent, as some handbooks on conducting ethnography suggest. 'When studying an unfamiliar setting, the ethnographer is necessarily a novice. Moreover, wherever possible they must put themselves into the position of being an "acceptable incompetent"' (Hammersley and Atkinson 1995: 79). Interlocutors often ascribe researchers a role, as Hirsch and Gellner remind us, and often it is the role of a student: 'It may be, however, despite the ethnographer's attempts to explain him- or herself, he or she continues to be slotted into the easily understood category of student, a role sufficiently close to the researcher's that it can conveniently be accepted; in many cases, of course, researchers actually are students' (Hirsch and Gellner 2002: 6).

The notion of research traineeship implies the ascription of a student category. However, since it is also a broad and vague concept, it also allows for some flexibility and open-endedness in terms of what role I would acquire. Sometimes trainees can achieve a more instrumental role in an organization, while at other times they remain mere observers and/or may even become a nuisance. My role in the field not only depended on the ways in which I presented myself, but also on the role that my interlocutors allowed me to play. Rather than knowing beforehand whether I would study up, down or sideways, the research traineeship left it up to the interaction with the diversity officers, and together we would define my role. After the first day in the field in Leeds, I wrote the following in my fieldwork journal:

The team head, who was clearly leading the meeting and who did most of the talking, brought up my presence at the very start. She asked every team member to give a short introduction of themselves. Yet she did not provide a space for me to present myself. I felt unsure whether or not I should speak, which would have meant interrupting her. Why didn't she provide that space? Did she think that I am not comfortable speaking in front of everyone? Should I have interrupted her?

I was clearly being slotted into the category of a student in Leeds, which was how diversity officers in Leeds made sense of my presence, as my fieldwork journal entry documents. On my first day in Leeds, my interlocutors gave me a day-by-day plan that they had compiled for me, which outlined what meetings and events I could participate in during my stay. Of course, there was still some leeway: I could organize the interviews with team members and my activities as I saw fit. I was first amazed and pleased by the amount of preparation that they had done for me and thought this was a great service and very helpful. Yet, I also realized that it was predefining where I was supposed to go and where they did not welcome my presence. This limitation became evident when, one afternoon, everyone in the team seemed to leave for a meeting that was not on my itinerary, without inviting me to come along. In my field journal, I noted:

> In the afternoon, suddenly everyone seemed to head to a meeting in the small meeting room. I was unsure if I could go there as well, as the meeting was not on my itinerary. When I approached the team head to ask if I could come along, she responded that they would be talking about something that they would prefer me not to take part in. Of course, I accepted, and I think that it is good that she was very clear about this preference. I am also glad that I asked, and did not just walk along, which could have resulted in a very awkward situation. I guess I could have anticipated this answer, but still, being left behind in the now empty open-plan office, I found it hard to deal with the feeling of exclusion that crept in. It made me reflect on the fact that my inclusion in the team is temporary and partial. These moments of exclusion, when the team protects some areas of knowledge and demarcates the boundary against me as an outsider, are intelligible but tricky to deal with.

It was an advantage that they perceived me as a student, legitimizing my presence in the team, and facilitating my access to meetings and the organization of interview – but it also felt limiting. It made it very difficult to create a situation where reciprocity was possible: I was given information because I was meant to learn, but I was not supposed to investigate too much into what was preconceived as non-relevant information for me. When the head of team introduced me without giving me the chance to speak for myself, I felt this under-mined my agency and created a hierarchy, putting me into a position of 'studying up'. Excluding me from the meeting reflected a strategy keeping me at a certain safe distance, making sure the researcher does not come too close or become too intrusive. As a result, I often felt in Leeds that I was perceived more as a student than a researcher. It therefore was difficult to access information that diversity officers had not planned to offer to me.

While this creation of a hierarchy between the officials and me, as the student, was present in the Leeds fieldwork, in Antwerp I felt from the very beginning that the officials accepted me as a temporary colleague. My main intermediary there was crucial in allowing me to attain this role, as she had recently completed her PhD and she was interested in engaging with her own organization from a researcher's perspective. The team respected her, and once she had introduced me to them, it was easy to build up relationships with the other team members. The feeling of sharing a similar mind-set and of being met with some trust from the outset clearly provided a very easy starting point for my research, and gave me access to many insider stories in the field. In one of the team meetings, the head of the team initiated a group exercise in interviewing. As some of the team members frequently had to interview people as part of their job and had reported some uncer-tainty as to how best to do this, they formed several working groups for the exercise and assigned me to one of these groups. It struck me that none of the team members mentioned my role as a researcher or the fact that I may have had some more experience with interviewing; instead, they accepted me as one of them. Therefore, I gave feedback to team members and received feedback from them, just as if I had been a member of the team. So in the case of Antwerp I could research sideways, and the interviewing exercise demonstrated a window of opportunity for exchanging information and feedback.

Their acceptance of me as a temporary colleague was not without challenges, however. Towards the end of my stay, the head of team asked me whether I would be willing to present my findings from my project to a high-level manager of the city administration, as he was in the process of deciding over the unit's future reorganization. I had interviewed many senior officials about their perception of the unit by then and had heard some positive and some not so positive accounts of the diversity unit and its importance for the local orga-nization. My project and its findings had suddenly acquired central strategic value, as plans to reorganize the unit arose. The fact that the team asked me to present to their manager on such a sensitive question, without having an idea of my findings, demonstrated again that they saw me as a sort of insider and as someone to trust. I became very conscious of the weight of my words. Should I be talking as a researcher, who presents whatever the findings were? Alternatively, should I be talking as someone from the team, taking the interests of my temporary colleagues into account? I could resolve my conflict by first presenting my findings to some of the team members, to see their reaction to my assessment, and only then deliver my presentation to the manager. While everything worked out well, it became clear to me that combining different roles could create some conflicts of loyalty, as my presentation could potentially have worked to the detriment of the unit.[3]

In Amsterdam, my interlocutors defined my role again very differently. In my first conversation with my main intermediary, he drew a clear boundary between the logic of being an official and that of a researcher. He repeatedly posited a fundamental difference in the aim of our work: while researchers could always question underlying paradigms, policy officials needed to decide on the nature of problems and then come up with some possible solutions. He also was very critical of initiatives in which research and policy link up. This boundary making was a constant element in our interactions over the following weeks, and I sensed that slotting me into the category of 'researcher' was an important way for him to negotiate my presence. In his view, I was not of too much use to him in terms of getting work done, but I was pleasant to chat with and could bring in an outsider perspective. My chance of getting a role was thus limited to becoming a welcome addition to the social interactions he had at work. I was at first somewhat puzzled by what I felt was a rather delimiting view on our respective roles, but as long as it did not prevent him from interacting with me, I could accept this stark differentiation. I conceive this as 'studying across', given the emphasis of dialogue based on similar capacities but across different roles and work logics. However, at the end of my research stay, there was one situation when my ascribed role was destabilized and a window of opportunity for studying sideways occurred. I had presented some of my initial findings from the project, in return for which I had interviewed different team members on their impression of the team dynamic after a merger of two separate units. After the presentation, I wrote the following in my field journal:

> He emphasized that my presentation had given him a lot of food for thought. He said he was impressed by the depth of my understanding of

what is at play in the unit. Suddenly he seemed to understand what my research was about, and he acknowledged that I had been able to capture their reality in a way that, being 'inside', they often felt hard to capture. However, when responding that I was glad and thankful for his feedback, he was quick to emphasize that of course this is not going to contribute directly to their work. It was only interesting from a broader perspective. So he immediately returned to his clear separation of the logics of policy work and research, a paradigm that I think has strongly informed the way he has perceived my role. It can also be seen as an exercise of power, that he wanted to keep control of what he sees as his professional boundaries, which I guess is fair enough.

But at the end of our conversation, he did suggest that maybe we could together conceptualize a workshop at an international conference of researchers and practitioners they were organizing. Even though we never implemented this idea, a short window of opportunity had opened for a potential collaboration.

From these experiences, I can identify three findings on the potential of going beyond participant observation and entering into a more collaborative mode of ethnographic work in para-sites.

My first finding is that officials adjusted their own roles when they saw fit. My interlocutors shifted, for instance, from their role as an official into the role of a researcher or a role of an activist. The performance of these different roles highlights a practice of consciously shifting positionalities as research subjects in order to inform the research in specific ways. It opened a window of opportunity for collaboration as fellow researchers or fellow activists.

My second finding is that I was not necessarily free to define my role in the field, but that I was ascribed a role. Thus, the concept of a research traineeship allowed the definition of my role and relationships to become an interactive and flexible process. A different category was foregrounded in each of the cities: as 'student', I was studying up in Leeds; as 'temporary colleague' I was studying sideways in Antwerp; and as 'researcher' I was studying across in Amsterdam. There were some moments when the dominance of one category was destabilized, as I have demonstrated with the example in Amsterdam. The three field sites thus provided very different opportunities for collaboration due to the different roles my interlocutors allowed me to play in each of these sites.

My third finding is that with my 'research traineeships' in the professionalized context of municipal organizations, I embarked on a 'fieldwork experiment', since I conceived of the openness of my roles and relationships in the field as an element of my research design. I have been reflecting on this experimental character of my fieldwork, trying to make sense of my experiences and interactions. Through the research traineeship, I was able to make the ascription of different roles an element of what I observed. Indeed, the ways that my interlocutors slotted me into one or other category became an important aspect of my findings. The ways in which my main intermediaries made sense of my role and assigned me roles revealed important information about their self-conception as bureaucrats, their own power positions and local organizational cultures.

In Antwerp, where I acquired the role of a temporary colleague, my intermediary had a very similar background to my own, having recently completed a PhD at a British university, and also had a strong understanding of what I was doing and why I was asking certain questions. As such, she was very much a 'peer'.

In Amsterdam, my intermediary was a more senior official, who had worked as a manager in the arts sector before joining the city a few years ago. At the time of my research he was operating in a climate of strong pressures on the department from politicians. He clearly emphasized the differences between us, highlighting the freedom of researchers to keep asking questions without needing to provide practical answers. Our relationship shifted over the course of the fieldwork, from studying across to studying sideways, and back again to studying across.

In Leeds, the relationship with my intermediary was again different, as I had acquired the role of a student in the field, and so was studying up. The case of Leeds stuck out with the clear hierarchies within the city council, which I saw reflected in our relationship.

Differentiated Para-sites

The research traineeship revealed to me the shared analytical capacities with my interlocutors, who could easily themselves switch into the logic of a researcher and were eager to inform my own research from their individual perspectives. However, the potential to collaborate differed across para-sites.

In my fieldwork, I was able to collaborate in some situations. This was the case when I sat together with my interlocutors to discuss the possible project of return that I could carry out for them. I experienced other moments of collaboration when I exercised interview techniques with my interlocutors and provided feedback on the position of the diversity units in Antwerp, and when being invited to conceive of a workshop in Amsterdam. However, I have also shown that the different contexts of diversity departments in Amsterdam, Antwerp and Leeds provided different para-sites and different positions that I was able to take vis-à-vis my interlocutors, sometimes defining our relationship in more collaborative terms, and on other occasions confining my research to a more conventional participant observation. The research traineeship method allowed me to experiment with my role as a researcher, and my interlocutors actively negotiated my role in the research.

My experiment of research traineeships in state organizations can serve to develop the nuances of the notion of para-sites and para-ethnography. While Holmes and Marcus's proposal of para-ethnography suggests that the optimal way to do fieldwork in expert sites is by collaborating, my fieldwork demonstrates the possibility that collaboration also depends on our interlocutors, and the possibilities may differ from one context to another. The 'research traineeship' illustrates the opportunities and challenges of para-sites, as sometimes I was studying up, sometimes across and sometimes sideways in the diversity departments. As I have shown above, collaboration was more complicated when my interlocutors made a clear differentiation between our respective roles, as was the case in Amsterdam and Leeds. Collaboration was most likely when I was able to study sideways, as was the case in the interactions with my interlocutors in Antwerp.

I suggested that research traineeships have some potential for defining an ethnographic stay in the field of modern organizations in ways that go beyond classic conceptions of participant observation. They are an experiment that provides a rather open and flexible self-definition of the role of the researcher, and leaves the interpretation of the researcher's relationships to the interactions in the field. The process of being ascribed a role in the field was itself an important element of my observations, and I found that I was often unable to determine whether I would study up, down or sideways. As I have illustrated with my own research experience in municipal organizations, interlocutors in modern organizations perceive us as learners, as allies, or as people to be kept at distance – in short, they take part in shaping our role and position in the field. Thus the researcher defines the role he or she wants to play in the field. By carrying out a 'research traineeship' one can leave one's own role sufficiently open and access and study state bureaucracies, which have rarely been studied from within, and tease out some moments when collaboration with local officials becomes possible.

 the

I started out from the question of what we could learn from contemporary ethnographies for the methodology of participant observation. Based on my own experiences of conducting participant observation in local state organizations, I can confirm that interlocutors in large modern organizations often have the capacity to make abstractions, to analyse and reflect. However, the three diversity departments in Leeds, Amsterdam and Antwerp provided decisively different para-sites, and my interlocutors differed in their positioning towards me and in their ascription of my role. This difference was due to the particularities of the position, image and way of working of these departments, as well as the individual self-images of diversity officers. This finding allows us to call for a differentiated understanding of para-sites, as officials with similar training and capacities did not all necessarily allow for cooperation. In order to arrive at a more nuanced concept of para-ethnography we need to take into account the different self-conceptions of our interlocutors, their different positions within organizational hierarchies, and the different organizational cultures in different field sites.

Maria Schiller (Max Planck Institute for the Study of Religious and Ethnic Diversity) is a postdoctoral research fellow at the Max Planck Institute for the Study of Religious and Ethnic Diversity, in Göttingen, Germany. She has published a monograph entitled *European Cities, Municipal Organizations and Diversity: The New Politics of Difference* with Palgrave Macmillan, and articles in peer-reviewed journals including *Ethnic and Racial Studies, Journal of Ethnic and Migration Research* and the *International Review of Administrative Sciences*. Maria holds a PhD in migration studies from the University of Kent and an MA in anthropology from the University of Vienna. In the past, she has held teaching positions in Germany, Austria and the UK.

Notes

1. City administrations installed diversity officers to implement newly introduced local diversity policies. This included the management of a range of projects, liaising with local civil society initiatives as well as with local politicians, and the administration of subsidy schemes.

2. I established these links by way of a traineeship at the Council of Europe, where I could attend several meetings of the Intercultural Cities Network, as well as through participation at meetings of the Eurocities Working Group on Integration.
3. This feeling of double loyalty is reminiscent of conceptions of 'anthropologists as spies' (Boas 1919).

References

Bate, S.P. 1997. 'Whatever Happened to Organizational Anthropology? A Review of the Field or Organizational Ethnography and Anthropological Studies'. *Human Relations* 50(9): 1147–75.

Boas, F. 1919. 'Scientists as Spies'. Letter to the editor, *The Nation*, 20 December.

Coffey, A. 1999. *The Ethnographic Self*. London, Thousand Oaks, CA and New Delhi: Sage.

Czarniawska-Joerges, B. 1992. *Exploring Complex Organizations*. Newbury Park: Sage.

Czarniawska, B. 2007. *Shadowing and Other Techniques for Doing Fieldwork in Modern Societies*. Copenhagen: Liber.

Flick, U. 2009. *An Introduction to Qualitative Research*. Thousand Oaks, CA: Sage.

Hammersley, M., and P. Atkinson. 1995. *Ethnography: Principles in Practice*. London: Routledge.

Hannerz, U. 1992. *Cultural Complexity: Studies in the Social Organisation of Meaning*. New York: Columbia University Press.

Hauser-Schäublin, B. 2003. 'Teilnehmende Beobachtung', in B. Beer (ed.), *Methoden und Techniken der Feldforschung*. Berlin: Reimer Verlag, pp. 37–58.

Hirsch, E., and D.N. Gellner. 2002. *Ethnography of Organizations and Organizations of Ethnography*. Oxford: Berg.

Holmes, D.R., and G.E. Marcus. 2005. 'Cultures of Expertise and the Management of Globalisation: Toward the Re-functioning of Ethnography', in A. Ong and S.E. Collier (eds), *Global Assemblages: Technology, Politics and Ethics as Anthropological Problems*. Malden, MA: Wiley-Blackwell, pp. 235–252.

———. 2008. 'Collaboration Today and the Re-imagination of the Classic Scene of Fieldwork Encounter'. *Collaborative Anthropologies* 1(1): 81–101.

Malinowski, B. 1922. *Argonauts of the Western Pacific*. New York: Dutton.

Mayring, P. 2002. *Einführung in die qualitative Sozialforschung: eine Anleitung zu qualitativem Denken*. Weinheim: Beltz.

Nader, L. 1974. 'Up an Anthropologist: Perspectives Gained from "Studying Up"', in D. Hymes (ed.), *Reinventing Anthropology*. New York: Random House, pp. 284–311.

Shore, C., and S. Wright. 1997. *Anthropology of Policy: Critical Perspectives on Governance and Power*. London: Routledge.

Watson, T. 2011. 'Ethnography, Reality and Truth: The Vital Need for Studies of "How Things Work" in Organizations and Management'. *Journal of Management Studies* 48(1): 202–17.

3

Finding One's Rhythm

A 'Tour de Force' of Fieldwork on the Road with a Band

Anna Lisa Ramella

'Is not experimentation … as fundamental to anthropological inquiry as
it is to the ways of life it seeks to understand?'
—T. Ingold, *Being Alive*

Introduction

This chapter deals with the experiences of a fieldwork on the move,
namely touring domestically and internationally with the band *Two
Gallants* from San Francisco. A music tour is a highly structured,
tightly paced endeavour in which fixed, assigned roles are at constant
interplay with yet to be negotiated functions and responsibilities.
Ostensibly stable entities – like music venues, stages, and the tour
van – are repeatedly being played on, equipped and constituted by
practices that are always partly subject to improvisation and experimentation. Yet a rigid tour schedule allows for few open arrangements, and the smallest ruptures can easily unsettle a functioning
mechanism – one that might need to be regularized in a period as
brief as that between a sound check and a show. I will describe this
specific form of travelling together with the metaphor of rowing
a boat, where a general movement is *determined by* as much as it
determines individual actions.

But what does it mean to carry out ethnographic fieldwork in a
context such as this one that is constantly negotiating itself? Before
joining the tour, I had prepared for participant observation and

armed myself with a video camera, hoping to engage visually and physically in a mobile field. Fitting an anthropologist into the boat, however, meant not only moving along and filming the repetitive actions that shaped the process of touring, but gradually learning to become part of this overall movement by finding my way into the structure – through my own camera practices. Studies on mobile methods have sought to find novel ways of studying people on the move (cf. Pink 2008; Büscher and Urry 2009); however, in this chapter I will not focus on methods or methodologies of studying mobility as such, nor on conducting visual research, but rather on coming to understand the linkages between the practice of touring and the practice of doing (visual) research on touring. Apart from a constant positioning of being an anthropologist and not a groupie, a journalist or a member of the crew, this ethnographic labour required the mobilization of my methods towards an experimental mode similar to what drives the endeavour of touring as such. Going beyond the negotiations of closeness and distance as discussed broadly for participant observation, getting involved in the overall rhythm meant experimenting with the practice of 'doing fieldwork' in relation to 'doing touring'.

Experimentation, as pointed out in Tim Ingold's epigraph, is part of the anthropological inquiry as much as it is, in this case, of touring. What I will develop in this chapter is how the practices on a music tour – on one hand prescribed, on the other experimental – and the practices of fieldwork find their way (or not) into an overall, collective rhythm. By ethnographically describing both the rhythmic practices of my counterparts as an empirical object, and my own rhythmic form of fieldwork, I will consider how sensitivity towards experimentation may be used to frame the process of 'rhyming along' with the band.

Beginning with the preparation of my fieldwork, which took over a year and included many attempts at communication, as well as several trips traversing Europe to schedule a meeting to plan my involvement in the tour, it became apparent that my interlocutors and I were not only used to different temporalities, but also had a different take on making arrangements. Here, a main discrepancy was that of the bureaucratic formalities researchers are subject to, such as funding application deadlines and the expectations of single-site research locations. These did not always mesh well with a yet-to-be announced tour schedule that would cover over thirty cities across Europe and the United States in less than two months, and would constantly be subject to alterations.

But also *during* this fieldwork, the effects of such movement became noticeable to me: I soon became a person who did not know where she was, or when and where she was going – something I had wondered about throughout my dealings with the musicians prior to touring. This fieldwork was a 'tour de force' in two ways: not only did it bring to light various aspects of extensive movement, but also of ethnography itself. By demanding to comply with a structure, a schedule, a rhythm, which is synchronously developed through experimentation, the fieldwork experiences conveyed similar struggles and ambiguities to touring itself. The presence and handling of my video camera finally helped me in this endeavour – though in a quite unexpected way.

Excessive touring, for musicians, has become crucial in order for them to be considered successful and economically sustainable; the band I travelled with had been on and off tour for a total of about fifteen years at the time of the fieldwork/tour, spending most months of each year on the road. This shows how tightly a music career is connected to mobility, and it can be considered a job where '[it] is no longer a question of being allowed or able but rather of *having* to be mobile' (Kesselring 2014: 8; emphasis added). I would even argue that musicians' lifeworlds could be related to all five 'mobilities', as identified by Büscher and Urry: travel of people, movement of objects, imaginative travel, virtual travel and communicative travel (Büscher and Urry 2009: 101).

Although, as Stith Bennett writes, '[m]usicians have always been travellers, and road musicians have always been auto-mobile' (Bennett 1980: 71), research on musicians has barely touched upon issues of movement, but rather focused on media and music (Mjøs 2012), as well as on music in relation to identity (Molitor and Pierobon 2014), image and travel (Ottosson 2009), and music scenes (Bennett and Peterson 2004) – not to mention music production (Bennett 1983) and the dynamics of becoming a musician (Bennett 1980). Existing research on touring, however, has much more examined the impact on identity (Nóvoa 2012), the diffusion of music, the means to convey a political message or the economies of music tours (see Johansson and Bell 2014: 314), rather than focusing on musicians as mobile actors; although musical jargon has a remarkable stance in the studies of routinized practices with regards to movement and mobility, terms such as 'rhythm' (Lefebvre 2004; Edensor 2010), 'beat' and 'orchestration' (Potts 2008), 'flow' and 'synchronization' (Edensor 2010), 'choreography' (Cresswell 2006; Haldrup 2011; Merriman 2011) and 'place ballet' (Seamon 1980) have rarely been applied to the mobile practices of musicians and performers themselves.

Work on mobility, on the other hand, has been dedicated to various aspects of mobile work (Clifford 1997; Urry 2000, 2007; Cresswell 2001, 2006; Larsen, Urry and Axhausen 2006; Sheller and Urry 2006; Elliott and Urry 2010; Salazar and Glick Schiller 2012; Kesselring 2014), to research in mobile contexts (Frello 2008; Pink 2008; Büscher and Urry 2009) and to the intersections of movement and place (Appadurai 1996; Massey 2007; Bærenholdt and Grånas 2008; Mazzullo and Ingold 2008; Ingold 2009, 2011; Kirby 2009; Cresswell and Merriman 2011; Harvey and Dalakoglou 2012) as well as of space, place and (mobile) media (Morley 2003, 2011; Cresswell 2004; Thrift 2006; Larsen, Urry and Axhausen 2006; Pink 2008; Elliott and Urry 2010; Moores 2012) but, again, it has mostly been ignored to consider musicians in relation to these aspects.

My research on touring musicians examines the practices developed for this particular form of mobility and seeks to contribute to anthropological work on media, place-making and a rhythmic structuring of practices in relation to music tours. By participating in such a radical form of travelling together during my fieldwork, I was able to experience how the imperative of moving along in order to anthropologically 'capture mobility' (Nóvoa 2012: 351) means not merely learning to travel, but being closely connected to becoming part of the dynamic constitution of touring. This may demand to move, but at times to be still, to know where to stand and how to speak, to learn when to leave and where to stay. A few months after the tour, I talked to the sound engineer of the band on Skype. 'You kind of had a difficult role', he told me. 'You somehow had a role, but somehow you didn't. For us you didn't. I mean, you weren't part of the crew or the band, nor were you one of our girlfriends.'

I was naturally meant to follow the same pace and conditions as the musicians, yet my presence did not serve a clear function within the tour as a whole. Being a 'sojourner of the "between"' (Stoller 2009: 4) in such an exhausting environment impacted my fieldwork in a way that transcended temporal, spatial and social realms, because knowing 'when to be where' was closely connected to knowing 'what to do'. In addition to the increasing exhaustion that everyone of us experienced, the search for a role within a system that has no apparent need, space or time for an extra person became a tiring challenge, having to go through multiple episodes of trial and error before I got my footing. At the essence of the process of trying to fit in lie various spatio-temporal experimentations, which I will frame as the conditions for reaching a sense of 'rhyming together'.

The first section of this chapter focuses on the specificities of touring as a fieldwork site 'on the move'. Then, demonstrating how daily life on tour is structured by a set of routinized practices and choreographic arrangements, I will attempt to unravel the interplay of rhythms – individual and collective, prearranged and unforeseen, personal and professional – as main determinants of travelling together. The musical performance itself, which obviously lies at the heart of every tour, will not be explicitly analysed in this chapter, but rather considered part of the overall chronology of events. I shall also address my own practices of 'doing fieldwork' as part of my effort to find a place within this tour, and elucidate the way 'learning to rhyme' has been crucial to the constitution of my research. Understanding how this form of travelling is a condensed example of situated mobile practices (for the musical performances as much as for the fieldwork methods of a researcher) allows reflection on how the disposition of certain skills may heavily influence the experience in the field, but also how this can be counteracted through one's own fieldwork practices. As a concluding note, I will refer to the particular relations of rhythm and place, and discuss how in highly mobile settings of travelling and working together, rhythm may even supplant the spatial and temporal metaphors that have been broadly used to describe mobilities.

Touring and Researching

A music tour is a field site with a number of particularities. It is a multi-local site that involves traversing fixed localities such as venues and hotel rooms, while moving in a van, which itself can be considered a stable yet mobile space. Drawing from Jirón's description of transient places, they 'involve those fixed spaces [that] people signify while moving through them' (Jirón 2010: 132). As part of a larger route, they must be considered through the lens of movement and paths (Morley 2000: 14; Massey 2007: 13; Ingold 2007: 2). Routines and repetitive practices are being developed and carried out 'in situ' throughout the course of a whole or many tours, actually contrasting the apparent transience of being 'in motion'.

Routes of a tour are usually planned out by a conjunction of the label, managers and booking agents, where the profit of tour histories will be combined with the mapping of financially sustainable drives (see also Johansson and Bell 2014: 316). The musicians themselves usually have little say in this process, though they can express preferences. It is not uncommon, as shown by my research, for the musicians to be unaware of the exact tour dates until a few weeks prior to departure. The route of a tour, however, is not only economically relevant, but fundamental to the experience within the van; to give an example, while the North American leg of the tour I participated in led us 16,000 km through the United States in a circular shape, the band's later tour throughout Europe rather resembled a zigzag line on the map, which proved to be even more exhausting for the members, as the singer Adam Stephens told me after a concert in Düsseldorf in November 2015.

Touring – and, therefore, moving spatially – is necessary for one of the main activities of a musician: performing live. In a phone conversation during a tour break, the drummer Tyson Vogel told me he was glad to be home for a while, but regretted that he would not be able to go to Europe anytime soon. In interviews, members of the band would insist on celebrating the fact of being able to do what they love, and therefore would not want to complain about their frequent travels.

Ottosson has given an interesting account on the 'touring discourse at home' of Australian aboriginal musicians (Ottosson 2009: 102), where the positive image of touring among friends often justified the occasional discomforts experienced when touring. My research relates that my interlocutors generally felt little understood by those at home, and therefore conversations on travel would mostly be held with other musicians and crews on tour. As Kesselring points out, 'the normalization [of being mobile] also appears as a "disenchantment" of the modern promise of mobility' (Kesselring 2014: 8). There are certain moments when touring can become a rather tedious experience, such as when one falls ill. When touring the United States prior to my fieldwork, Adam sent me an email in which he recounted: 'We're out on tour right now. I miss home. Tyson is really sick. Living the glamorous life of a traveling musician'. He was pointing out that touring is not all about having fun and seeing the world, but rather it can turn into a burden that disregards one's physical state.

Apart from being hard work, for some musicians touring is even seen as a threat to their physical and mental health. In a journalistic interview published in the *Guardian* (Britton 2015), various accounts of musicians deconstruct the notion of a romanticized version of travel, as for example singer Meredith Graves plainly notes: 'Being confined to the van for a 10-hour drive … You can't sleep, you can't move, you can't do anything. It's like a recipe for a breakdown for me'. However, among the musicians I have worked with, although they pointed out the struggles connected to their mobility, it was considered to be the price one pays for playing music; complaining about mobility was largely seen to be taboo.

Through a common friend, I had the chance to interview the French punk drummer Laurent Pataillot, who teaches at a music conservatory in part to prepare the music students for their future mobility. He showed me a presentation he uses in his talks in which he relates the success and flow of a tour to Abraham Maslow's (1943) 'Hierarchy of Needs' (see Figure 3.1) to underpin his statement about the lack of the fulfilment of needs on a tour.

If we consider the day-to-day of touring, Laurent told me, Maslow's pyramid is rather inverted: a combination of lack of rest, irregular meals and changing environments are the general components of a tour. Tensions that arise from these factors often compromise needs such as relationships and the achievement of one's full potential. On the other hand, attention and admiration reach their peak on stage almost every night.

Laurent's accounts draw out quite well the physical and social circumstances of a tour. If we were to apply this pyramid to anthropological fieldwork, we would rarely achieve any of the self-fulfilment or psychological needs while in the field – most of us are confronted

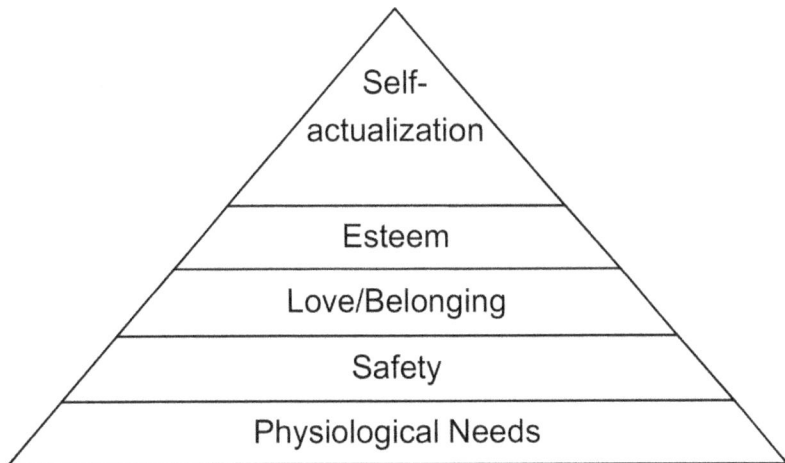

Figure 3.1 'Hierarchy of Needs' by Abraham Maslow (*A Theory of Human Motivation*, 1943). Image by Anna Lisa Ramella.

with struggles for roles and self-legitimization rather than noticing our accomplishments, which tend to appear only afterwards. As an anthropologist on a music tour, however, this only adds to the unfulfilled basic needs one is facing as much as everyone else in the van, thus making the pyramid, rather than inverted, simply a thin line. Ultimately, it is a 24/7 endeavour, where intervals of fieldnote writing, reflection and temporary distance from the field are close to impossible.

My fieldwork experience was impacted by this in a way that made me constantly feel as though I was running out of time or misusing my methods – while only afterwards realizing that for me, like for everyone else, the most crucial consideration was just to *exist* in these environments, and to simply keep 'rowing'. Touring itself became the method to go by, and learning to effectively tour from my own mistakes materialized some of the conditions underlying this endeavour – spatially, temporally, as well as socially.

Structuring and Experimenting

With regards to Edensor's description of 'mobile experiences of place and belonging [as] transient and fleeting' (Edensor 2010: 6), we may identify repetitive practices like the loading of the van or the setting of the stage as substantial moments of experiencing place on tour. Transient only in terms of being carried out at points of transition, which for a moment become fixed points before one moves on; fleeting, because they establish a scene for a short time before it is dismantled again by a reversion to the same practices.

However, we should keep in mind that 'claim[ing] that a certain activity is "mobile" can be seen as a performative act that constitutes what it names' (Frello 2008: 31). It certainly is problematic to call touring routines 'mobile' regarding the unclear contours of what is 'at the other end' (ibid.: 45). Rather than simply categorizing the practices as mobile activities themselves, they could be understood as determinants that 'structure' and 'fixate' a mobile undertaking.

There are very basic reasons for the spatio-temporal structuring of a music tour through a rhythmization of practices, even though it may mean giving up autonomous decisions. The timing on tour is generally determined by a schedule. On the tour I followed, a regular day began by meeting everyone at the van at some point between 9 and 11 a.m. to start driving towards the next city. The day would be spent driving, stopping along the way to get coffee and snacks, and switching drivers now and again. We would usually arrive at the venue around 4 or 5 p.m., and start loading equipment onto the stage. After set-up and soundcheck, we would have approximately one hour of free time (usually while the support band soundchecked and performed) before stage-time at 9 or 10 p.m. After the concert we would load the van, maybe have some drinks, and go back to the hotel to be in bed between 1 and 3 a.m.

There were six of us travelling together: two musicians, a sound engineer, a tour manager, a merchandise manager and myself. Each person in the van, except for me, had a prescribed role for the tour. The tour manager coordinated routes, accommodation and communication with the venues, assembling everyone at a fixed time at the van and usually leading the navigation to the next city. At the venue, all members unloaded the van and carried the equipment on stage. Once the instruments were on stage, each band and crew member would start unpacking the cases and assembling the contents. While in the early part of the tour some logistical arrangements would still be discussed, everyone would gradually allow their hands to dive into developed automatisms. Quickly and skilfully, fingers would slide over guitar cases, turn screws on the drums, move carpets, and stick plugs into microphones. The stage was now divided into small zones of apparent chaos, but it was obvious that hands, fingers and eyes moved in very predetermined ways, almost automatically.

Conversations were held through the sound of the individual practices; it seemed as if the repetitive ritual of setting the stage enabled a relaxation of the mind. Edensor (2011: 196) has phrased '[t]he daily apprehension of regular features [as providing] a comforting reliability, fostering a mobile homeliness and a familiarity with space'; indeed, the drummer Tyson once told me that setting the stage was the moment of the day when he felt most at home, assembling his drums and crafting a familiar place around himself. I perceived the set-up of the stage as a calming situation, a moment of stillness within the fast pace of the everyday. A chain of performed routines seemed to appropriate these apparently 'transient' places through practice.

After the set-up of the stage, the merchandise manager would prepare his vending table and the tour manager would use the venue's Wi-Fi in the backstage room to map out the next route, or take care of accounting and communication. Once the sound engineer had equipped all instruments with microphones, the band would start their soundcheck. By watching and filming the soundcheck many times on tour, the ambivalent role of the sound engineer became quite visible to me: while he is not a formal member of the band (in terms

of decision making or playing an instrument), he plays an important part in composing the live performance of a song. Also during
the show, he maintains constant eye contact with the band from his
stand at the back of the venue. The musicians will give him signs for
retuning the separate microphones of the instruments (e.g. pointing
at the guitar and lifting the finger in order to pitch up the sound).
Vice versa, if the sound engineer needs the attention of the musicians,
he will twist a thin flexible lamp on the mixing board towards his face
to light it up in the dark of the room. If we include him in the performance, the common frontal perception of a performance becomes
triangular throughout the space of the venue.

Within the tight margins of a music tour, these moments show how
experimenting still remains integral to the endeavour. Although a
tour itself, in the life of musicians and their crew, consists of singular,
repetitive practices throughout the day, it is far from an immutable
undertaking; while there are fixed practices and responsibilities, each
tour is subject to many unpredictable factors that demand flexibility
and improvisation – not only during the musical performance, but
also around it. At the beginning of the tour, for example, instruments and luggage need to be fitted into the back of the van in a
space-efficient and systematic order. While at first it seemed like a
puzzle, trying one way then another, after a few days of loading in
and loading out, a clear and optimized placement structure appeared
to carve itself out of the empty space. We would all gradually become
aware of the best order, calling out loud invented short names for
each of the objects as they were being loaded before or unloaded after
the show: 'skin tone' for the guitar case with the soft pink colour;
'coffin' for the big heavy case that carried microphone stands and the
feet of the drum set.

Within the musical performance, but also around it, continuous
attuning plays a significant role in producing the routines that then
became 'familiar spatio-temporal experience[s]' (Edensor 2010: 8).
Another example shows how a sensitive attention to the spatio-
temporal situation influences adjustments on a very practical level.
During the first week of the tour, we would share a three-bed room
between the six of us. Throughout the course of the tour, it was
observable how the need for space increased, and with it the number
of beds. In the last week of the tour, everyone was eager to have a
queen-size bed to themselves. These arrangements seemed necessary
in order to comply with the tensions and pace that arose as the tour
progressed, like rowers need to change their pace according to the
varying currents of the river.

Arranging and Choreographing

I will here elaborate on the idea that a structuring of time and space may be read as a choreography of paces in the sense of a measure to make things work collectively, '[relying] upon the synchronization of practices that become part of how "we" get things done' (Edensor 2010: 8). Considering the physical and mental conditions of a tour, as explained above, I suggest that this idea lies at the root of developing routines with the goal of stabilization.

The practices on tour can be divided between those falling within a professional bandwidth (setting up the stage, sound-checking, discussing the show, etc.), and those relating to the very personal – coping with mobility as a singular emotional being (phone calls or communication on social media, sleeping needs, socializing, activities in the van). However, as Edensor writes, 'repetitive, collective choreographies of congregation, interaction, rest and relaxation produce situated rhythms through which time and space are stitched together to produce what Seamon (1980) calls "place ballets"' (Edensor 2010: 8), touring may be understood as a negotiation of travelling together that accounts just as much for collective as for individual, for professional as for personal practices and needs.

Imagining the course of a tour as a rhythm, being on the road appears as being both mobile and immobile at the same time: a vehicle, while itself mobile, becomes a stable and confined space for those inside. While some bands travel in nightliners (buses equipped with bunk beds) and others in vans, both types of vehicle become a home base for a while and the place where most free time is spent. Nightliners are usually driven at night, leaving more time during the day in each visited city. Vans on the other hand, equipped with regular car seats, are usually driven during daylight hours, which limits the time in each city to a few hours. Our van was equipped with nine individual seats, and the three extra seats in the back row were generally out of use in order to tilt back the two seats located just in front for sleeping more comfortably. The pace of the journey as well as the means of transport influence the experience of the journey and of place: '[T]he speed, pace and periodicity of a journey produce particular effects through which space and place are known and felt – a stretched out, linear apprehension shaped by the form of a railway or road, the qualities of the vehicle and the time and pace of the journey' (Edensor 2011: 191).

In my own work on the mobility of railway employees on a West African train (Ramella 2013), I have described their sleeping and sitting positions on the train seats, which seemed much more elaborate compared to passengers who travelled on the train irregularly. In a similar manner, van seats are personalized by transforming objects and other features in a way that makes one's sitting position more comfortable, adding to the appropriation of a 'familiar … mobile environment [that] lull[s] drivers and passengers into a state of kinaesthetic and tactile relaxation' (Edensor 2010: 6).

When Ursula Biemann speaks of a 'contained mobility', she comes to describe a particular mobile situation as a 'trans-local state of *not* being of this place' (emphasis in original), which is characterized by taking part in a 'site of … existence [that] is connected but segregated' (Biemann 2008: 56). Looking at the group inside the van that is roaming through states and cities, stopping at predetermined locations where the crew go about their routinized practices and move on afterwards, we may perceive a tour as a containerized experience of 'being in movement', but never really 'being in one place'.

However, some practices common in touring help to appropriate the visited anonymous spaces prior to arrival. Riders are sent to the venues in order to prearrange drinks, food and dressing rooms. The cables for microphones are aligned on stage following a 'stage plot' (a visual map of the stage in the technical rider), which predetermines the particular position of each instrument. 'Set lists' are written out in order to preconceive a dramaturgy of the show. These practices may be considered in terms of Edensor's 'prescribed rhythms' (Edensor 2010: 11), Thrift's 'cartographies [as] not only dynamic but also strategic arrangements' (Thrift 2006: 145), or Merriman's account on 'choreographing … spaces *and* movements, … environments *and* actions' [emphasis in original], which he concludes with the statement that '[s]paces and *practices* [emphasis AR] must be seen as intricately intertwined' (Merriman 2011: 113). Those prearrangements or choreographies only materialize through the repetition of practices and an ongoing process of adjustments through experimentation.

Specific practices of constructing stability on tour, however, transgress the professional arrangements described here. The individual 'repertoire of mobility' (Nóvoa 2012: 362) of a touring musician develops through place-making practices on a very personal level. Each of the people I was travelling with had their own, idiosyncratic way of installing themselves in the various locations, and each brought along particular objects: some would put clothes into the closets of the hotel room, others would set up their speakers and turn on music. The van seats would be equipped with books, stuffed animals or pillows, depending on the personal habits, but were also subject to adjustment during the course of the tour.

Rowing and Steering

When a rowing boat moves forward, the individual movement of each oar is what enables the progression. When looking closely at the very movement of oars, we can make out an individual rhythm of different paces within the singular stroke as well as a displacement of each stroke due to the overall progress of the boat in the water. However, only when the strokes of the oars are synchronized will the overall movement be performed smoothly. This synchronization underlies a rhythm that structures the individual movements: the coxswain, responsible for steering the boat and setting the beat of the rowers, coordinates the power of the team. On a music tour, there is also one person responsible for mediating most of the regularizations and negotiations: the tour manager. He is responsible for programming, for example by allocating time to eat, drink, shower or rest for the whole crew – including the anthropologist.

When I first started talking to the musicians who became part of my research, it often struck me that being aware of the travel route was quite peripheral to most of them. Being used to travelling self-reliantly and independently myself, I came to realize that certain skills are redundant on tour. There was someone here with the specific function of taking care of the coordination for everyone else, in order for them to be able to focus on their own work. Tyson once told me: 'When you travel and the outside is constantly changing, that's how you really get to know the people. Really experience their presence. Get to know what they demand. Like Georg [the tour manager on European tours], he just demands that you relax in his presence'.

The drawing out of personal negotiations under mobile conditions is closely connected to the use of mobile media. Media practices form part of what shapes these fragile, mobile choreographies. Shared location apps and group messaging are used to coordinate the members of the travelling group. Not only the 'interaction[s] with spatial absentees' (Kesselring 2014: 9) through mobile devices (or 'miniaturized mobilities', see Elliott and Urry 2010: 27), but also the actual production and performance of music, as well as the peculiarities of media choice in the van, play a role in keeping the situation steady. While, as Reißmann argues, communication spaces are hybrid and cannot be separated into 'real' spaces vs. network platforms (Reißmann 2013: 92), I do suggest that specific media practices are part of the negotiation of space in mobile environments. This may refer to how electronic devices of communication served as regulators that negotiated privacy in the van, but also to how physical and mental rest was protected by a specific apportioning of the common space. The atmosphere in the van was intentionally characterized by quiet music and restful activities in line with everyone's need for down time. It offered a necessary break from the stressful and exposed times at the venues (see Bennett 1980: 4), which were full of social interaction with press and fans even before the actual performance started. Being in line with these agreements was expected from me as much as from everyone else, however they were not articulated explicitly.

If '[m]obile ethnography draws researchers into a multitude of mobile, material, embodied practices of making distinctions, relations and places' (Büscher and Urry 2009: 105), then travelling under the dictate of someone else as well as respecting unwritten rules were factors that contributed to becoming part of this rhythmic undertaking. My path towards becoming a good rower was marked by coping with this unknown condition, mainly through the experience of ruptures. If space among disparate social actors is constituted through a collective of rhythms, arrhythmic practices must however also be considered (Edensor 2011: 191). On tour, a number of moments can be identified as such: incidents such as car accidents, theft of equipment, or emergencies within personal surroundings, but also simply breaking or ignoring agreements can disrupt the progress of a touring rhythm. I would even argue that it is through those ruptures that a rhythm and its value become most visible.

Ruptures on tour exemplify a transgression of personal and professional spheres. When a relative passes away or a girlfriend is badly missed, it has an effect on performing one's profession. Indeed, life-course changes (Hockey and James 2002) may influence the personal perception of touring, and consequently change the pace of a tour. Both Gibson (2012) and Bennett (2012) have described the physical and social challenges of age as a key factor in music communities, while Ottosson's aboriginal musicians have complained about not being able 'to do this anymore' (Ottosson 2009: 104). Those cases show that adaptations are made in order to integrate lifestyle and, for example, family life or physical constraints, while the business of touring still demands a similar dedication to mobility as at a younger age. The participants of my research were mostly over the age of thirty, and have addressed questions regarding the negotiations of changing personal priorities and the responsibilities that a mobile job entails – from reflections on starting a family to negotiating the length of a tour in order to get home earlier.

Rhyming and Filming

In conceiving accounts on the practices of musicians, we must consider that 'the conscious focus of group interaction is sound' (Bennett 1980: 4). No movement of musicians would materialize if it were not for the (performance of) music. There is, however, coherence in the consideration of music as a 'collective – not an individual – endeavour' (Bennett 1983: 216ff.), and the practice of touring as a collective 'rhythm of mobilities' (Edensor 2010: 5). By turning our attention to the actual production of music, it shows that the experience of touring is articulated in manifold ways; it is commonly seen as part of the lifestyle of a musician and can be discovered as a motif in many songs. The mobile situation of touring during most of the year may be a factor that inspires certain on-the-road themes, but there are certainly also music genres with a long history of travelling and touring songs – for example, in blues and folk music.[1] It is not without reason that Tim Cresswell, who has worked on academic understandings of mobility for more than three decades, wrote his doctoral thesis on metaphors of travel in the lyrics of Bob Dylan (Cresswell 2006).

Songs that address notions of 'dwelling-in-motion' (Sheller and Urry 2006) or 'dwelling-in-travel' (Clifford 1997) are the musical equivalent to what Crouch identifies as a representation of mobility (in painting; Crouch 2010: 10ff.). However, when asking musicians for a concrete description of how a home on a tour can be shaped, this often proved impossible for them to articulate. For most of my interlocutors, it was something that involved no specific knowledge. Nóvoa makes a similar observation: '[S]omething … was so naturalised in their practices and representations that they did not feel the need to stress it' (Nóvoa 2012: 357). What becomes visible here is an adjustment to what 'align[s] the body with place' (Edensor 2010: 9): an embodied regularization of swaying in movement, or the production of collateral knowledge through embodied practice.

Getting there as a researcher on a tour is marked by the initial difficulty that my role had no technical function for the touring process. As Tyson explained to me before the tour, 'another person on tour means another body that breathes, takes space and changes the relations between the individuals'. On tour, we often had a similar conversation in which he tried to explain to me that it was crucial to 'respect each other's space'. This made clear that I was not merely participating to do my research, or to observe their practices, but was actually involved in a fragile environment in which every movement counts. Finding the movements that would fit into the overall rhythm that we were shaping together primarily meant finding a role within the group, and balancing between being useful and not being in the way. This search materialized in manifold ways, positive and negative. At a music festival in Amsterdam, for example, a friend of the band shouted out: 'You have an anthropologist on tour? That's awesome. Who can say that of themselves? Everyone should have that'. On another occasion, however, the merchandise manager, Steve, said to me that he was happy I was there, as it meant that he was no longer going to be the 'weakest' member of the tour.

With the method of participant observation, which involves living with a group of people under their day-to-day conditions, we are confronted with the interplay of categories such as closeness and distance, while endeavouring to be both within and without, together and apart, emic and etic – all simultaneously. In conditions of intense time–space constraints, however, those spatial categories are often challenged, as we are forced into a physical intimacy at a high pace.

This fragile distinction between intimate spaces (the van, the backstage room) and public spaces (the venue, the stage) complicated the rhythm I was attempting to develop for myself, especially with regard to the use of a camera. The time when they relaxed was when I was working. Conversely, during the concerts, when they were working, was usually the time I could write and reconstruct.

The task I set myself was to navigate within and become a rower in a boat where people, objects and practices were constantly being negotiated. During the activities that I could participate in, I would switch between helping and filming. After a few days of watching and filming the unpacking of the cases on stage, I gradually learned the positioning of each of the instruments and, after another few days, I would even dare to open a box and try to assemble the instrument it contained. This showed in several instances that, while having a function on tour was a substantive condition for being on tour, ethnographic fieldwork was by and large not considered to be work. Participating in practices as mentioned above, however, was not considered to be the reason I was there. It was, after all, the use of my camera that negotiated and justified my presence: whenever I was filming, I was accepted as someone doing work. By combining the film work with helping out where I could, I gradually became part of the group.

While in visual anthropology, the camera is often considered an actor that shapes the situations in which it is used (Pink 2007: 48), in my case it was substantial in defining my role and function within the tour. Most importantly, filming was considered to be work.

The practices connected with the camera became the key to rhyming along. It was not just that the handling of this object determined my relationship to the subjects, but also that my habitual practices with the camera made me feel most comfortable. Although my role could never have included the bodily experiences of playing at a concert, writing a song, adjusting sound levels or blindly fiddling a plug into a microphone, my camera and my movements with it evolved into a mediating instance of including me in the chain. Without directly participating in what everyone else was doing, without the disposition of a particular skill related to playing or setting up music, and without technically being part of the overall endeavour, there was a way to become part of the rhythm. The routine of setting up my camera was *my* setting up a drum set or adjusting sound. My camera bag was *my* guitar case, and I relished the feeling when it became one of the objects that had a specific place in the back of the van. It helped me to understand the value of routines and habitual practices for feeling in one's place. Through harmonizing my own work within the practices of a music tour, I came to feel as though we were 'rhyming together', and through this experience I came closer to understanding how the collective rowing changed one's perspective of being out of place.

Conclusion

Frello defines place as 'never-ending becoming' (Frello 2008: 26). I have claimed that the practice of touring, for band members, crew members and anthropologists, is a collective practice that co-creates its rhythm between prearrangements and experimentation. In this chapter, I have come to conceptualize this with the image of rowing, which describes a structuring and distributing of responsibilities in order to make a collective movement work. However, it is a movement that evolves with the individual movements of each 'rower' and is always in part subject to improvisation.

There are a number of similarities between touring and doing fieldwork on touring – in the rhythmic practices of 'making place', but also when it comes to the image of touring; 'the touring discourse in academia', an equivalent perhaps to the 'touring discourse at home' (Ottosson 2009) described earlier, confronts the researcher with similar positive imaginations regarding the fieldwork site and situation. Additionally, in the way that traditional ethnographic fieldwork methods such as participant observation are not considered work on tour, nor is touring considered proper or real work for many people outside the music industry.

In my endeavours to understand the mobile environment of touring, I have had to let my body discover and locate a performance of routines that stabilized the moving world around me. Leaving aside the crucial dichotomies of movement and stability, as well as of closeness and distance, what I have tried to argue is the perception of a more rhythmic, dynamic figure, which is shaped by both mobile and immobile aspects in a temporal, spatial and social interplay.

Musicians are neither constantly touring nor constantly in one place. While they tour, they traverse and craft 'place' with their routinized practices. And while they are at home, they might also be moving around. I therefore argue for a concept of 'mobilit[y] in which migration and stasis are seen as interconnected aspects of the human condition' (Salazar and Glick Schiller 2012: 5). Maybe it is even a case for moving beyond those categories.

In the aforementioned article in the *Guardian*, the producer Matan Zohar states that within a touring lifestyle, '[r]elationships are compromised, partly because it becomes difficult to relate to people with a more stable lifestyle. Your problems and cares become radically different to the other people in your life' (Britton 2015). Having arrived in the group as a moderately mobile person, I cannot rule out the influence that this difference might have had on my fieldwork. However, because the mobile environment and authoritative organization of a tour regularizes even the personal interactions, this chapter only peripherally touches upon the influence of touring on playing out social relations. Rather, it focuses on the functions of a rhythmic structuring for a music tour and its effects on ethnographic fieldwork, both driven by the search for place, for making a home in movement.

When Frello suggests that '[e]ven a seemingly quintessentially sedentary phenomenon such as "home" can and should be studied in the light of "movement"' (Frello 2008: 29), we must take a close look at the practices involved in the making of a 'mobile' or 'transient' place. In the case of the field presented here, a rhythmic structuring of practices and spaces seems a fundamental factor of travelling together on a music tour, with the very ethnographic practice of a fieldwork being the rhymed effect of such.

Finding a rhythm may in this sense be considered the basis of finding one's place within movement, but the necessity of 'rhyming along' also mobilizes fieldwork to assume different modes: to experiment with rhythm. Rhythm is a term that describes temporal and spatial negotiations, but it is also related to the involvement of a function or role. A tour, just as much as a fieldwork, may be described as negotiations of exactly those three dimensions. I have related this notion to the specific practices that are being performed in 'transient places' (Jirón 2010: 132): setting up the stage, installing the instruments, inhabiting the van or the hotel room in *touring*, and, in parallel, setting up the camera, filming the instalment of the instruments and inhabiting the seemingly fleeting spaces in *fieldwork*.

In the field of music tours, travelling and working together is, as I have tried to show, a negotiation that depends as much on prescribed structures as on open arrangements and experimentation. By linking the practices of fieldwork to the practices of touring, we may be able to combine the temporal, spatial and social dimensions that shape the movement of such a rowing boat and determine finding one's place within its rhythm – for the members of a music crew as much as for the anthropologist following them.

Anna Lisa Ramella (University of Siegen) is a doctoral researcher in the 'Locating Media' DFG Research Training Group at the University of Siegen, Germany. Her anthropological research examines the mobility of musicians with a focus on place-making, rhythm and media practices on tour. Employing mobile, digital and audiovisual ethnographic methods, her work takes into account the impact of the digitization and mediatization of music on the everyday experiences of touring musicians. She co-convenes the EASA Networks Anthropology and Mobility (ANTHROMOB) and Collaboratory for Ethnographic Experimentation (COLLEEX). Her audiovisual work can be found at www.laviedurail.net and www.vimeo.com/annaramella.

Note

1. For example, Blind Willie McTell's 'Travelin' Blues' (1929), Geoff Mack's 'I've Been Everywhere' (1959), Roger Miller's 'King of the Road' (1965), Bob Seger's 'Turn the Page' (1973), and Willie Nelson's 'On the Road Again' (1979).

References

Appadurai, A. 1996. *Modernity at Large: Cultural Dimensions of Globalization*. London and Minneapolis, MN: Minnesota University Press.
Bærenholdt, J.O., and B. Grånas (eds). 2008. *Mobility and Place: Enacting Northern European Peripheries*. Aldershot, Hants: Ashgate.
Bennett, A. 2012. 'Dance Parties, Lifestyle and Strategies for Ageing', in A. Bennett and P. Hodkinson (eds), *Ageing and Youth Culture: Music, Style and Identity*. London and New York: Berg, pp. 95–104.
Bennett, A., and R.A. Peterson (eds). 2004. *Music Scenes: Local, Translocal, and Virtual*. Nashville, TN: Vanderbilt University Press.
Bennett, H.S. 1980. *On Becoming A Rock Musician*. Amherst, MA: University of Massachusetts Press.
———. 1983. 'Notation and Identity in Contemporary Popular Music'. *Popular Music* 3: 215–34.
Biemann, U. 2008. 'Suspended in the Post-humanist Lapse: Contained Mobility', in *Mission Reports: Artistic Practices in the Field/Video Works, 1998–2008*. Bildmuseet: Umea University, pp. 55–61.
Britton, L.M. 2015. 'Insomnia, Anxiety, Break-ups … Musicians on the Dark Side of Touring', *Guardian*, 25 June, at http://www.theguardian.com/music/2015/jun/25/musicians-touring-psychological-dangers-willis-earl-beal-kate-nash (last accessed 8 Nov 2017).
Büscher, M., and J. Urry. 2009. 'Mobile Methods and the Empirical'. *European Journal of Social Theory* 12(1): 99–116.
Clifford, J. 1997. *Routes: Travel and Translation in the Late Twentieth Century*. Cambridge, MA: Harvard University Press.
Cresswell, T. 2001. 'The Production of Mobilities'. *New Formations* 43: 11–25.
———. 2004. *Place: A Short Introduction*. Oxford: Blackwell.
———. 2006. *On the Move: Mobility in the Modern Western World*. New York: Routledge.
Cresswell, T., and P. Merriman (eds). 2011. *Geographies of Mobilities: Practices, Spaces, Subjects*. Farnham, Surrey: Ashgate.
Crouch, D. 2010. 'Flirting with Space: Thinking Landscape Relationally'. *Cultural Geographies* 17(1): 5–18.

Edensor, T. (ed.). 2010. *Geographies of Rhythm: Nature, Place, Mobilities and Bodies*. Farnham, Surrey: Ashgate.

———. 2011. 'Commuter: Mobility, Rhythm and Commuting', in T. Cresswell and P. Merriman (eds), *Geographies of Mobilities: Practices, Spaces, Subjects*. Farnham, Surrey: Ashgate, pp. 189–203.

Elliott, A., and J. Urry. 2010. *Mobile Lives*. London and New York: Routledge.

Frello, B. 2008. 'Towards a Discursive Analytics of Movement: On the Making and Unmaking of Movement as an Object of Knowledge'. *Mobilities* 3(1): 25–50.

Gibson, L. 2012. 'Rock Fans' Experiences of the Ageing Body: Becoming More "Civilized"', in A. Bennett and P. Hodkinson (eds), *Ageing and Youth Culture: Music, Style and Identity*. London and New York: Berg, pp. 79–91.

Haldrup, Michael. 2011. 'Choreographies of Leisure Mobility', in M. Büscher, J. Urry and K. Witchger (eds), *Mobile Methods*. London: Routledge, pp. 54–71.

Harvey, P., and D. Dalakoglou. 2012. 'Roads and Anthropology: Ethnographic Perspectives on Space, Time and (Im)Mobility'. *Mobilities* 7(4): 459–65.

Hockey, J., and A. James. 2002. *Social Identities across The Life Course*. Basingstoke, Hants: Palgrave Macmillan.

Ingold, T. 2007. *Lines: A Brief History*. London: Routledge.

———. 2009. 'Against Space: Place, Movement, Knowledge', in P.W. Kirby (ed.), *Boundless Worlds: An Anthropological Approach to Movement*. New York: Berghahn Books, pp. 29–43.

———. 2011. *Being Alive: Essays on Movement, Knowledge and Description*. London and New York: Routledge.

Jirón, P. 2010. 'Repetition and Difference: Rhythms and Mobile Place-Making', in T. Edensor (ed.), *Geographies of Rhythm: Nature, Place, Mobilities and Bodies*. Farnham, Surrey: Ashgate, pp. 129–43.

Johansson, O., and T.L. Bell. 2014. 'Touring Circuits and the Geography of Rock Music Performance'. *Popular Music and Society* 37(3): 313–37.

Kesselring, S. 2014. 'Corporate Mobilities Regimes: Mobility, Power and the Socio-geographical Structurations of Mobile Work'. *Mobilities* 10(4): 571–91.

Kirby, P.W. (ed.). 2009. *Boundless Worlds: An Anthropological Approach to Movement*. New York: Berghahn Books.

Larsen, J., J. Urry and K. Axhausen. 2006. *Mobilites, Networks, Geographies*. Aldershot, Hants and Burlington, VT: Ashgate.

Lefebvre, H. 2004. *Rhythmanalysis: Space, Time and Everyday Life*. London: Continuum.

Maslow, A. 1943. 'A Theory of Human Motivation'. *Psychological Review* 50: 370–96.

Massey, D. 2007. *World City*. Cambridge: Polity Press.

Mazzullo, N., and T. Ingold. 2008. 'Being Along: Place, Time and Movement among Sámi People', in J.O. Bærenholdt and B. Grånas (eds), *Mobility and Place: Enacting Northern European Peripheries*. Aldershot, Hants: Ashgate, pp. 27–38.

Merriman, P. 2011. 'Roads: Lawrence Halprin, Modern Dance and the American Freeway Landscape', in T. Cresswell and P. Merriman (eds), *Geographies of Mobilities: Practices, Spaces, Subjects*. Farnham, Surrey: Ashgate, pp. 99–118.

Mjøs, O.J. 2012. *Music, Social Media and Global Mobility: MySpace, Facebook, Youtube*. New York: Routledge.

Molitor, V., and C. Pierobon. 2014. 'Identities in Media and Music: Case-studies from National, Regional and (Trans-)local Communities'. *InterDisciplines* 5 (1), available at http://www.inter-disciplines.org/index.php/indi/article/view/105/85 (last accessed 8 Nov 2017).

Moores, S. 2012. *Media, Place & Mobility*. Basingstoke, Hants: Palgrave Macmillan.

Morley, D. 2000. *Home Territories: Media, Mobility and Identity*. London: Routledge.

———. 2003. 'What's "Home" Got to Do with It? Contradictory Dynamics in the Domestication of Technology and the Dislocation of Domesticity'. *European Journal of Cultural Studies* 6: 435–58.

———. 2011. 'Communications and Transport: The Mobility of Information, People and Commodities'. *Media Culture Society* 33: 743–759.

Nóvoa, A. 2012. 'Musicians on the Move: Mobilities and Identities of a Band on the Road'. *Mobilities* 7(3): 349–68.

Ottosson, Å. 2009. 'Playing with Others and Selves: Australian Aboriginal Desert Musicians on Tour'. *The Asia Pacific Journal of Anthropology* 10(2): 98–114.

Pink, S. 2007. *Doing Visual Ethnography: Images, Media and Representation in Research*. London: Sage.

———. 2008. 'Mobilising Visual Ethnography: Making Routes, Making Place and Making Images'. *Forum Qualitative Social Research* 9(3), available at http://www.qualitative-research.net/index.php/fqs/article/view/1166 (last accessed 8 Nov 2017).

Potts, T. 2008. 'Orchestrating Chaos: Clutter, Rhythm and Everyday Life'. *Keywords: A Journal of Cultural Materialism* 5: 88–105.

Ramella, A.L. 2013. 'La Vie du Rail: A Railway Line as Transitory Space'. Interactive website, http://www.laviedurail.net (last accessed 8 Nov 2017).

Reißmann, W. 2013. 'Warum Netzwerkplattformen (keine) Räume sind: Ein Beitrag aus medienökologischer Perspektive', in T. Junge (ed.), *Soziale Netzwerke im Diskurs*. Hagen: Medien im Diskurs.

Salazar, N., and N. Glick Schiller. 2012. 'Regimes of Mobility Across the Globe', *Journal of Ethnic and Migration Studies* 39(2): 183–200.

Seamon, D. 1980. 'Body-Subject, Time-Space Routines and Place-Ballets', in A. Buttimer and D. Seamon (eds), *The Human Experience of Space and Place*. London: Croom Helm, pp. 149–165.

Sheller, M., and J. Urry. 2006. 'The New Mobilities Paradigm'. *Environment and Planning* A 38(2): 207–26.

Stoller, P. 2009. *The Power of the Between*. Chicago: University of Chicago Press.

Thrift, N. 2006. 'Space'. *Theory, Culture & Society* 23(2–3): 153–55.

Urry, J. 2000. *Sociology beyond Societies: Mobilities for the Twenty-First Century*. London: Routledge.

———. 2007. *Mobilities*. Cambridge: Polity Press.

Music References

Mack, Geoff. 1959. 'I've Been Everywhere'. Courtesy of the Artist.

McTell, Blind Willie. 1929. 'Travelin' Blues'. Columbia Records.

Miller, Roger. 1965. 'King of the Road'. Sony/ATV Music Publishing.

Nelson, Willie. 1979. 'On the Road Again'. Columbia Records.

Seger, Bob. 1973. 'Turn the Page'. Universal Music Publishing UK.

Two Gallants. 2007. 'Seems Like Home to Me'. Saddle Creek Records.

4

Idiotic Encounters

Experimenting with Collaborations between Ethnography and Design

Andrea Gaspar

> We must never forget that human motives are generally far more complicated than we are apt to suppose, and that we can very rarely accurately describe the motives of another.
> —Fyodor Dostoevsky, *The Idiot*

My ethnography is about a design company whose motto is 'Form Follows Fiction', but usually the fictional is something they work out conceptually in advance, which is an aspect that intrigued me throughout my entire fieldwork. The fact that concepts in that context are worked out in advance of situated experiences, places and materiality, and that narratives are usually created around objects, prompted me to engage in intense discussions, one of which occurred during my participation in the creative process for a conceptual design object. This project started with a call for a competition for an object of leisure for the domestic space, which had been launched by an important furniture company of Milan, which organizes this competition every year. The theme of the competition was 'Places for relaxing: Decorative objects for the domestic space'. The call for proposals invited applicants to invent new domestic objects for relaxation. All the questioning that I generated during the design process had an assumption in mind: I assumed that 'real' design objects – in the sense of material objects, either conceptual or not – were at stake. Only at the end did I realize they were not. These competitions and their conceptual design objects had a performative (in the sense of dramatized) function that I had ignored – no material objects of any kind were to be produced beyond the prototype, which was an end in itself. This was a relevant misunderstanding that prompted me to work as an 'idiot' – an unexpected and annoyingly resisting 'other', able to disturb the normal course of life and especially 'what I was busy doing' (cf. Michael 2012b) as an ethnographer.

The disruptive/creative character of the idiot is a widely used device in design, either intentionally and explicitly, through methods such as probes (Bohener, Gaver and Boucher 2012),[1] which are material practices specifically used to elicit new insights and inspiration during the design process (usually unfinished and open-ended devices or prototypes that are given to people without any instructions in order to learn from their reactions), or implicitly, such as in the practices that I found among the designers with whom I was trying to engage. Somehow inspired and contaminated by their practices and their more implicit ways of 'devicing' idiocy, I explore what idiocy does, if it may be taken to the practice of ethnography, discussing the potential of idiotic encounters to rethink the collaborations between ethnography and design.

Collaborations between Anthropology and Design

Although the relationships between design and anthropology assume many different forms, none of those forms seem to explore the productive potential of such idiotic resources. Some of the more institutionalized modes of collaboration are participatory design and the 'relatively recent shift in design and business', called 'user-centred' design, 'a practice that foregrounds the needs and wants of the end user as central to the development of new products and services' (Hunt 2011: 33–34). These institutionalized modes of collaboration have been described as instrumental relationships, where ethnography is used to provide data about user behaviours and preferences (Wasson 2002; Wilkie 2010; Dourish and Bell 2011), but where ethnographers are rarely invited to participate in the creative processes of design. The potential of ethnography is not explored as a contribution to those design processes (Crabtree and Rodden 2002). There are, however, other relationships between anthropology and design that are intended as non-instrumental: for example, critical anthropology of design (Suchman 2011). This approach, however, is based on a conventional ethnographic relationship: ethnographers doing critical anthropology of design would work with experts in these disciplines for producing an anthropological understanding (and critique) of design, but would use their usual methodological tools without necessarily seeking to change them by the contact with designers' 'other' ways of knowing.

A transdisciplinary field called design anthropology (Clark 2011; Gunn, Otto and Smith 2013) emerges precisely as an alternative to such available approaches to the relationships between anthropology and design, redefining the traditional relationship between the ethnographer and her/his 'objects' of study. Design anthropology's explorative work challenges the conventional distinctions between social science and design research: it is presented as 'a distinct style of knowing' that emerges from the connection between anthropology and design. The ethnographers who engage with this interdisciplinary mode of knowledge production aim to do ethnography *with*, or through, rather than *of* design. Their intention is to do 'design by means of anthropology, and anthropology by means of design' (Gunn and Løgstrup 2014: 7).

But while design anthropology is a mode of collaboration that puts into relation the two *different* disciplinary cultures of knowledge making for explicitly exploring common questions and common aims, the kind of engagement with design that I explore affords a different relational arrangement: an arrangement that departs from the unpredictable encounters between epistemic differences. Those encounters open up the possibility of destabilizing each discipline's tacit ways of bringing the new into being, thus creating the opportunities for performing them differently.

'Bringing the new into being' is an analytical expression that I use to refer to the specific ways of generating knowledge or creativity according to a discipline or an epistemic culture (Knorr Cetina 1999), where 'new' is produced not only in the sense that it is fabricated or assembled by a multitude of agencies, but in the sense that it is performed. With this expression I refer to the 'performativity of the new' – new knowledge, new ideas, new objects – a performativity that is situated in different epistemic cultures and their respective communities of practice (Lave and Wenger 1991). As a performative practice, bringing the new into being is also a tacit, non-explicit process, something that one does without necessarily being conscious about how one does it or what the processes and operations involved are – as if, for example, riding a bicycle (Polanyi 1958). The ways of bringing the new into being involve different relationships and prioritizations that are put to work between subject/object, inside/outside and abstract/specific, which are themselves specific according to the community of practice in which we are disciplinarily or epistemically enculturated. But the 'new' is not reduced to the epistemic practices that we may be able to observe 'out there' – the 'new' is also an event or 'the coming into existence of something that has got the power to produce agreement among competent colleagues' (Stengers 2008: 47). What I wish to explore is if idiocy, if taken to ethnographic relationships, could work as an epistemic event. That is, exploring how idiocy as a source of unpredictable effects could help to bring the new into being through/in fieldwork. If, as Anna Tsing puts it, friction is a mode of cultural encounter that is creative, this idiotic proposition means taking into consideration the possibility of exploring fieldwork itself not so much as 'a zone of cultural friction' (Tsing 2005: xi) but more as a 'moment' of cultural friction.

Engaging with Designers' 'Conceptuality' Making

In 2009, I started my ethnographic fieldwork for my PhD thesis at an Italian firm in Milan dedicated to Interaction Design (IxD), a sub-discipline of design concerned with the usability of things, whose emergence had been enhanced with the development of digital technologies. The studio was a spin-off from a well-known IxD institute, which had been the first IxD graduate school in Italy, where 'experimental' work had been developed in that field – but it had closed in 2005. That studio was the heir of that school, as well as of the 'hopes and dreams' of IxD, a hype that by then was already fading. My acceptance to the studio was easy: it was facilitated by the fact that it was a very loose structure – a network of people from many different places and fields organized around 'projects'. From that perspective, I was just one of the many students and interns who had sought out the studio for some short-term experience, in exchange for nothing more than CV enrichment at the beginning of a career. Becoming a participant observer, however, was not as easy: although I eagerly struggled to get involved, it was very difficult to figure out the terms of that involvement and what my 'role' could be, since I lacked any kind of design skills. The conceptual stage of projects was one of the few opportunities I had for participating in the studio's life, where I ended up developing a strange mode of participant observation – an observation that was not as detached as it should be, and where I found it difficult, beyond my ethnographic role, to leave myself behind as a person. There was no pure 'ethnographic' without interference from my personal and embodied sensibilities, and for this reason what you will find here is inevitably a very personal, embodied account.

Since the structure was so loose I ended up following mostly the project leaders, who were also the founders and the most stable workers in the design studio. There was one in particular with whom I ended up developing a more frictional interaction: Osvaldo,[2] one of the founders, the 'brain' and the leader of the company, despite saying that they were 'a non-hierarchical organization'. The company had a CEO, but his role was akin to a design director of the company. Even though Osvaldo is someone who is open to participatory design and participatory architecture (and would later develop an interest in 'community design'), he had a strong position about user-centred design, often declaring it useless and 'an obstacle to progress'. On my very first day of fieldwork, when handing them a sheet of paper on which I had prepared the presentation of my project, I innocently revealed that I had assumed a direct relationship between interaction design and user-centred methods. 'If you are looking for user-centred design, you have knocked at the wrong door', he abruptly told me, advising me to consider other places for doing my fieldwork, since they were opposed to that approach. From then on, a very frictional kind of relationship unfolded: even though I immediately clarified that I did not necessarily subscribe to user-centred design, I too often found myself objecting and reacting to their design-centred mode of creativity. This frictional relationship, taken into the ethnographic realm, is what I would call 'idiotic'.

The Idiot and Speculative Design

Inspired by Stengers' figure of the idiot, Mike Michael discusses the potential of 'idiotic objects' for social research and proposes proactive idiocy as a way of interrogating 'what we are busy doing' as social researchers (Michael 2012a, 2012b). His proposal is based on his engagement with the practices of speculative design.

Speculative design is a specific practice of design research developed by Anthony Dunne and Fiona Raby, a provocative and fictional approach intended to open up spaces of debate and discussion within an attempt to extend design's boundaries beyond the strictly commercial. Inspired by radical architecture and fine art, speculative design is based on 'an intention to change reality' rather than simply describing it. As a practice, it often starts with a what-if question as a means of speculating how things could be, through the use of trigger devices such as probes and scenarios.

This form of design thrives on imagination and aims to open up new perspectives on what are sometimes called 'wicked problems', to create spaces for discussion and debate about alternative ways of being, and to inspire and encourage people's imaginations to flow freely. Design speculations can act as a catalyst for collectively redefining our relationship to reality. (Dunne and Raby 2013: 2)

Michael considers the speculative practices of design research as 'a chronic invitation to, indeed as a mechanism for, the proliferation of idiots', stressing that these practices enable unforeseen participant actions – that is, misbehaviours (Michael 2012b: 537). In Michael's use, the figure of the idiot is inspired by the Deleuzian concept of event: the event as something that emerges out of the coming together of different entities, a mutually transformative effect that generates 'inventive problem making' – the opening up of a space for a reframing of the research issues. Among the idiotic situations, he points to the 'disastrous engagement events' within research (misbehaviours, unpredictable reactions, unpredictable participation). My experience in the studio and the specific ethnographic relations that I had developed led me to think about the kind of opportunities that idiocy as an event-making phenomenon opens up for ethnographic practice.

Although my fieldwork was not done in a 'speculative design' context, I am interested in using that vernacular vocabulary to relate not only to my field but also to what it might bring to ethnographic modes of bringing the new into being. That is, rather than idiocy being something that works for speculative designers, here I am interested in how it might work to define the idiotic ethnographic encounters with interaction designers.

Form Follows 'Friction': Performing Idiotic Encounters

In order to participate in the conceptual design project for an object of leisure that I referred to at the opening of this chapter, one afternoon in the studio I joined the designers in brainstorming, where an idea for a 'conceptual' object was to be produced. Silvana and Luna, two interns, and I, were expected to produce some proposals. The 'project leaders' gave us instructions that we should think of an object beyond its functionality: it should be an object that would 'tell a story' about the contemporary situation, using the topical economic crisis, which was severely affecting the design industry. Osvaldo suggested we think of alternative uses for a domestic object – a chair or a table, for example – and transform it into an object of relaxation. He intended to frame the object around this idea, which confirmed my perplexity about their prioritization of abstract concepts over objects, materiality and the concrete empirical, sensuous world. The challenge was to think of an object that would somehow refer to this scenario of contemporary crisis with irony and a sense of humour: 'The studio is interested in things that speak to contemporary problems,' he stated, 'so instead of creating a new object, it would be more interesting to reinvent one already in use'. By that time, I had also learned about an aspect that they usually stress: the idea that 'we don't need new objects, we need stories for the existing ones' – in this case, the story we would convey with the reinvented 'object' would be something around the economic crisis. Apparently, the object would not add anything new to it – it would just be a semiotic vehicle of a previously defined concept. It intrigued me that the object would not be a way of opening up questions but would rather be used as an answer to, or vehicle of, a conceptual problem.

Having this brief from Osvaldo in mind, I spent that entire afternoon with Luna and Silvana thinking about possibilities. The creative process in the studio usually starts with looking for 'references' on the Internet, which means other design projects. Therefore, it struck me that inspirations come from inside this world of design references and never from the 'outside'. I was surprised that the possibilities that my colleagues insisted on were categories of objects – such as *a* table, *a* chair, *a* sofa, *a* bathtub – rather than specific situations or objects. In the brainstorming I raised the question as to why we were working on abstract categories instead of 'concrete' objects. Silvana explained their point of view to me: 'obviously what matters for us is the general object', not any specific table as 'each table can be different, [and] we are not interested in behaviour [either, because] of course, each one can do whatever one wants with a table, [and] the different uses people may make of a table are not important for us'. The intention, she stressed, was rather to work on the concept of 'table'. Troubled by the realization that they did not see any generative power in concrete physical things, and that these were being excluded from the creative process, I asked: 'Couldn't the experience of the specific and concrete be a way of thinking about what a table can make us do? And wouldn't that potentially open possibilities for other ideas?'. These questions did not even work as an objection – something that would nevertheless have had a rational possibility of discussion. According to Stengers, the idiot 'cannot be taken into account' because the idiot neither objects nor proposes anything that 'counts' (Stengers 2005: 1001). Too alien to make sense, my questioning worked rather as a resistance to these designers' 'normal' ways of doing their business. Whenever I asked these kinds of questions, it was likely to be interpreted as if I were straightforwardly concerned with technical and boring functionality – too concerned with documenting the 'existing', without getting to the point of conceptual design.

My suggestion, though, was not to make a study on how people use tables, as I clarified, but rather to get inspiration from it. However, that was not the aim: for them that is not where 'inspiration' comes from, in general. Their argument for this was already familiar to me by then: they wanted to create something 'new', and for that reason the 'existing' is not important – as Osvaldo used to say, 'if we always asked users what they wanted, we would probably still be living in caves'. 'User-centred' design is often interpreted in this context as synonymous to a 'consumer-centred' approach to innovation, and so it is an approach that is truly 'the other' – and they somehow regarded me as representative of that. In their eyes, I belonged to the people (social scientists) who usually conduct those studies. Thus, despite the fact that this design-centred position can easily be regarded as a cultural domination process that despises 'the people', it should better be seen as a reaction to a market culture that puts the consumer at the centre of the creative and innovation process. The point, for Osvaldo, was that creativity and innovation are unpredictable processes that can never be achieved through devices such as consumer studies, as shown by an email exchange between us on 28 May 2009: 'Most of the things I believe important get transferred in a very subtle and invisible way', said Osvaldo, replying to my insistence on departing from 'the practices' and 'real life'. I replied: 'Hum, I didn't quite get it. What do you mean – that important decisions [in the creative process] are not formalized?' Osvaldo responded: 'Never. Generally, relevant decisions do not follow very formalized patterns. If things are relevant, it is always better not to formalize them. In this respect, I am curious to see your findings'. Unpredictability may in fact be embraced, actively stimulated in their creative practices, but what puzzled me was the way they derive it from the 'conceptual' rather than from concrete social life.

As Osvaldo also made clear to me in his email, 'normal design does fix a problem, but conceptual design puts you to thinking. Conceptual design can be made with the same tools as normal design, it is just not meant to fix the world satisfying material needs'. In another email a few days earlier, he said: 'Design can be understood as a response to a question. I have a question = I want to sit down. The response = I design you a chair. The more interesting design, however, is the one that makes you generate *new* questions'.[3] But precisely concerned with that, my problem was how could design generate interesting questions from inside its own self-referential process – if they are born from themselves only, how could they be new? We can also argue that a good ethnographic process is one where we arrive at new questions. It was as if we were talking about the same thing, but just departing from opposite points without reaching any understanding. In these kinds of conversations, we were idiots to each other: we generated misunderstandings that somehow ended up being productive both for ethnography and design, although productive in different ways and transformed into different kinds of 'new' things.

The interns and I ended up excluding other categories and chose a table as 'our' object, because a table strongly relates to the imaginary of an Italian way of life (food, family, gregariousness) and thus was also an easier point to trigger associations to the cultural transformation associated with the crisis. The project leaders liked the idea but we then needed to find a way to transform the concept of the table: how to make it an object for relaxing and at low cost – a table that would not just be used for its expected functions but that would invite other alternatives. Again I tried to object, stating that alternative functions could always be found for any object – those depending on the 'use', rather than the conception.

My own disciplinary way of 'bringing knowledge into being' was colliding with another radically different disciplinary way of 'bringing the new into being', and from there an insight started to emerge that while ethnographers usually derive their knowledge from a describable 'outside', designers apparently do the opposite, performing creativity as an internalized, intellectualized process (Leach 2007). Can these confrontations that I am referring to, and their related misunderstandings, disturb this sort of disciplinary way of generating the new, opening up space for *new* ones?

Departing from the ideas that we collected during our brainstorming, we proposed work on some objects that would have other symbolic functions: among these, we thought about a table-*tapis-roulant* for aspiring models, a table-golf set for businessmen in crisis, a table-with-airbag for the heavy drinker, and a table with an inflatable friend for depressed singletons – although not explicit in the proposal that we circulated, this last idea was my modest contribution.

We gathered these ideas and sent them by email to the project leaders as our 'conceptual' proposal. Osvaldo reacted very quickly, immediately suggesting that we work on the idea of a tablecloth

instead of a table, and to create a set of tablecloths for different functions. Inspired by the Lars von Trier's film *Dogville*, he wanted these
tablecloths to have instructions drawn on them for the different
activities:

> The principle should be that of *Dogville*: a series of tablecloths, indicating
> the positions to put various items (glasses, cutlery, bottles, etc.) and then,
> each tablecloth instructs us (to do) a different thing: it can urge us to play
> golf, perform a concert (with glasses, full of water, etc., etc.) and so on …
> Reference: four tablecloths: one for positioning golf paraphernalia; one
> for positioning apparatus for producing music from glasses and bottles;
> one for positioning the items for making a piece of Giorgio Morandi;
> one for positioning the material for making a language course; another
> tablecloth could be dedicated to the garden. Place the plates on it, the
> glasses, and then, instead of eating on it, put soil on it and start cultivating
> flowers or stuff to eat. (Osvaldo, email to 'All', 30 April 2009)

Everyone liked the idea of having a table that changes its meaning
according to the tablecloth it wears, including myself. Eager to
confirm my suspicion that this would end up being just another
self-referential project, I encouraged the idea and showed particular
enthusiasm about it. So we started working on the prototype: making
the musical tablecloth and then preparing the booklet of the project
with this example. The prototyping process brought about another
interesting event that illustrates what I define as 'idiocy'.

Wondering why they do not acknowledge the creative potential of things outside their own mindful creative processes, I asked
Osvaldo why we were integrating the object into a story and not
the other way around? Why were we thinking about general objects
for general categories rather than starting from the exploration of
specific material objects? Why was the idea coming from an abstract
process – an abstract table rather than a real one? From my point
of view, there was a lack of specificity that could have offered other
creative possibilities that I realized were not being fully explored.

The reason they depart from 'general concepts' is actually part
of a disciplinary practice commonly used in conceptual design – the
'intellectualization' turn in design (Naylor and Ball 2005). Much of
what they claim (for example, that we do not need new objects, but
stories for existing ones; or that design is not about materiality but
rather about fiction; or the idea of design as redesign) is already part
of a broader conceptual design discourse. Working on the 'conceptual
level' means working on abstract categories of things (archetypes),
and thus there is a name for what we were doing: it is called 'the

reinterpretation of the archetype' (Ferreira 2010), which is one of the most common strategies of formal concretization used in conceptual design, among others such as the paradox or the metaphor. Within a conceptual design framework, designers do not transform objects, they transform their meaningful archetype.

Reacting to my suggestion that their work was too abstract and general, and lacking specificity – something that Osvaldo regarded as a personal obsession – he promised we would make this project more 'specific'. My ethnography started becoming speculative here in terms of bringing hypotheses and ideas into the very articulation of fieldwork to see what they might bring and how potential conflicts such as these might be worked out in a non-consensual way. These somewhat frictional or problematic exchanges are interesting moments when, after these idiotic encounters, we started working on something seeking to understand each other's mode of relating to bringing the new into being.

In order to make the story 'more specific' as I had advocated for, Osvaldo invented a story in which to frame this tablecloth: he started to imagine the story of Beppe, the engineer, a depressed businessman who had been fired, and who was lonely, abandoned by his girlfriend. With nothing else to do, he would finally have a set of tablecloths that would promise to change his life. But this did not correspond to what I meant as 'specific', I told him, as it seemed to me that the story was based on a general (and gendered) stereotype, so I asked him why the character was a man. 'It is because the story is not general', he said. 'It is Romolo, acting as a loser but dressed in his usual way …' Romolo is an engineer from the studio, whom Osvaldo frequently drew attention to as someone who cared about his looks and dressed elegantly – in contrast to himself, who always looked very shabby. 'You see, he fits the Italian male stereotype, he likes wearing French cologne and so on'. Romolo inspired him, he said, 'because if the story has a character it is easier to identify with it, and so it has a stronger impact. If the story is general, then we won't identify … People would feel a lot of sympathy and emotion for this guy: he lost his job, he lost his girlfriend; he has no friends, nothing. Still, [he] is dressed in decent clothes, he tries to shape up, and finally finding himself using the table not to eat but to play music with glasses is a great vision'. This is the transformation of the 'everyday life' into design, he explained, giving an example: 'A boy and a girl who argue and split [up], [that] is everyday life. To transform everyday life into Romeo and Juliet is something different. My cousin is very jealous. So what? Are you interested in my cousin being very jealous? I don't think so. Then, if you have Shakespeare, this same (boring) thing, becomes Othello' (Osvaldo, personal email, 12 May 2009).

This story would give shape to the concept book, and the proto-typing would be based on the enactment of it. My questions about the lack of specificity seemed not only out of place in the context and situation I was in, but they were misinterpreted – and that mis-interpretation was transformed into inspiration for an ironic story that is produced out of these idiotic interactions made of mutual misunderstandings. If the story was not specific in the sense that I imagined, the effects of enacting the story started to emerge as a specific performative device that was partially intended to provoke me and what I represented in terms of a disciplinary stereotype: the 'people-centred', 'obsessed-with-the-specific' anthropologist, who is one of those people who usually conduct the user-centred studies.

To enact the story, we needed to create a tablecloth and the sce-nario in order to make pictures of it and then compose the concept book. So we gathered again, the interns and I, to work on these next steps of the prototype, and through trial and error we managed to make a functional musical tablecloth. We used the glasses in the studio to play a song – I took an active role in this process, which was particularly tentative and amusing as I actually managed to play music with them – and then we graphically represented the amounts of liquid that each glass would need to play a given song. Finally, we printed the tablecloth with those graphic instructions.

After having the prototype of the 'tablecloth-for-a-concert-with-glasses' made, we needed to photograph it, so we all met one Friday night, at the house of one of the other project managers from the studio, Lisen, where we cooked dinner and afterwards did the pho-tographic session with the tablecloth, improvising a scenario accord-ing to Osvaldo's instructions. Osvaldo had asked Lisen to convince Romolo to play the character.

While looking at the proofs of those pictures, and somehow deceived by the promise that it would finally be more 'specific', I commented to Osvaldo that the whole process ended up as a story, presented through text and images: information, rather than a mate-rial object. The object that we had been working on was not able to stand by itself without the story/text that accompanies it – the booklet with the pictures and the story that they produced around it. The tablecloth was informative; the whole project was ironic, sym-bolic and provocative – but it consisted of *words* – the images and objects were just instrumental to the story. There was no materiality, no new object, I complained, somehow disappointed with the fact that this did not fit into what I expected as 'specific'. In my view, we were prototyping nothing but 'meaning', which for me illustrated well their general design approach: there was no real change to follow apart from semiotic change. So in one email exchange I asked Osvaldo if 'the tablecloth' for him was 'an object or a sign'? 'The tablecloth ended up as an idea', I complained; 'it is abstract, used as just a vehicle of meaning. If objects are signs, then what difference do objects make in the stories that they create?' To Osvaldo, 'it is an ambiguous thing, because in one sense it is not an object, but rather a conceptual mask for the table, but at the same time, it is a true object: a tablecloth – like a mask. A mask is a conceptual device. Still, it is an object ... we could have done the same thing without a tablecloth. Still, we needed the object (the tablecloth) otherwise it wouldn't exist. ... The object (like the film, or the paper for a book) is the medium; it is the thing that makes our idea alive'. Once again, there seems to be no possible conversation. In a sense, Osvaldo was also resisting what I was trying to ask him – the possibility of deriving questions and concepts from concrete objects and specific relations. He was refusing to understand, acting as an idiot in that regard, but making me slow down: making me more reflexive about what I was doing with those questions and my embodied role in that process whereby I felt it impossible to separate myself with my reactive character and my emotions from my role as an ethnographer. Concerned with the practical utility of it as a future commodity – because regardless of being conceptual, I assumed that those tablecloths were going to be commercially produced at the end of the process – I wondered who would need 'a tablecloth that changes the use of the table' in a time of crisis (which was the frame of the story, the crisis). This did not make sense to me as an object, and it did not fit with the idea I had about a design product, albeit conceptual. My concern was with the 'real' effect of these objects in 'the world', outside the studio. I presumed the whole process had the purpose of conceiving new objects, and thus my questioning was about the role and reception of such an object in the 'real' world. I was embodying a very biased notion of change and innovation that departs from the assumption that there is 'a world out there' for these 'innovations'. That was not what was being performed there: change was rather being performed as a (self-referential) dramatization, as a fictional operation more akin to a critical or speculative design methodology (see Boehner, Gaver and Boucher 2012; Michael 2012a, 2012b, 2015) than to something actually intended to become an object with a life outside the studio. And to Osvaldo, that is the point: '[E]specially because we are in a crisis, stories, movies, love affairs, football games become incredibly important to us'. A 'realist' account of innovation processes, for example in an STS style (one that would look at the material, technical change in the making), would simply not fit into what was being developed here, as there was no material change in the making to follow, and no 'users', no people, for that innovation. This project was nothing more than a dramatic *play*, and as such it performed innovation as a dramatization of change.

An unexpected outcome of this idiotic encounter was that the project was evolving as a response to this ethnographic engagement, including my wrong assumptions about innovation: it was emerging out of the *specific* in that regard. It was a way of responding to it in an ironic way, mocking me and my anthropological assumptions about design, entrapping me in my own research. By coincidence or not, after this conversation Osvaldo decided to name the project 'NandoPessoa': some days before I had mentioned Fernando Pessoa as being my favourite poet. Fernando Pessoa was a modernist Portuguese poet with many pen names (masks) whose iconic image is introspective, and his poetry and his image work as the perfect caricature of intellectualization and abstract thought. This choice of name made that interaction between the project and my ethnographic expectations more explicit, assuming a personal provocation. Acting as a kind of a private joke (and therefore, 'specific'), the project ambiguously caricaturized a too-intellectualized situation – mine, them or general?

In the end, this project won the first prize of the competition (€5,000) for 'having interpreted with provocative irony the existential crisis of our times through a domestic alternative toy'. Excited with the idea that they would finally somehow produce this object, and that I would then have the chance to see what happens to such a self-referential object in the 'real' world – the change that I was expecting – I asked Osvaldo how it was. Sneering, he explained to me that the prize was attributed in a ceremony that was a party for business people where these projects are usually the '15 minutes of culture', among food, drinks and Russian prostitutes ... This surprising ending could not have been a more ironic confirmation to me of the intellectualized character of the work they do and the absence of material innovation. I was again disappointed with the abstractness of the whole thing and by the fact that there was no new 'object' (in the material sense) to follow. This was an unexpected kind of specific to me, and so I continued to be disdainful of this project precisely because now it was 'too specific' – not universal – and unable to make a difference to anyone's life. Strangely, somehow, we seemed to have changed roles – I found myself using their designerly criteria, and maybe they were using my ethnographic ones. The results of this process were as much 'bad design' (in my judgement), as 'lousy anthropology' (in Osvaldo's judgement). Albeit poor design and bad anthropology, it was nonetheless a design and an anthropology that travelled elsewhere, that transgressed their own boundaries. Idiocy was productive in that regard and I believe that is its power for the design and anthropology relationships.

While Michael's account on idiocy is intentionally on how it can be proactively 'produced' through speculative design projects, the idiotic encounters that I explored open up a different, perhaps more implicit, unintended, way of generating idiotic events. These idiotic events result from the ethnographic encounter, therefore offering the opportunity to rethink the relations between anthropology and design. Idiocy resulted from the confrontation between embodied disciplinary epistemic differences: through my questioning, I seemed to be constantly accusing them of performing a very abstract kind of design process and outputs (deriving the new from themselves), so they decided to use this project to mock my own 'too-abstract'/ intellectualized questioning process, which seemed to them so disconnected from their world through this project, therefore accusing me of performing the same kind of process. While I transformed these 'disruptions' into moments of reframing my anthropological questions about innovation and the new, refocusing them on the ways in which ethnographers, in opposition to designers, usually generate 'new' questions from (an interaction with) the outside, Osvaldo would transform these specific 'disruptive' interactions into inspiration for new design.[4]

The project that I have referred to is one of those examples of an idiotic event transformed into a new idea, although the process between one thing and the other is difficult to trace because, as Osvaldo himself explains, that trajectory is never a direct one. This means that they practice idiocy as an implicit device for bringing new ideas into being, and there is something we can learn from that that is useful for ethnography. The lesson is that there can be no creativity without the 'other'; there can be no creativity without difference. The encounters between design and anthropology can thus be thought as ways of bringing difference into being, and therefore as frictional events. As Anna Tsing reminds us, "[a] wheel turns because of its encounter with the surface of the road; spinning in the air it goes nowhere. Rubbing two sticks together produces heat and light; one stick alone is just a stick. As a metaphorical image, friction reminds that heterogeneous and unequal encounters can lead to new arrangements of culture and power" (2005: 5). This is precisely what design anthropology lacks: in their departing from common questions and common projects, there is no friction; there is no 'other'. The idiot opens up other kinds of collaborations between anthropology and design – collaborations that depart from these frictional disciplinary and epistemic differences, which in turn create the conditions for a more speculative ethnography.

Conclusion: Speculative Ethnography?

The figure of the idiot, if taken to the field of ethnography, affords a mode of 'engagement' that resonates with the methodological proposals of other traditions in anthropology – namely, the collaborative interdisciplinary fields of design anthropology (Clark 2011; Gunn, Otto and Smith 2013) – for it opens the possibility of forging other relationships with other ways of knowing. However, while design anthropology puts the epistemic practices of design and anthropology into relation developing a 'collaborative' and 'interdisciplinary' kind of work, the figure of the idiot invites a step behind, by opening up the question of what collaborations may be between anthropology and design (or other areas of expertise). Idiocy opens possibilities of epistemic and disciplinary transformation that result from the confrontation – or even friction (Tsing 2005) – between anthropology and design as two distinct epistemic cultures. Idiocy can thus be thought of as a frictional device, the very condition of possibility for epistemic and creative transformation between anthropology and design.

In this chapter I have explored how idiotic encounters can be potentially generative for both disciplines by affording non-explicit ways of 'bringing the new into being'. Idiotic moments bring a disruption into the 'normal' flow of epistemic performances, making us more conscious and reflexive about those otherwise invisible processes that are involved in the bringing of different disciplinary 'news' into being, and therefore offering an opportunity to imagine how to generate them differently. The design story that I recounted provides an example of this, where it was not my questions explicitly that became integrated in the fiction that was being created; but the idiotic encounter provided difference to designers, and therefore new creative material was able to be translated into a new story. The same event, however, was transformative of different things; it was generative of different kinds of 'new': while the designers transformed the specific (a specific interaction, a private joke) into the general (an ironic fiction about the crisis; a conceptual design project), through the same event, I transformed the general (my 'general' assumptions on 'where the new comes from') into the specific (producing a cultural relativism of those assumptions). There are, however, no direct links we could trace between the event and the transformations generated by it. It is in this sense that idiotic ethnography can be understood here as a device for producing events, (moments of) radical difference that open up the possibility of performing ethnography in a different way: a kind of 'speculative' ethnography, an ethnography that intervenes in the field through a sort of technology for making (idiotic) events.

The figure of the idiot resonates also with the practices of critical and speculative design (Dunne and Raby 2013), and in particular with Mike Michael's sociological inspirations on the materialities of it (2012a, 2012b; 2015). However, while Michael is concerned with idiocy as something referring to the role of objects in the design – albeit objects that generate events – I turn the attention to how the idiot can be useful for designating (or maybe actively experimenting with) a specific kind of ethnographic encounter, and how relationships may be performed to intentionally generate certain kinds of events. Although the ethnographic relationships with design that I have analysed did not perform this gesture intentionally, it affords the possibility of doing so. Those ethnographic relationships open the question of what a design anthropology would look like if based on idiocy as something explicitly devised in the ethnographic encounter with design: what would a collaborative ethnography look like if we use the idiot as a technique for producing epistemic frictions?

Andrea Gaspar (University of Coimbra) is a lecturer in social anthropology at the University of Coimbra, Portugal. She holds a PhD in social anthropology, awarded by the University of Manchester in 2013. Her research addresses innovation practices in design, and the relationships between these practices and knowledge making in anthropology. She has also worked as a postdoctoral researcher at CES (Centre for Social Studies, University of Coimbra) in an STS research project focusing on digital scholarship and digital methods.

Notes

1. 'The probe process on a whole is judged in terms of whether it opens up conversation, provides inspiration, and results in innovative ways of thinking about and designing for a particular context' (Bohener, Gaver and Boucher 2012: 197); 'their purpose is not to capture what is, so much as to inspire what might be' (ibid.: 185).
2. For identity protection, the names I use for fieldwork characters are fictitious.
3. 'Il design può essere inteso come una riposta a una domanda. Ho una domanda = mi voglio sedere. La risposta = ti disegno una sedia. Il design più interessante é quello che ti fa venire in mente nuove domande'.
4. In another situation, he even invited me to play that idiotic role in a more intended way: he needed to convince the managers at the art academy, where he was in charge of the design department, that a new master's course on 'community design' would be preferable to one on 'exhibition design', and thus he invited me to be part of the process. Trying to learn about what I should do and what task I would have, I understood that there were no specific tasks assigned to me: what he wanted from me was simply to be there, questioning him in the way I usually did as a way of generating good ideas and arguments for him to negotiate with the design department. He did not even want me to help him to prepare those arguments explicitly, nor did he introduce me to the people he was trying to convince: what he really wanted from me was the possibility for discussion and this sort of frictional, idiotic interaction (cf. Gaspar 2013).

References

Boehner, K., W. Gaver and A. Boucher. 2012. 'Probes', in C. Lury and N. Wakeford (eds), *Inventive Methods: The Happening of the Social*. New York: Routledge, pp. 185–201.

Clark, A.J. (ed.). 2011. *Design Anthropology: Object Culture in the 21st Century*. New York: Springer.

Crabtree, A., and T. Rodden. 2002. 'Ethnography and Design?' http://www.mrl.nott.ac.uk/~axc/documents/papers/IAW02_1.pdfhttp://www.mrl.nott.ac.uk/~axc/documents/papers/IAW02_1.pdf (last accessed 12 May 2014).

Dostoevsky, F. (1868–1869) 2012. *The Idiot*. New York: Vintage Classics.

Dourish, P., and G. Bell. 2011. 'A Role for Ethnography: Methodology and Theory', in P. Dourish and G. Bell (eds), *Divining a Digital Future: Mess and Mythology in Ubiquitous Computing*. Cambridge, MA: MIT Press, pp. 61–89.

Dunne, A., and F. Raby. 2013. *Speculative Everything: Design, Fiction and Social Dreaming*. Cambridge, MA and London: MIT Press.

Ferreira, P. 2010. 'Design Conceptual na era pós-industrial: "A forma segue o conceito"'. Master's dissertation, Faculty of Architecture, Universidade Técnica de Lisboa.

Gaspar, A. 2013. '"Where does the new come from?" An Ethnography of Design Performances of "the New"'. PhD dissertation, University of Manchester.

Gunn, W., and L. Løgstrup. 2014. 'Participant Observation, Anthropology Methodology and Design Anthropology Research Inquiry'. *Arts and Humanities in Higher Education* 13(4): 428–42.

Gunn, W., T. Otto and R.C. Smith (eds). 2013. *Design Anthropology: Theory and Practice*. London: Bloomsbury.

Hunt, J. 2011. 'Prototyping the Social: Temporality and Speculative Futures at the Intersection of Design and Culture', in A.J. Clark (ed.), *Design Anthropology: Object Culture in the 21st Century*. New York: Springer, pp. 33–44.

Knorr Cetina, K. 1999. *Epistemic Cultures: How the Sciences Make Knowledge*. Cambridge, MA: Harvard University Press.

Lave, J., and E. Wenger. 1991. *Situated Learning: Legitimate Peripheral Participation*. Cambridge: Cambridge University Press.

Leach, J. 2007. 'Differentiation and Encompassment: A Critique of Alfred Gell's Theory of the Abduction of Creativity', in A. Henare, M. Holbraad and S. Wastell (eds), *Thinking through Things: Theorizing Artefacts Ethnographically*. London: Routledge, pp. 167–188.

Michael, M. 2012a. 'De-signing the Object of Sociology: Toward an "Idiotic" Methodology'. *The Sociological Review* 60(S1): 166–83.

———. 2012b. '"What Are We Busy Doing?": Engaging the Idiot'. *Science, Technology, & Human Values* 37(5): 528–54.

———. 2015. 'Ignorance and the Epistemic Choreography of Method', in M. Gross and L. McGoey (eds), *Routledge International Handbook of Ignorance Studies*. London: Routledge, pp. 84–91.

Naylor, M., and R. Ball. 2005. *Form Follows Idea: An Introduction to Design Poetics*. London: Black Dog.

Polanyi, M. 1958. *Personal Knowledge: Towards a Post-Critical Philosophy*. Chicago, IL: University of Chicago Press.

Stengers, I. 2005. 'The Cosmopolitical Proposal', in B. Latour and P. Webel (eds), *Making Things Public*. Cambridge, MA: MIT Press, pp. 994–1003.

———. 2008. 'Experimenting with Refrains: Subjectivity and the Challenge of Escaping Modern Dualism'. *Subjectivity* 22: 38–59.

Suchman, L. 2011. 'Anthropological Relocations and the Limits of Design'. *The Annual Review of Anthropology* 40: 1–18.

Tsing, A. 2005. *Friction: An Ethnography of Global Connection*. Princeton, NJ: Princeton University Press.

Wasson, C. 2002. 'Collaborative Work: Integrating the Roles of Ethnographers and Designers', in S. Squires and B. Byrne (eds),

Creating Breakthrough Ideas: The Collaboration of Anthropologists and Designers in the Product Development Industry. London: Bergin & Garvey, pp. 71–90.

Wilkie, A. 2010. 'User Assemblages in Design: An Ethnographic Study'. PhD dissertation, Goldsmiths, University of London.

5

Fieldwork as Interface

Digital Technologies, Moral Worlds and Zones of Encounter

Karen Waltorp

In the summer of 2015, a Danish journalist contacted me by telephone. She asked whether I could confirm that even though a growing number of young second-generation immigrant women were pursuing higher education, they were still victims of social control. She had written the story and was looking for an expert to quote. I asked what she understood by social control, as I myself had used the term previously (Waltorp 2013) but had failed to interrogate it in depth. She replied that many colleagues of mine had no problem with calling 'what was taking place' social control. I reiterated that I would love to talk to her should she be interested in critically engaging the concept of 'social control', but if she needed someone to confirm it before a deadline she was welcome to call someone else. I was surprised that she did actually call me back, and a dialogue by mail then ensued.

In the meantime, I discussed the term and its use with a number of my interlocutors – young Muslim women, mostly second-generation immigrants. I was a bit irritated on their behalf that the journalist had not questioned the term 'social control', but simply assumed it to be a dynamic endemic to Muslim immigrant families, while Danes were understood to raise their children to be responsible individuals who make 'free choices'. I felt that ideas about freedom, autonomy and the collective were at stake. Over the following weeks, exchanges of views with interlocutors followed in a WhatsApp group, on Facebook, and over the telephone. The WhatsApp group was initiated by me, and included Henriette,[1] an ethnic Danish woman of 23 who had converted to Islam; Samah, 26, of Palestinian–Jordanian origin; and 25-year-old Yasmin, of Iranian origin. The latter quickly responded:

> Hi Karen, don't get it. Want to help out … What do you mean – what is social control? Can't you describe it in street slang [*gadesprog*]?
> Karen: That ethnic minority girls are controlled by their family … says the journalist.
> Yasmin: Not all of us, no. I'm Muslim, my mother is religious, but we come from a very open family and have the same opportunities as everyone else. But you know immigrants [*indvandrere*] are always more afraid that people are going to talk. They think more about the neighbours than making themselves happy.

Samah entered the discussion on WhatsApp with a formulation that was strikingly close to the formulation in a particular leaflet from a government-funded organization called Etnisk Ung (Young and Ethnic). The example described a young woman who was not allowed to choose whom or when to marry, not allowed to decide where to go, and her parents would check the messages on her telephone. The discussion in the WhatsApp group continued, but Samah chose to call me up also, and talk privately about her views on social control.

What I wish to direct attention to with this opening vignette is how digital technology enabled the iterative formation of knowledge and continued feedback in specific ways. It easily disappears from view how a knowledge-making process is entwined with specific digital technologies and platforms. In the example above, there was communication via landline, mobile telephone, email, Facebook's Inbox, and WhatsApp. These digital technologies and platforms contributed in various ways to the interactions, both to what was communicated and how. These mediated interactions were in turn shaped by the face-to-face relations existing prior to and alongside the communications via media. I have elsewhere discussed how reciprocity and mutuality are necessary in qualitative research in the private spaces in social media, as in all other anthropological fields (Waltorp 2016).

With a starting point in fieldwork and filmmaking (2010–11, 2014–15) with and about young Muslim women on a social housing estate in central Copenhagen, I argue that the use of digital technologies such as smartphones and video cameras allows for particular interfaces in fieldwork. I had set out to explore place-making and belonging with a focus on the affordances of smartphones for women who had transnational networks and lived in a local immigrant neighbourhood in Nørrebro. The term 'affordances' is used here in a relational sense,

rather than as the properties of an object (Gibson 1977). My interlocutors' smartphones shaped, registered and impacted on what they
communicated, 'did', and made through them and with them, just as
my video camera also impacted on the knowledge created between
us. Using video and social media platforms as part of being 'in the
field' resonated with my interlocutors' ways of being and sharing
moments; and while my research looks at affordances in the broadest
sense of smartphones for my interlocutors, in this chapter I seek to
draw out the affordances of smartphones and a video camera for the
anthropologist as knowledge-making devices that allow for specific
interfaces in fieldwork, through describing a few such interfaces in
my fieldwork.

Both viewing fieldwork as interface and drawing on the concept
of affordances imply certain ideas about agency, the relationality
between human and non-human actors, and between interior worlds
and the environment of which we make up part. Attempts to understand the relation between inner worlds, cognition, and the 'outer'
phenomenal world of objects have been at the centre of inquiry
and theory building for centuries. I see affinities between Gregory
Bateson's ecological systems theory and his notion of 'distributed
mind' spanning brain-body environment, on the one hand, and post-
Gibsonian approaches underscoring the relational property as shared
between object and agent, on the other – as well as the idea that 'the
information specifying where the situation can lead is not entirely
within the agent's head, but is in some way also held within the
object (itself within an environment)' (Knappett 2004: 46). I quote
Bateson's example of the blind man and the stick as an analogy for
my interlocutors and their smartphones.

> ... when we seek to explain the behavior of a man or any other organ-
> ism, this "system" will usually *not* have the same limits as the "self" – as
> this term is commonly (and variously) understood ... If you ask anybody
> about the localization and boundaries of the self, these confusions are
> immediately displayed. Or consider a blind man with a stick. Where
> does the blind man's self begin? At the tip of the stick? At the handle
> of the stick? Or at some point halfway up the stick? These questions
> are nonsense, because the stick is a pathway along which differences are
> transmitted under transformation, so that to draw a delimiting line *across*
> this pathway is to cut off a part of the systemic circuit which determines
> the blind man's locomotion. (Bateson 2000: 317–18; emphasis in original)

In this chapter, I introduce two examples of fieldwork as interface:
Interface 1, a participatory photo-diary project turned collaborative exhibition-making titled 'Ghetto NO Ghetto'; and Interface 2,

participant observation with smartphone and video camera as integral components. Digital technologies formed part of the object of study and were also integral to the applied methodology, intertwined with other contexts and practices (Ardévol 2012). I trace how digital technologies have gradually come to work more intentionally as fieldwork devices for me. This has happened as a response to previous fieldwork experiences, and points to an iterative movement of collaboration between anthropologist, interlocutors and, not least, 'field'. While acknowledging that there are already interfaces in place everywhere, the interface I conceptualize here as a methodological device is one that is changed and repurposed with the inclusion of the anthropologist – one that has been devised through a constellation of digital technologies that bring into existence an encounter in specific ways.

The conception of the interface as I use it here is not restricted to the well-known graphical user interface between humans and computers alone, but also indicates critical points of intersection between lifeworlds, social fields, and moral and value systems, made possible in a specific way through digital technology. The interface is defined as 'a zone of encounter that actively extends into and conditions that which it separates' (Hookway 2014). The interface has an ambiguous condition because it simultaneously links together those things that it separates. As such, it can be conceived of as a 'productive moment of encounter embedded and obscured within the use of technology' (ibid.: ix). Hookway continues: 'It is a disputed zone, a site of contestation between human beings and machines as much as between the social and the material, the political and the technological'. Research in the humanities and social sciences arguably depends increasingly on digital technologies, affecting how research is conducted and the knowledge that it produces, so that specific forms of technology reconfigure the relation between researcher and object in any field of study (Law 2004, 2016). Here I describe vignettes from an ethnography where the field takes the form of an interface: a field of ambiguous condition because it links together those things that at the same time it separates.

Interface 1: Photo-Diary Project Turned Exhibition

In 2010–11, I carried out a participatory photo-diary project in Blågården, a social housing estate, which transformed into a collaborative exhibition titled Ghetto NO Ghetto (Waltorp 2011). I invited young people (between 15 and 25 years of age) from the Blågården area to participate in a photo-diary project. It is notoriously difficult to engage this age group in this area. My point of entry was the work I had done previously with young people in the so-called coloured township of Manenberg outside Cape Town (Waltorp 2010, Waltorp and Jensen, forthcoming), and in the Parisian suburb (*banlieue*) Saint-Denis (Waltorp 2011), which resonated with some of the young people in Blågården. Through NGOs and personal contacts in the area, I invited as many as possible to attend a free screening of the film 'Manenberg' (Waltorp and Vium 2010) at the Empire cinema near Blågården. There was a Q&A session after the film, at the end of which I invited the young people attending the screening to a workshop introducing the photo-project. The 'inaugural meeting' was held at the facilities of Rabarberlandet (part of the social housing association FSB), located in a corner of the central square, Blågårds Plads. In this sense, media products, photographs and film made up part of the interaction from the start.

The young participants would take photographs with a disposable camera every week as a form of visual diary. I would develop the film and meet them individually to discuss their pictures, and then once a week we would all meet at the Rabarberlandet meeting spot. The weekly gatherings took the form of workshops, where there would either be a talk by a photographer or filmmaker to inspire their practice, or hands-on training in techniques like picture editing or framing. When inviting the young people, I framed the project as one of documenting from the 'inside' what living on the Blågården social housing estate was like, as a response to the heavy stereotyping of the area, which the young people talked a lot about. It is important to be critically aware of such a 'politics of inviting', as it frames how issues are allowed to emerge – or rather, if issues are treated as pre-given through the framing of a project, it shapes both how people engage with it, and who becomes concerned. As soon as I had invited them and instigated the photo-project, though, the participants, technology, and 'outside' circumstances started to reshape it.

First of all, none of the participants found the particular aesthetic or process of the disposable analogue cameras appealing. Instead they brought their smartphones with them and showed the pictures they had taken with those – they had their phones with them all the time anyway, and they preferred the instant editing that a digital camera affords. In October 2010, two months after I had initiated the project, Blågården, along with twenty-eight other areas in Denmark, was identified as a ghetto by the centre-right government as part of its new 'ghetto strategy'.[2] This topic dominated the discussions in the group, and shaped how the ten participants and I presented the photos and narratives: we formulated a reply countering the ghetto stigma. Practically, it created an interest in the project from the Copenhagen municipality and a few local NGOs, which helped to fund the exhibition. When we were invited to exhibit the outcome of the project at the Nørrebro Theatre, we jumped at the opportunity. This was a chance to generate data for me, and a way of working together that arguably involved a moment of cultural critique (Marcus and Fischer 1999) for anthropologist, audiences and participants. The exhibition juxtaposed the pictures and narratives from Blågården alongside pictures and narratives from young people in Manenberg (South Africa) and Saint-Denis (France), and asked of its audiences: What is a ghetto? Who decides? For what purpose and with what effects?

At the exhibition opening, several politicians and stakeholders from the various organizations in the area were present. Rania, a 22-year-old participant in the project of Syrian descent, with braces on her teeth and a veil covering her hair, took the microphone and welcomed people:

> I am so tired of turning on the television and listening to Pia Kjærsgård (influential Danish right-wing politician). She doesn't know anything about living in our neighbourhood, and I wonder why she doesn't come to this event. I am tired of hearing all the prejudices against us wearing a scarf, or Blågården being called a ghetto, which it is not. It is actually very multicultural, like Syria in the old days, which is why it had such an amazing culture, and artistic styles developed. This is what can come out of this place too.

The above quote from Rania points to a way of being able to 'talk back' through media, entering into a public space of appearance (Arendt 1998). Through exhibition-making, questions were raised about how the young, mostly Muslim, people living in the area were seen as a group, and the power of mainstream media in this.

According to Hannah Arendt, plurality is a precondition for being a public agent; without the presence and acknowledgement of others, action would cease to be a meaningful activity. To the extent that action requires appearing in public, making oneself known through words and deeds, and receiving the consent of others, it can only exist in a context defined by plurality (Arendt 1998: 177–79; Waltorp 2013). Stereotyping of the area, and of Muslims, by mainstream

Danish media were addressed through the analogue medium of disposable cameras, the digital video camera and smartphones, and through interviews and stories broadcast about the exhibition in local newspapers and online. I bear in mind James Weiner's reminder that we cannot consider visual representation apart from the particular metaphysics that is deposited in our image-producing technology, a metaphysics that is just as much part of our culture and the social relations through which we live it (Weiner 1997: 198), and there is consequently reason to be critical when working together with groups of people with implicit ideas of 'giving voice' to them. The framing rests on my (Western) values of democratic politics and a public space of appearance. The staging of the exhibition, to me, formed part of an exploration of the relation between ascription and self-ascription of (ethnic) minority identity, rooted in place – and the role played by media and media representation in this dynamic. To the participants, I guess it implied various things, and the conversations around that subject are ongoing with those participants with whom I am still in contact.

I interacted with participants on Facebook and via text messages, and – at the participants' suggestion – organized a Facebook group where we could all post information and remarks, yet 'private' communication was still possible through the Inbox function. This latter function was used by almost all participants discerning what they wanted to disclose to me but not necessarily to other project participants or followers of the group on Facebook. In this sense, the affordances of the digital technology of cameras, smartphones and the social media platform Facebook (trans)formed the way we worked together and how knowledge was created. Furthermore, this online communication with participants and other people interested in the project was a source of data creation in itself around the diverse issues that could be made public, and those that ought not to be. It sparked my interest in boundaries between intimate, private and public spaces, and between visibility and concealment, which I elaborate on elsewhere (Waltorp, forthcoming).

In the case of the photo-project, which transformed into the Ghetto NO Ghetto exhibition, we set up photographs by participants and a twelve-minute video shot by two of the participants and me to dialogue with the written texts displayed next to the photographs and in the exhibition catalogue. The 'representations' shaped by the participants and anthropologist were visual products full of excess that intended to evoke the multiple experiences and narratives coexisting and contesting each other.

Framing, Feedback from 'the Field', and Reiterations of Fieldwork

The project Ghetto NO Ghetto, described above, was framed 'derivatively' in the sense that George Marcus speaks of when he says, in conversation with Paul Rabinow, that any anthropology of the contemporary is fated to be derivative since it covers the ground that others – the media, other disciplines, the 'natives' themselves – have already represented, written about, described and analysed (Marcus, in Rabinow et al. 2008: 68). We are working derivatively, they say of anthropologists, in that we depend on actors and their already constituted discursive realms:

> Fieldwork evolves these days as an engagement with found imaginaries ... This found imaginary could begin anywhere – with experts, or migrant workers – and eventually these sites or positions will be connected if they are relevant to each other. Sometimes the ethnographer defines this relevance as her argument and makes connections between overlapping worlds that may only be indirectly perceived by the actors/subjects, or not at all. It is not only the native point of view that is operative ... You develop this design as you find yourself in situated engagements with epistemic partners, but you are constructing it for your own purposes, which are those of making the tools, the concepts that permit the exploration of the kinds of relations that a distinctive anthropology of the contemporary approaches. (Marcus, in Rabinow et al. 2008: 70–71)

They call for experimenting with the design of techniques and equipment for research that 'face up to anthropology's present condition of distinction and derivativeness, and the tension between the two' (Marcus, in Rabinow et al. 2008: 91). The interface that I describe here, as a fieldwork device, is a contribution towards this. It is an interface that may lead to transformations of the self of the ethnographer, who is engaged in playing new roles within the frame of fieldwork, and experimenting with new statuses in the different contexts he or she takes part in, while at the same time representing other moral worlds to her interlocutors. Ideally, our anthropological fieldwork and analysis is an interface that takes the form of a 'mutual interrogation, which can reveal "our" traditions to ourselves, as much to the other' (Verran 2013: 154). Norms, or particular values of the host society, can often become part of the anthropologist's self (which is hybrid, multiple, situated, and shifting), or come to form new social repertoires (Maskens and Blanes 2013: 261). This is a peculiar case, when the 'host' society is at the same time also one's own 'home' society.

In the time between the photo-diary project and collaborative exhibition-making in the Blågården area in 2010–11 and my fieldwork in 2014–15, I kept in contact with a number of the participants through social media and face-to-face meetings. Some of the initial participants from the photo-diary project went on to become interlocutors in my PhD fieldwork. Other interlocutors became involved in my research through the network I had developed; in other words, friends of friends or acquaintances became my interlocutors through the snowball method. Without people in the area to introduce me, access would not have been easy, and keeping in contact with people, while still working full-time and meeting family obligations, was made possible through social media. During these intermediate years I increasingly came to see the digital technologies as a fascinating object of study, as well as a promising fieldwork device.

In the next section, I argue that participant observation is both experimental and collaborative at its core. This potential is arguably lost when coupled with a strictly positivist analytical framework. If the anthropologist is restricted to 'being there' to document, when there are other modes, and experimentation could go beyond mere observation, then once again the potential of anthropology is lost. There is no 'outside the frame'; instead there are situated and partial knowledges (Haraway 1988) with the anthropologist always included in her/his experimental material (Law 2004, 2016; Mol 2008). Such an experimental approach, to me, is qualified by generating questions and answers in an iterative movement, through reiterations. To get at something, we have to accept that getting it right the first time may not be a criterion of success but an indication of a lack of sensitivity to the feedback in the field.

Interface 2: Participant Observation with Smartphone and Video Camera

The places that comprised my field were the social housing estate Blågården and the larger Nørrebro neighbourhood, the online sphere, and some of the (transnational) spaces that are assembled by this technology. I conducted fourteen months of fieldwork: eight months of fieldwork in situ in Blågården between February and September 2014, which included participant observation and collaborative video making; and six months of subsequent online fieldwork conducted via smartphones and the social media platforms that my interlocutors used – most importantly Snapchat, Facebook, Instagram, WhatsApp, text messaging, telephone conversations and video calling applications like Skype and Viber. At the time, the WhatsApp application only supported photos, text and small videos; Facebook was the largest social (networking) site and, as mentioned above, afforded both public displays on 'the wall' and private communication via an inbox. The Snapchat application allowed users to take photos, record videos, add text and drawings, and send the so-called 'Snaps' to a controlled list of recipients. The content was then automatically deleted after a set time limit of maximum ten seconds (see Waltorp 2016). FaceTime was a video-telephony application that made it possible for the parties – as long as they were both using Apple products – to see each other while talking on the phone; Skype and Viber also offered video and audio calling but across a wider range of operating systems than Apple and, as Voice over IP (VoIP) applications, they also supported instant messaging and exchange of images, video and audio media messages.

I stayed at interlocutors' homes for two to three days at a time once or twice a month during the six months when I did, primarily, online fieldwork. I interchangeably conducted participant observation (sometimes with a video camera), shared physical space and time, and shared moments in online media physically removed from the interlocutors. I also achieved the view on communication from the United Arab Emirates and Iran to others 'at home' in Blågården, Nørrebro, as I accompanied two interlocutors on trips to their parents' country of origin, Iran, and to visit a potential future husband of an interlocutor in Dubai, where several interlocutors had married and settled.

Below I present a vignette from fieldwork, a situation where values were probed at various levels, and bodily and aesthetic norms discussed. Simultaneously those norms were expressed and transformed through a continuous, effortless discerning between what to share via which media channels or platforms, and with what audiences. My presence, and that of my video camera, invited a questioning of the deep-seated values of the anthropologist, those of the interlocutors, and potentially those of the audiences of the textual and audiovisual outputs from the interface, in the future.

It's a late summer afternoon in 2014 in an interlocutor's living room on the outskirts of Copenhagen. Together with a group of interlocutors, I took the bus from the neighbourhood of Nørrebro to visit

Khadija, who moved here from Nørrebro with her husband and son, pregnant with their second child. We brought along cakes, bread, humus, olives and other snacks.

I film lips. Smoke is inhaled and exhaled. I film the table full of plates of cake, the colourful mix of fresh and dried fruits, candy and soft drinks. I zoom in on a Coca-Cola can. I hear the light summer rain on the windows because my hearing is augmented, courtesy of the technical extensions to my body that is the camera equipment. Nour grabs her phone and says: 'Come, we do a selfie'. We move closer together, eyes to the tiny lens on her smartphone. The picture she takes is quickly decorated with a few emoticons and sent as a Snap to girlfriends who are not there with us in the moment – and who only see the picture in the moment they receive it (see Waltorp 2016). Other pictures are arranged in montages of pictures of the cakes, the fruit that is arranged on the table, and us smiling to the camera. A filter is added and the photo is put on Facebook, receiving comments from friends and acquaintances. In these pictures, the hijab is worn, as a very different audience is able to look at what is uploaded to Facebook. It is a semi-public space, as opposed to the private space of the living room, and the private space of the Snapchat platform.

I pan over the four women sitting on two black leather sofas around a glass table. Although they go veiled in public spaces, here in the private space of the home they remove the veil, long cardigans, and the 'outer layer' of clothes they are wearing. This is safe and allowed as long as no men except those from the immediate family are present. Nour sits in her black leggings and tight black blouse. She has removed just part of the hijab from her head, and keeps on the inner part that functions like a hairband. Khadija is wearing a short, comfortable dress in a stretchy jacquard material, and her hair is in a ponytail. She is five months pregnant and the bump shows clearly now. Jamila does not remove her headscarf – 'bad hair day' – she sits legs curled up under herself on the sofa, in elegant trousers and a small jacket. Mona arrives late, with a water pipe wrapped in two H&M plastic bags, and arranges it on the table. She is wearing jeans and a tunic top. I am in tight jeans and a T-shirt, seated next to Nour. My thoughts are drifting, until they are called back by the women's voices getting louder:

> Khadija: If you're psychologically tired of your breasts, then it's allowed, I'd say it's allowed.
> Mona: Depends on your husband.
> Jamila and Khadija protest: No, no, no, no, no not the men.

Khadija: I'd do it for my own sake. My husband says, no, that he doesn't want me to do it. But I want to do it – why: because I feel uncomfortable when I'm naked and my breasts are small.
Jamila: Listen, if your husband tells you to do something that is really wrong and lousy, would you still do it just because then he would be happy?
Mona: No, I'm just saying …
Nour: If it's for him, and he's happy about it, he won't look at other women!
Jamila: Even if it's haram, you'd do it?

Voices overlap and interrupt each other as the discussion heats up, and my camera follows the discussion, zooms in on facial expressions and the simultaneous handling of messages on the smartphones. Soon, I am actively drawn into the discussion and asked why I do not use push-up bras. This is something several interlocutors have been discussing among themselves, and the discussion follows around what my thoughts are on beauty ideals, 'being natural', whom one should attempt to look good for, and so on. My camera grows unsteady as I defend my choices and ideals, so embodied and taken for granted that I rarely question the deep-seated values in which they are embedded.

The above case unfolds an everyday social situation among the women, slightly altered and made into an event by an anthropologist being present with her video camera. In the situation, the smartphone is used in various ways: to take selfies and share them on the Snapchat platform with friends, to take other pictures for a different audience on the Facebook platform (wearing the hijab in the pictures for Facebook), and for texting and talking with friends and family. The video camera helps in focusing on the many simultaneous (inter) actions, and in handling both on- and offline dimensions – it is an interface that extends into the on- and offline spheres, which it at the same time brings together and separates. In situations like the one described above, the tactility of hands touching and handling the smartphone is kept on record because of the video camera.

I consider devices and technologies in terms of their affordances – the actions they make possible, or the opposite, those that they constrain. Yet my focus is not on technologies or agents alone, but on the fundamental interactions between the two and on how the relational property shared between an object and agent is at once highly situational, socially negotiated and contested (Knappett 2004: 46). In the conversations we would have around topics such as gender roles and beauty practices and ideals, I was interchangeably identified as a separate individual and a representative of Danes at large. We were each other's interlocutors, probing each other and ourselves around body aesthetics, maintenance and alteration, and gender relations. I observed, filmed and participated in their everyday lives and activities, as well as staged more particular events through my presence, my questions and my camera – and my interlocutors shared thoughts, videos, photos and texts with me when I was physically present, as well as through the smartphone when I was physically absent.

Moral Worlds and Zones of Encounter

In the above vignette, Interface 2, conceptualizing fieldwork as interface has helped me to draw nearer to understanding practices, logics and values as experienced and lived by the interlocutors, as well as turn a critical gaze back upon my own culturally taken-for-granted ideas, morals and values. My interlocutors and I belong to the same nation, share the city of Copenhagen and the neighbourhood of Nørrebro, and belong to various other collectives reaching beyond the Danish borders. We are each other's interlocutors – with various stakes, from various class backgrounds and social positions, differently positioned in terms of religion, secularism, politics and ideology. The interface between us is made up of resonances, contestation and critique. Our (moral) worlds are not 'wholes', but rather composites (Waltorp 2015). We may disagree with some aspects of each other's moral stances, and ethical and normative practices, without dismissing or holding in disrespect each other's worlds, and our shared reality, altogether.

My interlocutors formulated in various ways a wish to counter the stereotyping of immigrants and Muslims that they experienced in Denmark, as well as to show people in the Middle East what life in Europe is 'really like' – and in this endeavour, they envisaged me as a partner. This focus on minority–majority relations occurred often, although only when I initiated those discussions, and mostly at the beginning of the fieldwork. It also came up when we were doing feedback sessions, when I would ask for their opinions on and critiques of my tentative analyses (see Waltorp 2016).

In the vignette that opened this chapter, a journalist's question made me revisit the concept of 'social control' with my interlocutors. In this instance, there were three main themes that emerged from their responses: irritation at being uniformly represented by mainstream media as subdued Muslim women with headscarves, discontent about having less control over their own affairs than they wished for, and a questioning around freedom, secularism and religion, and what this entailed for each of us (see Asad et al. 2009; Fernando 2013). I argue that, as anthropologists, we should subject our own moral positions and assumptions to the same kinds of analysis we use on others in the process of asking 'what is it that counts as morality in the various social worlds we and our interlocutors inhabit, and what are the processes by which this morality comes to matter?' (Zigon 2010: 13; see also Fassin and Stoczkowski 2008). Anthropologists are always already entwined in power relations, political agendas and the public debate; ethnography cannot be disconnected from political morality.

To reiterate, the interface is 'a productive moment of encounter embedded and obscured within the use of technology. It is a disputed zone, a site of contestation between human beings and machines as much as between the social and the material, the political and the technological' (Hookway 2014: ix). 'Most human encounters … occur in this in-between space of partial evaluations, translations and contestations' (Benhabib 2002: 41).

Conclusion

It is the fieldwork as mutually produced interface instigated by the curiosity of the experimental anthropologist that I have sought to tease out here. There is no doubt it can be demanding and tiring work to make up part of an interface. The interface, in its provision of an augmentation, Hookway argues, 'requires an extraction of work, and for this work a cost must be paid' (Hookway 2014: 7). The augmentation comes at a cost, which many a fieldworker who could not easily exit the field might agree with. Also, an interface, once established, is not just eradicated when the fieldworker physically leaves the field site. One can encounter emotional and physical fatigue when continually being made to question one's values and morals, perhaps encountering 'epistemic disconcertment':

> 'Epistemic' refers to knowledge and how we account for what it is: our story or theory of knowledge. 'Disconcertment' conveys the sense of being put out in some way, and when qualified by the term 'epistemic' it implies that our taken-for-granted account of what knowledge is has somehow been upset or impinged upon, so that we begin to doubt and become less certain. (Verran 2013: 144–45)

We implicitly invite our interlocutors to do this work as well. Yet working with epistemic disconcertment might allow us to grasp 'generative possibilities for going on together doing difference' (ibid.: 146).

In the examples offered above, I first described (in the opening vignette) how a journalist's question about social control led to a discussion in social media with interlocutors on freedom, autonomy and control. In Interface 1, a photo-diary project turned exhibition allowed for a fieldwork interface, which then led to the more intentionally created fieldwork as interface described in Interface 2. Sensitivity to the interfaces that emerge, and an intentional crafting or devising of such interfaces in fieldwork, allow for unforeseen experiments into moral behaviour, and a new range of moral possibilities (Zigon 2009) are opened up (for study) in this process, implying a cultural critical potential (Marcus and Fischer 1999). We cannot afford to ignore spaces, practices, or technological devices that are significant to our interlocutors, or to neglect seeking to qualify these as they make up part of our fieldwork and knowledge making. My efforts here have been towards showing how tracing the affordances for my interlocutors of technological devices have entailed an increased awareness and employment of those same technological devices in pursuing fieldwork as interface – as a device and a conceptualization that we can draw on, not instead of but alongside other methods and practices, whether experimental, interventionist or classical.

Karen Waltorp (Aarhus University) is assistant professor at the Department of Anthropology, Aarhus University, Denmark. Her interests span digital and visual anthropology, social media, gender, kinship, the (urban) environment, and Islam and the West. She teaches in the Eye and Mind MA specialization in visual anthropology and design anthropology. Her PhD Mirror Images entailed a thirty-minute film as part of an exploration of the smartphone as relational device and real virtuality with young Muslim women in Copenhagen. She is currently part of the three-year research project ARTlife: Articulations of Life among Afghans in Denmark.

Notes

1. Names of interlocutors have been changed.
2. Denmark is a small country of 5.6 million people where first and second generation immigrants currently constitute around 11% of the national population, and approximately 22% of Copenhagen's population (Danmarks Statistik 2014:11). The definition of a ghetto was according to such criteria as the percentage of residents unemployed, the percentage of immigrants from non-Western countries, and the percentage of inhabitants with a criminal record (Ghetto Strategi 2010: 5).

References

Abu-Lughod, L. 1986. *Veiled Sentiments: Honor and Poetry in a Bedouin Society*. Berkeley, CA: University of California Press.
Arendt, H. (1958) 1998. *The Human Condition*. Chicago, IL: University of Chicago Press.
Ardévol, E. 2012. 'Virtual/Visual Ethnography: Methodological Crossroads at the Intersection of Visual and Internet Research', in S. Pink (ed.), *Advances in Visual Methodology*. Anderson, SC: Parlor Press, pp. 74–93.
Asad, T., et al. 2009. *Is Critique Secular? Blasphemy, Injury, and Free Speech*. Berkeley, CA: University of California, Townsend Center for the Humanities.
Bateson, G. (1972) 2000. *Steps to an Ecology of Mind: Collected Essays in Anthropology, Psychiatry, Evolution and Epistemology*. Chicago, IL: University of Chicago Press.
Benhabib, S. 2002. *The Claims of Culture: Equality and Diversity in the Global Era*. Princeton, NJ: Princeton University Press.
Danmarks Statistik. 2014. 'Indvandrere i Danmark'. Available at http://www.dst.dk/pukora/epub/upload/19004/indv.pdf (last accessed 2 April 2017).
Fassin, D. 2008. 'Beyond Good and Evil?: Questioning the Anthropological Discomfort with Morals'. *Anthropological Theory* 8(4): 333–44.
Fassin, D., and W. Stoczkowski. 2008. 'Should Anthropology be Moral? A Debate'. *Anthropological Theory* 8(4): 331–32.
Fernando, M.L. 2013. 'Save the Muslim Woman, Save the Republic: Ni Putes Ni Soumises and the Ruse of Neoliberal Sovereignty'. *Modern & Contemporary France* 21(2): 147–65.
Fischer, M.J. 2009. *Anthropological Futures*. Durham, NC: Duke University Press

Ghetto Strategi. 2010. 'Ghettoen tilbage til samfundet'. Available at www.
stm.dk/publikationer/Ghettostrategi_10/Ghettostrategi.pdf (last
accessed 2 April 2017).

Gibson, J.J. 1977. 'The Theory of Affordances', in R. Shaw and J.
Bransford (eds), *Perceiving, Acting, and Knowing: Toward an Ecological
Psychology*. Hillsdale, NJ: Lawrence Erlbaum, pp. 67–82.

Haraway, D. 1988. 'Situated Knowledges: The Science Question in
Feminism and the Privilege of Partial Perspective'. *Feminist Studies*
14(3): 575–99.

Hookway, B. 2014. *Interface*. Cambridge, MA: MIT Press.

Klintefelt, T., L. Lavrsen and D. Larsen. 2014. 'Indvandrere i Danmark'.
Copenhagen: Danmarks Statistik.

Knappett, C. 2004. 'The Affordances of Things: A Post-Gibsonian
Perspective on the Relationality of Mind and Matter', in E. DeMarrais,
C. Gosden and C. Renfrew (eds), *Rethinking Materiality: The
Engagement of Mind with the Material World*. Cambridge, MA:
McDonald Institute for Archaeological Research, pp. 43–51.

Law, J. 2004. *After Method: Mess in Social Science Research*. London:
Routledge.

———. 2016. 'Modes of Knowing', in J. Law and E. Ruppert (eds), *Modes
of Knowing: Resources from the Baroque*. Manchester: Mattering Press,
pp. 17–56.

Marcus, G.E., and M.J. Fischer. (1986) 1999. *Anthropology as Cultural
Critique: An Experimental Moment in the Human Sciences*. Chicago, IL:
The University of Chicago Press.

Maskens, M., and R. Blanes. 2013. 'Don Quixote's Choice: A Manifesto for
a Romanticist Anthropology'. *HAU: Journal of Ethnographic Theory*
3(3): 245–81.

Mol, A. 2008. *The Logic of Care: Health and the Problem of Patient
Choice*. London: Routledge.

Rabinow, P., et al. 2008. *Designs for an Anthropology of the Contemporary*.
Durham, NC: Duke University Press.

Robbins, J. 2009. 'Value, Structure, and the Range of Possibilities: A
Response to Zigon'. *Ethnos* 74(2): 277–85.

Verran, H. 2013. 'Engagements between Disparate Knowledge Traditions:
Toward Doing Difference Generatively and in Good Faith', in L.
Green (ed.), *Contested Ecologies: Dialogues in the South on Nature and
Knowledge*. Cape Town: HSRC Press, pp. 141–61.

Waltorp, K. 2010. 'Uddannelse & Opposition'. *Antropologi: Skole* 62:
127–51.

———. 2011. *Catalogue: Ghetto NO Ghetto*. Copenhagen: Avant Afro
Micro Press.

———. 2013. 'Public/Private Negotiations in the Media Uses of Young
Muslim Women in Copenhagen: Gendered Social Control and the
Technology-Enabled Moral Laboratories of a Multicultural City'.
International Communication Gazette 75(5–6): 555–72.

———. 2015. 'Keeping Cool, Staying Virtuous: Social Media and the Composite Habitus of Young Muslim Women in Copenhagen'. *MedieKultur: Journal of Media and Communication Studies* 58: 49–67.

———. 2016. 'A Snapchat Essay on Mutuality, Utopia and Non-innocent Conversations'. *Journal of the Anthropological Society of Oxford* VIII(2): 251–73.

———. Forthcoming. 'Intimacy, Concealment and Unconscious Optics: Filmmaking with Young Muslim Women in Copenhagen'. *Journal of Visual Anthropology*, special issue on 'Camera as Cultural Critique'.

Waltorp, K., and S. Jensen. Forthcoming. 'Awkward Entanglements: Kinship, Morality and Survival in Cape Town's Prison-Township Circuit'. *Ethnos: Journal of Anthropology* (http://dx.doi.org/10.1080/001 41844.2017.1321565).

Waltorp, K., and C. Vium. 2010. *MANENBERG: Growing Up in the Shadows of Apartheid*. London: Royal Anthropological Institute. Available at www.therai.org.uk/fs/film-sales/manenberg/ (last accessed 2 April 2017).

Weiner, J.F. 1997. 'Televisualist Anthropology: Representation, Aesthetics, Politics'. *Current Anthropology* 38(2): 197–235.

Zigon, J. 2009. 'Within a Range of Possibilities: Morality and Ethics in Social Life'. *Ethnos* 74(2): 251–76.

———. 2010. 'Moral and Ethical Assemblages: A Response to Fassin and Stoczkowski'. *Anthropological Theory* 10(1–2): 3–15.

6

Thrown into Collaboration
An Ethnography of Transcript Authorization

Alexandra Kasatkina, Zinaida Vasilyeva and
Roman Khandozhko

This chapter is an account of our fieldwork experience as researchers and interviewers in the Obninsk project – a large-scale collective enterprise aimed at collecting a corpus of in-depth biographical interviews with scientists and engineers who lived and worked in Obninsk, one of the science cities constructed as part of the Soviet nuclear programme. Once it was decided to publish the corpus of transcribed interviews online in an open digital archive, we had to consider getting agreements from our interlocutors to publish, or, as we came to call it in the project, to *authorize* the transcripts (translators and journalists use Russian term *avtorizatsiia*[1] when they show translated texts or edited interviews to the authors or interviewees in order to get their consent for publication). Although the collaborative paradigm was not part of the initial research design, we experienced and learned it from practice and, hence, were thrown into collaboration.

Our intention is to compose an ethnography of authorization. After discussing the project, the field and logistical details, we will describe our journey through three personal cases of authorization, and reflect on how that experience influenced and was influenced by the disciplinary views of the three of us – two anthropologists (Alexandra and Zinaida) and one historian (Roman); and how the dynamics of our relationship with our field partners were shaped and transformed in those negotiations.

The Obninsk Project

With a general orientation towards the oral history practice of collecting narrative biographical interviews (Thompson 1978), the Obninsk project was designed with the aim to approach a particular ethos of the Soviet scientific elite that emerged in the post-war era: nuclear scientists and engineers. Intellectually, this interdisciplinary initiative was open to any and all research methods and theoretical approaches. The only feature of the research design established beforehand was the basic method of data collection: in-depth biographical interviews. This meant that along with conducting interviews, the participants were free to pursue their own research on the data they collected. Between 2012 and 2015, twelve individuals were involved in conducting interviews. Among them were anthropologists, historians, psychologists, sociologists, philosophers and philologists. Most interviews were collected between 2012 and 2013, though single conversations are still being recorded. The corpus now contains 500 hours of interview (about 250 different conversations) with 151 long-time residents of Obninsk.

Authorization: Initial Debates

Because of our different academic backgrounds, we all entered the Obninsk field with diverse understandings of interview methodology and how the 'final product' of an interview should look. However, while we were conducting interviews, these epistemic differences were pretty manageable: each of us worked individually and we did our best to conform to the standards appropriated during our previous training. It was in the debate over transcription standards that our disciplinary divisions became critical. In that discussion, philologists advocated for literary editing of transcripts deposited online to make them more readable for a wider audience; however, a discourse psychologist objected that her analysis is impossible without detailed documentation of verbal and non-verbal speech events in the transcript, and that literary editing is a strong outer interpretation distorting the meaning of speech (on the interpretative significance of transcription, see, for example: Bucholtz 2000). After some heated debates, we agreed on a kind of soft verbatim mode of transcription with word-for-word documentation of oral speech, including lapsus linguae, paralinguistic elements and unfinished syllables.

The intention to publish the transcripts of the interviews as an open online archive was occasionally articulated, even at the beginning of the project (for a discussion on digital archives in anthropology, see Fabian 2002; Kelty 2009; Fortun et al. 2014). The challenge this would cause led to scepticism among some researchers of the team, who anticipated difficulties obtaining informant consent to publish unedited transcripts within the timeframe of the project (negative experiences of showing unedited transcripts to interviewees have been reported by, for example, Turnbull 2000; Mero-Jaffe 2011).

At some point, however, the initial idea to create an online archive of Obninsk interviews[2] was confirmed to be one of the main goals of the project, along with the printed volume,[3] and the protocol of authorization was set up. Now the interviewers faced the fact that they had to obtain signed consent from their interlocutors, not just for working with collected documents but for open digital publication, as well and bring transcripts back to them to negotiate the content, if the interviewees so wished.

Authorization turned out to be a challenge. Many interviewees were upset by seeing their oral speech carefully rendered in written form. The negotiations were often complicated, followed by misunderstanding, disappointment or even conflict. Some people demanded that their texts be edited, while others refused to have their transcripts published at all. Some took their texts for review and kept them for a year or more, being reluctant to agree to publish them, or even to decide to refuse (cf. Carlson 2010).

Obninsk: The City of Science

Obninsk is a small provincial town with about 105,000 residents. It is situated 100 km south-west of Moscow and is easily accessible from the Russian capital by train or car in just under two hours. However, unlike many other Russian provincial towns, Obninsk holds the special status of 'science city' (*naukograd*), boasting thirteen major scientific research institutes.

Like many scientific settlements, Obninsk was founded during Soviet times as part of an atomic project launched by Stalin after the Second World War to develop nuclear weapons and counterbalance US post-war military leadership. In 1945, it was set up as a nameless settlement surrounding the so-called 'Laboratory V'. The main goal of the nuclear project was achieved in 1949, when the first Soviet atomic bomb was tested successfully, marking the beginning of the Cold War. In 1956, Obninsk became known worldwide as the cradle of the first nuclear power station in the world, and was officially put on the map.

Until the end of the Soviet Union, Obninsk remained an important centre for nuclear science and radiation research. Its population mainly consisted of highly qualified experts, engineers and scientists, employed by local research centres and institutes. The best graduates from all over the country came to Obninsk to work on cutting-edge Soviet science and technology, and benefited from good wages and material privileges, such as better provisions and housing conditions. As an urban setting, Obninsk has produced a specific social environment: it is a relatively small territory with a highly skilled and well-networked population, which can be described as a tight-knit community of people connected through personal neighbour-like and professional relations. Moreover, scientists enjoyed a high level of social prestige, constituting one of the Soviet elite strata. The post-Soviet sociopolitical and economic crises challenged this privileged position: funds for state-sponsored research centres were cut drastically, and many Obninsk residents, including leading scientists, found themselves in poverty. However, most of them remained faithful to knowledge, loyal to the glorious scientific and technological achievements of the Soviet Union, and proud to belong to the history of the USSR and Obninsk, the city of science.

After landing in Obninsk in 2012, we found that our interviewees were far from being marginal and voiceless subjects. Instead, many of them had their own critical arguments, and historically grounded opinions. They reflected on their community, its place in the Soviet past and in the contemporary Russian social and political order, and its moral right to be a part of History. Moreover, our field counterparts were often active gatekeepers of local history, building their own archives and even writing and publishing their findings. Indeed, they 'share some of the same privileges and modest empowerments as those of us who interview and write about them' (Marcus 2001: 523).

The Interview Protocol of the Obninsk Project

The flexibility of the Obninsk project's overall research design did not apply to the protocol of recording interviews, which was set up from the beginning. For each recorded conversation, a letter of consent was to be signed by the interlocutor, where they could decide how the interview would be used in the future. Signing a letter of consent is quite a rare practice among contemporary Russian anthropologists; however, it is a routine practice for oral historians (Kalendarova 2006: 207). In our case, two additional points were at stake. First, Obninsk is not a typical city: during Soviet times, it was a strategically important research centre, so many of our potential subjects used to work under various levels of secrecy. In this context, our interlocutors were likely to consider formal regulation to be an important condition of our information exchange. Second, a recent Russian law on personal data (No. 152 of the Federal Law) requires a written agreement for it to be used, and personal data obviously forms part of any biographical interview.

The structure of our letter of consent offered four choices to the interviewee: (1) to allow/forbid using their real name when publishing the interview and/or particular quotations; (2) to express/decline a wish to read the transcript before publishing; (3) to express/decline a wish to introduce changes into the transcript; (4) to grant the right of interpretation of the transcript to the researchers of the project.

In practice, many of our subjects (128 of 151) chose to keep their real names, being aware that in a small city inhabited by a tiny community of professionals it is almost impossible to give a biographical narrative anonymously. The majority (107 of 151) wanted to read the transcripts before publishing.

The preparation of a verbatim text was a demanding task; it was time consuming, expensive, and labour intensive. In our project, over sixty individuals were involved in transcription, mainly Russian-speaking students from Belarus, Lithuania, Russia and Ukraine, but their labour was rather poorly paid due to funding limitations, which resulted in a less than ideal standard of work. To minimize mistakes and inaccuracies, the interviewers verified each transcript, which meant listening to the original recording again and comparing it to the text. Afterwards they contacted the interviewee and initiated the authorization process. Preparing a single transcript could take dozens of hours of work for two individuals, including one qualified researcher. This slowed authorization down significantly, adding to the length of time that negotiations might take. The first authorizations began in 2012, and the process is still continuing. By October 2017, five years after the project began, 91 of the 187 transcripts waiting for review have been authorized for publication (17 more are currently under review, and 3 have been withheld by interviewees).

This experience prompts important considerations for the institutional design and time frame of research initiatives willing to try transcript authorization. The Obninsk project was initially limited to one year; but while the interviewers were said to be responsible for authorization, it soon became clear that it was not possible to have all the interviews authorized for publication within one year. The three cases presented below took place when the three of us were still working for the project; yet, even now that our formal involvement with the project is long over, the authorization of our Obninsk interviews is still under way.

Zinaida, Alexei and Veronika

Interactions with seniors are common for the Obninsk project and the physical health of interviewees may decline dramatically over the course of two or three years. To our knowledge, 10 of the 151 subjects who took part in the Obninsk project have passed away. Alexei[4] (b. 1940) was the first among them. Since the decision on mandatory authorization of transcripts was made early on, the very fact of a subject's death brought up the question of who might be able to 'inherit' the right (or the responsibility?) to authorize the text. In what follows, Zinaida Vasilyeva analyses the process of authorization completed by Veronika, Alexei's widow.

On 8 August 2012, a brilliant, peculiar and rather caustic man met me in his office. During the first minutes of our talk, he ironically referred to himself as a 'lab rat' in our research – thus setting a barrier and constructing a hierarchy by choosing a subordinate and defensive position. Nevertheless, he eventually warmed to the topic, and the final length of the interview exceeded three hours. During our conversation Alexei expressed considerably straightforward judgements, criticism of academic praxis, and remarkable openness. He described conflicts with colleagues with irony, indulged in retelling delicate stories of some thesis presentations, and critically commented on the current state of affairs in the country and at his research institute. At some point I wondered if the interview in some way allowed him to get even with his past.

Building his career required a lot of effort, and his crowning achievement was when he became a laureate of the most prestigious international prize in his field. As a child during the Second World War, Alexei lost both of his parents and was seriously injured. This injury ultimately limited his career choice: after the war the so-called 'field' university departments (such as geology, geography, archaeology) were very popular, since they included field experience and participation in expeditions, and were associated with the romance of travel. However, enrolment required a general medical examination in addition to entry exams, and Alexei had no chance. Nevertheless, Alexei's remarkable commitment, outstanding intellect, fierce ambition and tremendous efficiency allowed him to build a successful career against all the odds.

Although his autobiographical narrative was full of sensitive details, Alexei expressed no intention to check the transcript when he signed the letter of consent at the end of the interview. Yet, I convinced him to select the option 'read the transcript' on the form. I thought he was likely to regret having conveyed such strong opinions after the fact, so I wanted to protect him in a way. When the transcript was ready, I called him back to arrange a meeting for authorization, but a woman's quivering voice answered that Alexei had passed away.

Alexei's death drastically changed the status of the interview. From then on, it was no longer just one of numerous interviews within the Obninsk project, but a memorial and final biographical document. Its destiny became of great interest and attention to the local community. To honour Alexei, his colleagues started preparing a commemorative volume, and the editor (who had also been interviewed for our project) asked if he could have a transcript (even a raw one) to use while working on the manuscript. But the transcript had not been authorized, and under these circumstances, the issue of authorization had become even more critical; at that moment, there was neither precedent nor any distinct protocol, so for the time being we had to deny his request.

After some discussion with colleagues I initiated authorization with Veronika, Alexei's widow, who was also a close colleague from his university days. Her deep professional and personal involvement in Alexei's life made her, in my eyes, an ideal successor in both the legal and ethical sense of the word. Moreover, being Alexei's colleague, she could assist us like no other in introducing context and detail to his narrative.[5] Veronika eagerly accepted my request; and on 11 June 2013 I sent her the transcript with a detailed commentary on how I would like her to work with the text.

The email contained a brief outline of the project and interview protocol, an explanation of the rules of transcription and a few lines emphasizing the importance of a verbatim record for our research. I hoped those lines would inspire her and help to preserve oral features in the text. I also offered a colour-coded system for editing: red would be used to block any parts she would prefer to remove, and any additions she wished to make would be in green.

A month later I received a heavily edited transcript – Veronika had accomplished a large amount of work, attentively checking forty pages of text, correcting misheard names of people and titles of books, seminars and conferences, specifying dates and a few biographical details, deleting repetitions of words and phrases along with the majority of vernacular expressions, and adjusting the transcript with respect to *her* understanding of how a written text should look. In addition, she had blocked a few (though meaningful) details. This editing was done accurately according to the mark-up system; hence Veronika demonstrated that she had done her best to meet the requirements of the project.

This version of transcript, however, challenged the very logic of authorization. In fact, the text had already been partially edited and, therefore, was not verbatim in a strict sense anymore. Moreover, it was now, to some extent, 'censored', because where Veronika had applied the red blocking colour, the whole meaning of some paragraphs had been changed. Interestingly enough, though, despite my expectations, she did not adjust the descriptions of social tensions within academia; but she did, for example, remove a passage describing everyday life during the war.

Alexei had spent his early childhood in Ukraine, the territory occupied by the Nazis during the Second World War. Many officers and soldiers had stayed at local people's houses, including Alexei's. Regardless of the difficulties of wartime, his memories of this period revealed not only tragic moments, such as the fatal shooting of his mother in the last month of the occupation, but also several bright events of everyday wartime life, like a New Year celebration with German soldiers. The climax of the story was the appearance of a German officer who enters the room, gets his gun, shoots a star on the top of the New Year tree, and leaves; the 'peaceful' celebration continues.

While working on this section, Veronika blocked any parts of sentences that could give the impression that life had remained relatively peaceful under occupation, and added words and characteristics emphasizing the terror of those times. By doing so, she undoubtedly intended to eliminate any details that (in her view) might damage the civil image of her spouse. Even today, the memories of a relatively calm coexistence with German soldiers contradict official and commonly shared Russian narratives of the war, which portray the Nazis as inhumane and cruel aggressors, and omit any unconventionally positive stories. Thus, Veronika's editing was to protect Alexei's story from any eventual critical reading. This is not particularly evident, as the narrated episode did not, in fact, present everyday life under occupation as idyllic. From Alexei's description one can understand why all the eyewitnesses of the New Year incident were horrified by the officer's arrival: nobody knew if the star would be his only victim. Moreover, the intensity of an ambivalent emotional experience, combining the joy of celebration and the fear of death, most likely became the main cognitive anchor in Alexei's memory. However, the mention of the fact of a common festivity obviously perplexed Veronika and prompted her to intervene by censoring the paragraphs containing minor ambivalence in moral evaluation of historical events. In her version, the story was adjusted according to the conventional description of the war drawn with unnuanced black and white. Moreover, Veronika added a few sentences describing their family trip to Belarus to find the grave of Alexei's father, who had been killed in battle during the war. Thus, not only did she restore a conventional narrative about the war but she even strengthened it by providing an image of a war hero commemoration. Because this intervention considerably modified the meaning of the story, I decided to remove the entire passage about the New Year celebration before submitting the transcript to the digital archive.

Working with the transcript, Veronika faced a task that was both ethic and epistemic in nature. She was caught between the will to keep the last words of her late spouse as intact as possible (in her first letter on 1 July 2013 she wrote: 'I do not dare correct the views, thoughts etc.'), and her wish to preserve memories about him in the most positive light. In some cases, this conflict prompted her to intervene. At the same time, Veronika's tactics were shaped by the rules of the project and the instructions I had given her in my email. Her subjective intention to keep the text intact complied with my expectation that she preserve as much of the original transcript as possible; yet the form of verbatim transcript contradicted her idea of a written text that was to become an important public representation of her spouse and even a memorial in Alexei's honour. Veronika felt responsible for the form and the content of this memorial, and my invitation for her to participate in authorization was a chance to contribute to Alexei's commemoration.

The deletions and additions introduced into the text were a compromise Veronika made when solving her ethic and epistemic dilemma. While using the toolkit offered by the project and accurately marking the sentences with red and green, she reinvented parts of it and, in a sense, rendered it an instrument of censorship, thus radically transforming (if not ignoring) the internal epistemic logic of verbatim records. Moreover, I believe that it had been my explicit instructions and my mark-up editing system that had enabled

Veronika to block the undesired passages and thus helped her to resolve her moral dilemma.

Although my interactions with Veronika can be described in terms of collaboration, they were not reflected as such in the process of authorization. Instead, as a member of the collective project with articulated collective goals, such as conducting biographical interviews and later on preparing data for the digital archive, I was forced to examine my personal and professional ethics. While my anthropological ethos called for the maximal insurance for the subject's comfort, the protocol of the project demanded preserving as much detail as possible. Under these circumstances, I tended to agree with the choice of my interlocutors. However, as Alexei had passed away I had to deal with two subjects: the narrator and the successor. Finally, I decided to accept all of Veronika's changes except those where Alexei's original meanings had clearly been modified; yet, to acknowledge Veronika's opinion, I chose to remove that whole section.

Today, I realize the authorization process had the potential to facilitate further eventual collaborations – with Veronika and other members of the commemorative community. However, this collaboration would hardly be possible within the same institutional framework of the project.

Roman and Pavel

The deterritorialization of an interview is one of the effects of authorization. Any version of a transcript is potentially non-final, just an element of a constantly evolving communicative ensemble including sound record, different editions of a transcript, original documents consigned to the project, and even drafts of future articles. Altogether, the unfolding process of building this ensemble can be interpreted as collaboration. In what follows, Roman Khandozhko would like to analyse his experience of collaborating with Pavel (b. 1942), an expert in the theory of atmospheric physics.

As a historian, I am interested in cases of political self-organization of scientists during the period of political instability in the USSR/ Russia of the late 1980s and early 1990s. Pursuing this agenda, I learned about Pavel via a chain of subjects who participated in creating the first democratic organization in Obninsk, the so-called Obninsk People's Front. I was particularly interested in meeting Pavel, because I knew he held a unique archive of documents of local non-official political activists. The interview was recorded in a hospitable home atmosphere: a three-hour-long conversation was followed by tea and ended by examining several boxes from the home archive. Pavel kindly offered me a significant portion of the documents to scan.

While the interview was being transcribed, we started exchanging emails. I scanned and sent Pavel the documents from his archive, which he later passed to the local museum. We regularly shared links to publications on the history of the Soviet atomic project. Three months after our meeting, the transcript was ready for authorization, and I gave it to Pavel during my next trip to Obninsk.

When Pavel signed the letter of consent, he decided to reserve the right to make changes to the transcript. Handing him the text for review, I reminded him about this option, but also emphasized that preservation of oral features would give the transcript additional value for the research tasks of the project. Like many other interviewees, Pavel was upset that his speech was not very eloquent and the structure of his narrative was rather incoherent. This did not prevent him from reviewing the transcript within a week, though. His general inclination for reflexivity and self-criticism probably motivated him to acknowledge his speech imperfections. The final text was partially spared of filler words ('you know', 'well', etc.) and some repeated storylines. Pavel also reformulated some of his judgements concerning the secret work of his institute, which he considered (after a discussion with his wife) to be too straightforward. At the same time, he added a large semi-memoir, semi-journalistic section, including a description of the mentality of atomic project employees living in closed settlements.

To understand the dynamics of our interactions it is important to note that Pavel is an amateur historian. Interested in the history of the Soviet atomic project, he follows memoirs and academic publications, and tracks life trajectories of people who lived and worked in Arzamas-16, a top-secret centre of nuclear weapons research, where his father worked as a building engineer and where Pavel himself spent his childhood. Therefore, his participation in the project became an opportunity to contribute to research on the subject in which he was already interested. It is likely that this context favoured the establishment of a collaborative spirit and facilitated the authorization process. One can guess that his own engagement in the historical inquiry and, therefore, his respect for scholarly methods helped Pavel to overcome the discomfort related to the public exposure of the awkwardness of his verbatim transcript and complete the authorization.

Pavel's editing tactics were influenced by his positivistic understanding of history as objective fact and his perception of his transcript as a historical document. He added modality markers such as 'it seems', 'likely', and 'as far as I understood' where he did not consider himself competent enough to judge 'objectively', as he wrote in one of his letters. I continued receiving emails from him clarifying this or that choice of modality long after the authorization was completed. Undoubtedly, the content of the transcript occupied Pavel's thoughts much longer than the authorization lasted. His clarifications evaluated the motives of certain people in his narrative, and the social parameters of his professional environment. Once he wrote: 'It was a wild guess to say that 30 percent of the people in my department were Communist Party members. That was clearly an overestimation – 20 percent is a more exact number'.

He felt responsible for the veracity of the historical document he was constructing, and did his best to attain fairness and objectivity, which is why he referenced external sources, like publications and consultations with former colleagues. In Pavel's case the situation of the interview – the first stage of our interaction – was only a prelude to further collaborative work on the production of memory. The following work with the transcript – a textual document – became a way to defamiliarize personal experience while transforming it into a 'historical document', which from now on did not belong to him personally but was part of history. Pavel often emphasized his 'interest in preserving the maximum amount of information possible', and he readily responded to my clarifying questions.

Pavel's positivistic understanding of history, his critical attitude towards his own memory, and his amateur interest in the history of everyday life, turned out to be an ideal basis for developing a collaborative relationship, which was extended in time due to the preplanned authorization of transcript.

Since one of my interests in the Obninsk project was the changing regimes of micropolitics and the structure of independent social actors under the influence of Gorbachev's reforms, it was very important for me to address not only individual experience, but the 'community of memory' that succeeds the narrow circle of democratic activists of the late 1980s. Collaboration with Pavel helped me to accomplish this. In addition to biographical interviews, I had an opportunity to observe how lost fragments of memory were restored as a result of communication between subjects. One can say it was a happy occasion of a mutually beneficial exchange, for I asked Pavel not only to specify the details of the interview, but also to provide commentary on information I had obtained from other sources, sometimes unknown to him. Thus, Pavel learned from my knowledge as well. For instance, we reconstructed details of the Obninsk election campaign of the 'first Soviet millionaire', Artem Tarasov, described rather one-sidedly in his memoirs. Pavel gathered memoirs of people who once attended Tarasov's election meetings and helped to clarify the importance of the city Komsomol committee for his nomination.

It is important to note that Pavel remains very self-reflexive and self-critical regarding the expertise he can provide. When talking about Arzamas-16, he positions himself as a competent connoisseur, if not an expert, but when it comes to the sphere of my own research interest, Pavel respects a conventional distance between the 'knowledge of witness' and academic historical knowledge. Although Pavel himself is an active author of journalistic reports for local newspapers, where he does not hold back from judging upon the Soviet past, he declined my attempts to discuss the latest academic publications on the history of Perestroika. Pavel said he doubted his abilities to adequately understand social science texts.

Thus, the transcript appears to be a meeting place for the interests of researcher and interviewee that may occasionally overlap, but never coincide completely. The collaboration between the researcher and informant is not, therefore, always limited to recording and transcribing an interview. These two might become only hubs in a network: more or less stable, though containing growing points for both accumulating factual material and sophisticating reflexive surfaces that allow a deeper grasp of the research. Moreover, an interview as an event turns out to catalyse social interactions re-establishing the structures of collective memory. The classic research interview, not meant for publishing, seems to produce similar effects. However, authorization, especially with the use of digital media, makes this reshaping visible to the researcher, thus enhancing their view of the field and stimulating deeper elaboration of the issues in focus.

Alexandra and Rimma

Classical literature on interviewing cautions against publishing and even showing verbatim transcripts to informants because it can hurt them (Kvale 1996). From this perspective, authorization of a verbatim text is a risky experiment, challenging both researchers and their field partners. Yet, from the perspective of collaboration as a form of joint research endeavour, it can be seen as an important condition of field partnership: by showing such transcripts, we honestly reveal our methods and admit our counterparts' intellectual ability to understand them. In what follows, Alexandra Kasatkina demonstrates the difficulties that arose when taking this stance while working with her informant, Rimma (b. 1935).

I was introduced to Rimma by Vera, an old friend of hers from the close-knit veterans' community of the oldest Obninsk research institute. She readily agreed to tell me about her life for our project: 'Come and we'll talk'. Our almost three-hour talk took place on 2 June 2013 on the terrace of her summer house. I started with the necessary formalities, introducing the project and giving Rimma a consent form to read and sign. Yet, the interview was very much like a heart-to-heart conversation. Slowly and thoughtfully my interlocutor developed the topics I offered, going deep into her memory. Never bothering to choose proper words, she talked about 'scoundrel husbands' and 'donkey bosses', made anti-Semitic remarks, shared gossip about her neighbours, and remembered the happy days of the past with dreamy smiles.

The transcript was ready after about six months. On 7 April 2014 I met Rimma again to give her the transcript. When signing her consent, she had selected the options to read and edit the transcript before publication. Yet, during our second conversation, Rimma seemed to be looking for an excuse for this choice, possibly fearing that I could take it personally as lack of trust. She shared her offence at a recent newspaper article by a journalist after an interview with their veteran medical gymnastics group. Then she dropped a couple of hints as to the roots of her caution about information: it was not just many years' working in the classified institute, but also the noble lineage of her grandfather – a circumstance that had made her family extremely vulnerable in the Soviet times.

I called Rimma several times to check her progress with the text. It was hard. My interlocutor was very proud of her writing skills. She proudly told me that when her husband had been writing his dissertation on nuclear physics, she had corrected his numerous spelling errors (even though she understood little of the content). A good command of standard literary Russian is highly regarded in Soviet-Russian culture as a sign of belonging to the educated class. As for many in her generation, Rimma had to struggle to gain her education. She had to start working right after finishing school. When her husband took her to Obninsk, Rimma managed to finish at technical school with honours, but she was not able to continue her studies because her husband was ill. Facing such a raw flow of oral speech as a verbatim transcript threatened her self-esteem as a language expert; publishing it would threaten her public face as an educated person. It is no surprise that Rimma did not like her transcript and asked me to turn it into a smooth written text, as journalists usually do, when they publish interviews.

Until that moment our interaction with Rimma had satisfied a fieldwork scenario I had learnt during my anthropological training: I had managed to establish a warm relationship and conduct our interview in a pleasant conversational mode. The ethos I adopted at my anthropology department prescribed doing my best to reduce my informant's discomfort during research and maintain a balance of power in the field. Therefore, when I became an unintentional cause and witness of Rimma's tension, I felt very uneasy, as if I had broken the professional ethical code. However, editing the transcript to meet the wish of my interlocutor would be a violation of the conditions established by my employer. By 2013, when I entered the project, the authorization policy prohibited literary editing of transcripts by a researcher to prevent outer interpretation. The interviewer's possible intervention was limited to removing most annoying and ethically threatening details, such as slips, repetitions, and personal names, and marking up their traces in order to preserve an image of an initial interview. Eventually I decided to follow my colleagues in the project in what seemed to be the only possible solution: to explain our methods of working with oral speech to my interlocutor and offer her a new approach to the transcript of her interview as a research document, not a biographical article.

In our long phone talks, I explained the principles of work with naturally occurring speech, and described its richness and heuristic potential. I expressed my sincere fascination with the beauty and melody of her speech. I shared my first experience of dealing with my own oral speech. I hoped that Rimma would share my position of a researcher, and realize the meaning and importance of her role as a co-producer of the research source. She, however, kept on failing to 'recognize herself' in her transcribed cues, and complained that it was difficult and unpleasant to work with such a poorly written text.

I was becoming more and more certain that the text would never be authorized. When I learned after another phone call that Rimma had lost the printed transcript, my pessimism was confirmed. Still, on 31 August 2014, I met her again and gave her another one. To my great surprise, when I called her on 1 December, she told me it was ready. She still could not accept the text, and yet she had completed the task, as she put it, to finish the business and not to let me down. A week later I came to take the transcript back. Rimma met me warmly and offered me tea with sweets. She brought a heap of pages, covered with notes that mostly consisted of crossed-out oral speech features – repetitions, discourse markers – and we discussed unclear details. The long process of authorization was finished at last.

When starting on the Rimma transcript, I had followed the common practice of social researchers publishing quotes from interviews and struggled to secure the privacy of anyone involved. I had excluded any bits that might threaten Rimma's social relations, as well as everything she had asked me not to publish. Hence, I took the responsibility for her statements, leaving her no choice. After almost a year, however, discussing the authorized transcript with Rimma, I recorded several extended versions of previously told stories. That time I decided to move 'ethical editing' into the dialogue zone and left an anti-Semitic remark unedited. Rimma did not pay attention to it. But as soon as I explained that it could insult a whole group of people, she asked me to remove it immediately. Thus, in the course of our long communication I gradually adopted the collaborative mode of field relations – the mode of equal dialogue. Eventually we came to joint reflection (however short and fragmented it was) with my field counterpart on the contents of her narrative and their effects, and we made joint efforts to elaborate a mutually acceptable public representation of the transcript.

Responding to my efforts to involve her in joint preparation of interview, Rimma built her own tactic of adaptation to authorization. She had had some experience of being interviewed by journalists as a local activist, so at first she thought of me as another press person, and was expecting a polished article. Having received the verbatim transcript, Rimma found herself in a quandary. She obviously did not want to refuse my request. One of the reasons, I assume, was her desire to introduce her view on city history to a wider audience through our open archive as a part of her lifetime struggle for her own voice in a patriarchal family and in male-dominated job environments. It was one of the leading ideas in her biographical narrative. And yet, the task I offered her to fulfil was unpleasant and completely unfamiliar. For all her life, Rimma had been verifying instruments for physicists, but now she faced the difference between oral and written language for the first time: 'When you speak, everything seems to be smooth, and then you look at it – and see only bits and pieces'. The experience of coming back to her words and the opportunity to change them was also new. To solve the contradiction, Rimma made explicit the third actor present in our relations – my employer – and framed our first meeting as a private talk ('you and me are just talking'), which I presented as an interview, seemingly following my job requirements. Then the unpleasant conditions of text production were dictated from above to us both, and authorizing it became an expression of solidarity with me. This position allowed Rimma to resolve her dilemma and save face.

Having yielded to our rules of text production, Rimma never accepted them. Empowering the field counterpart through her involvement in preparation of her interview for publication, developing partnership and sharing responsibility for the future publication are possible interpretations of authorization. Rimma rejected all of these interpretations by offering to have me edit her transcript. Her case may therefore be interpreted in terms of power and resistance: the researcher takes the dominating position, while the informant resists her well-intentioned efforts to empower her and insists on maintaining the status quo. I believe, however, that Rimma had enough of her own symbolic resources and agency in that situation: being a local activist with relatively easy access to newspapers, she seemed quite successful in her personal struggle for a voice. Moreover, she surely could have refused publishing her interview at any time. I would therefore argue for framing the case differently: not in terms of conflict, but as a complicated development of collaborative relations within authorization. Complicated – because for each of us it was a completely new experience, and we had to figure out on the spot how to act in the situation, and make sense of it. It means that the discomfort each of us felt can be regarded as a symptom of our shared resistance to entering the new order of field relationships and our mutual efforts to adjust, as well as a signal that the anthropological toolkit I had at my disposal did not provide me with appropriate instruments to participate in the authorization of interviews with educated professionals – that is, as a sign of a growing point.

Concluding Remarks

In Russian, the word *avtorizatsiia* connotes both the 'authority' and the 'author'. All our counterparts who chose and agreed to authorize transcripts became (at least to some extent) the co-authors of the texts to be published. Hence, the authorization turned out to be an 'experimental device' encouraging both researchers and research subjects to enter a previously unknown mode of interaction that can be interpreted as 'collaboration', comparable to 'joint production, but with overlapping mutual as well as differing purposes, negotiation, contestation, and uncertain outcomes' (Marcus 2001).

Engagement with this experimental device came, however, at a price. The institutional emphasis on preparing verbatim transcripts for open online archiving modified the logic of the fieldwork, shifting its focus from the contents of social experiences to the form and representational qualities of verbal exchanges. The interview became less a method to understand socialities embedded in individual experience, and more a way to co-produce specific textual autobiographical documents for open digital publication.

For the subjects, participation in our project mainly meant contributing to building the history of their community, which is also their own history. However, facing the prospect of open publication, they became concerned not so much with sharing their unique knowledge as creating appropriate public images. The discomfort of the counterparts, in turn, challenged the methodological and epistemic logic of the researchers, particularly of Alexandra and Zinaida. Trained as anthropologists, they tended to interpret the fieldwork dynamics in terms of political dominance, and were sensitive to power imbalances. This was not the case for Roman, who explored the interview method for the first time in the Obninsk project. Trained as a historian, he was used to working mainly with written sources and was more likely to agree with the logic of archiving interviews as historical documents; at the same time, interested in new knowledge produced over the course of co-production of the (non-)final texts of the transcripts, he was eager to pursue authorization.

With all the theoretical promises that such a digital archive may offer (Orlova 2016), rigid rules prohibiting literary editing of transcripts in order to preserve valuable features of verbatim speech inevitably privilege the needs of the researcher. Hence, as long as the design of a future archive is not discussed with the community from the very beginning, the final result will always be a rather asymmetrical compromise. As it turned out to be in the Obninsk project, the archive still remains a sophisticated database for researchers and the general public, while the local community is rather offered to extend its ideas of what a proper textual representation should look like. It may seem there is little space left for collaborative field relations.

The necessity to pass a verbatim transcript safely through authorization, however, prompted us to call on our field counterparts for even more intense collaboration. Through an explanation of the project goals and protocols we invited our field partners to engage critically with research methods and techniques, and to consciously participate in the co-production of a transcript as a form of knowledge about themselves and their communities. However, as the presented cases demonstrate, not every subject appears to be interested in such engagement. Rimma wanted to delegate the 'proper' editing of transcript to Alexandra, refusing to go so deeply into collaboration as to study our methods and become an active co-producer of the text. In contrast, Veronika and Pavel were eager to fulfil their task, but their level of cooperativeness was clearly shaped by their personal interests beyond the research itself.

We have never come to a consensus in evaluating our experiences of authorization. Neither are we sure that 'collaboration' is the most appropriate term to define our interactions with the field partners. Yet, we agree that these were *forms of partnerships shaped around knowledge production*. Given the diversity of these experiences and the ambiguity of feelings during and after authorization, today we prefer to ask the questions rather than give the answers.

What was authorization after all? Was it a right, a privilege or a duty? Was there in fact any collaboration? Did our field counterparts have tools to pursue their own goals through this mode of interaction? And if they did, to what extent? Was the engagement in authorization a free choice or a default necessity? Was the only free choice to decline any authorization and decide not to be part of the archive or, therefore, of the History of Obninsk? And who is to benefit from the digital archive?

Finally, does authorization offer a 'new epistemic order' or 'multiple orders' of field relations? Rather than seeing an established new epistemic order in authorization, we argue that it would be more justified to regard it as an open and uncertain *mode of knowledge production* that occurs through various differently shaped and (un)intended cooperative interactions. Authorization creates a new and uncertain communicative space, where all the participants constantly need to improvise and compromise. Navigating this terra incognita demands significant mutual efforts.

Acknowledgements

The work of the co-authors in Obninsk was generously supported by the Karamzin Fellowship Program of the Mikhail Prokhorov Foundation and the Administration of the Kaluga region in the framework of the following projects combined under the umbrella title of The Obninsk Project: 'Scientific and Technical Intelligentsia in Historical and Cultural Perspective: Shaping Environment, World View, and Work Ethics' (2012); 'Ideology and Practice of Technological Breakthrough: People and Institutions' (2013); 'Digital Scholarship: Humanists Creating Open Research Databases' (2014); and 'Crowdsourcing in Humanities: New Technologies and Communicative Modes of Knowledge Production in the Digital Era' (2015). The Obninsk project was implemented under the general supervision of Professor Andrei L. Zorin on the basis of the Russian Presidential Academy of National Economy and Public Administration (Moscow). Dr Galina A. Orlova joined him at the digitally focused stages in 2014 and 2015. The co-authors were employed as Karamzin research fellows at different times in these projects.

The draft of this chapter was considerably rewritten after a discussion at the graduate Writing seminar of Professor Stanley Brandes at the Anthropology Department of UC Berkeley. We thank all the participants of the seminar for their comments and questions. We are also grateful to Petr Safronov, Andrey Vozyanov and the editors of this volume for their valuable comments, and to Faye Gotlieb for proofreading the original text.

Alexandra Kasatkina (Museum of Anthropology and Ethnography, St Petersburg) is an anthropologist employed as a junior researcher at Peter the Great Museum of Anthropology and Ethnography (Kunstkamera) of the Russian Academy of Sciences, and a researcher in the Obninsk digital project. She is currently working on the dissertation about oral memories of the Perestroika age. Her research interests include field ethnography, cultural analysis of oral discourse, and digitalization of qualitative data.

Zinaida Vasilyeva (Université de Neuchâtel / European University at St Petersburg) is an anthropologist interested in historically grounded and ethnographically driven research of post-socialist societies. Her academic background includes training in history, anthropology, and science and technology studies acquired at the European University in St Petersburg, Université de Neuchâtel and UC Berkeley. She has participated separately in research projects focusing on post-Soviet memory and on techno-scientific communities in the former USSR. Her field of interests includes anthropology of knowledge and technologies, political anthropology, media and communications, subjectivity and the post-Cold war condition. She is currently finalizing her PhD thesis on DIY in post-Soviet Russia at the University of Neuchâtel.

Roman Khandozhko (University of Tübingen / Russian Academy of National Economy and Public Administration, Moscow) is a research fellow at the Institute for Eastern European History and Area Studies, University of Tübingen. He is a member of the collective project 'Nuclear Technopolitics in the Soviet Union', and concentrates currently on the history of the nuclear research centres in Dubna and Obninsk. Roman holds a PhD (kandidat nauk) in history awarded in 2010 at the South Federal University (Rostov-on-Don, Russia). His research addresses social and political networking in the late Soviet Union and post-Soviet Russia; intellectual anthropology of Soviet intelligentsia; and politics of history in the Soviet and post-Soviet context.

Notes

1. Hereinafter, for transliteration of Russian spelling we use the US Library of Congress standard (ALA-LC).
2. Forthcoming at: www.obninsk-project.net.
3. The volume is currently in progress.
4. All names in the accounts are fictional.
5. There were indeed many unclear fragments in the transcript, because during the interview Alexei had often got up and walked around the room, away from the recorder, while still talking.

References

Bucholtz, M. 2000. 'The Politics of Transcriptions'. *Journal of Pragmatics* 32: 1439–65.
Carlson, J. 2010. 'Avoiding Traps in Member-Checking'. *The Qualitative Report* 15(5): 1102–13.
Fabian, J. 2002. 'Virtual Archives and Ethnographic Writing: "Commentary" as a New Genre?' *Current Anthropology* 43(5): 775–86.
Fortun, K., et al. 2014. 'Experimental Ethnography Online: The Asthma Files'. *Cultural Studies* 28(4): 632–42.

Kalendarova, V.V. 2006. '"Rasskazhite mne o svoei zhizni": sbor kollektsii biograficheskikh interv'iu' ['Tell Me About Your Life': Collecting Biographical Interviews], in M.V. Loskutova (ed.), *Pamiat' o blokade: Svidetel'stva ochevidtsev i istoricheskoe soznanie obshchestva. Materialy issledovanii* [Memory of the Siege in Leningrad: Eyewitness Accounts and Public Historical Consciousness]. Moscow: Novoye Izdatel'stvo, pp. 201–29.

Kelty, Ch. 2009. 'Collaboration, Coordination and Composition: Fieldwork after the Internet', in J.D. Faubion and G.E. Marcus (eds), *Fieldwork Is Not What It Used To Be: Learning Anthropology's Method in a Time of Transition*. Ithaca, NY: Cornell University Press, pp. 184–206.

Kvale, S. 1996. *Interviews: An Introduction to Qualitative Research Interviewing*. London: Sage Publications.

Marcus, G.E. 2001. 'From Rapport under Erasure to Theaters of Complicit Reflexivity'. *Qualitative Inquiry* 7(4): 519–28.

Mero-Jaffe, I. 2011. '"Is That What I Said?" Interview Transcript Approval by Participants: An Aspect of Ethics in Qualitative Research'. *International Journal of Qualitative Methods* 10(3): 231–47.

Orlova, G.A. 2016. 'So-avtorizatsiia, no ne soavtorstvo: prikliucheniia transkripta v tsifrovuiu epokhu' [Co-authorization, Not Co-authorship: The Adventures of Transcript in Digital Age]. *Shagi/Steps* 2(1): 200–223.

Thompson, P. 1978. *The Voice of the Past: Oral History*. Oxford: Oxford University Press.

Turnbull, A. 2000. 'Collaboration and Censorship in the Oral History Interview'. *International Journal of Social Research Methodology* 3: 15–34.

7

A Cultural Cyclotron

Ethnography, Art Experiments and a Challenge of Moving towards the Collaborative in Rural Poland

Tomasz Rakowski

My aim in this chapter is to work on a possible experimental encounter of different fields of creation, stemming from the activities of the inhabitants of two Polish villages, and from the coming artists and ethnographers. One could say that I should go back at first, and refer to the moment of experimental 'replaying the field' as it was in Richard Schechner's and Victor Turner's laboratories, and in Victor Turner's words: 'Perhaps we should not merely comment on ethnographies but actually perform them' (Turner 1979: 80). Bryant K. Alexander's (2005) more contemporary experiments went further: together with his students they perform the field and its chaos within the academic halls and classes – they imitate, for example, the gestures of Mexican street traders in California and the noise they make. There is also the well-described work of Abdel Hernández and Fernando Calzadilla at Rice University (Calzadilla and Marcus 2006), who make an art installation inside the academic foyer, which brings about the embodied knowledge of the barrio's marketplaces in Venezuela and works more as an evocation of a certain sensibility/experience of these places, revealing an askance view of their ethnographic-like fieldwork. Yet, what I am particularly interested in is something different: it is not the situation of recreating or performing the ethnographic field within a seminar or within any artistic work. What is still to be discovered is moving and placing the art-related process right within the ethnographic site.

Going this way, I present and interpret a project realized by a group of ethnographers and artists, in which the ethnographic site was supposed to transform itself into an artistic action and vice versa – artistic exploration was supposed to build up the structures of the ethnographic scene. The project 'Prologue',[1] and its later continuation 'Ethnography/Animation/Art', were conducted between 2011 and 2013 in Broniów and Ostałówek in central Poland by a group called 'Field Collective', consisting mostly of ethnographers and community artists, who have been doing field studies in these villages since 2005. Then, after a few years of studies, the work expanded into a collaborative action realized together with the invited, usually critically oriented artists, who are well established in the Polish art scene. It was crucial here that the project took place in the vicinity of Szydłowiec in central Poland, an area of unprofitable, small-scale agriculture with high rates of local unemployment. The main purpose of this chapter is thus to explore how elements of art and community arts can be introduced into an ethnographic site, without establishing relations of symbolic inequality and building a fiction of intimacy achieved within the field – a quite conventional scene of ethnographic work, related to the other and often the underprivileged. By exploring the experience of the project I will argue that using a certain approach in both artistic and ethnographic situations we are able to step beyond this fiction, beyond the image of an outsider managing to get inside local life with ease and, at the same time, also beyond the artistic or scientific-interventionist engagement, aiming at causing any directed, mechanical or preplanned change. I argue instead that a certain effort to initiate the very specific encounter of all sides of the project was made, and also that the ethnographic work, artistic project, and participation of the addressed people have jointly opened a certain common field of creation and a series of unexpected probes performed by the participants on each other, and on their imaginaries.

Beyond the Perspective of Artist and Ethnographer

Here we should take a closer look at some present and recently particularly rich encounters of art and social sciences. The controversial curator of the Berlin Biennale in 2012, Artur Żmijewski, said in his manifesto (2007) that art can afford, like in social sciences, a certain political maturity. Art can demand, he claims, the role of refurbishing minds, creating new conditions of social life, and reaching towards what is 'efficient.' In this way, he struggles to transpose the arts into wholly new terrains, into places that offer very little safety for it, places not protected by the prestige of a gallery or official art institutions. Then art will be harnessed into directly acting towards people – with all the risks that such gestures entail. This change in emphasis is also stimulated by a broad understanding of art that grew out of the various traditions of participatory and collaborative art practices (Kester 2011; Bishop 2012), as well as out of the community art movement (Crehan 2011; de Bruyne and Gielen 2011). Even though especially the latter is an art practice that was once counter-cultural, anti-structural, militant or even punk, many of such participatory art practices have become increasingly pragmatic and institutionalized and, as it was put by a Polish art teacher, Grzegorz Kowalski, Żmijewski's mentor, they have been stretched out between 'duty and rebellion'. Yet, in its very sense, engaged art and the adoption of its tools in community arts have in their different ways striven towards acting in such a way as to bring about social change: leading to certain endpoints, meaning a new political situation.

Within the art-world environments, strong ethical motivations initiate and actuate this new methodological quest for engagement and collaboration. However, Claire Bishop (2012) sets a more critical depiction of many of the participatory and collaborative projects, and the drives and motivations behind them. From this moment on, this field is on the one hand developed in the name of the (subaltern) other, and on the other hand it is aiming to subvert the late-capitalist regime. Still, from the more precise perspective, we may see, as Bishop argues, that the ethical drive may transform here into a sort of regime (she refers to Jacques Rancière), and may hide or even devalue both the politic and the artistic dimension of such projects. In this sense the typical feature of the discourse around participatory art may bring about certain erosion of the political engagement/acting of the artists in favour of sustaining good, human relationships, and then, as she argues, 'an ethics of impersonal interactions come to prevail over a politics of social justice' (Bishop 2012: 25). On the other hand, the participatory art may seem to be withdrawing from reaching any 'aesthetic' effect, and she points here to her interviews with the Oda Projesi artist collective, working in an Istanbul neighbourhood, in which they indeed confirm very clearly that 'dynamic and sustained relationships provide their markers of success, rather than aesthetic considerations' (ibid.: 21). A well-known tension reappears here: reaching for experiences that are someone else's – that is, especially of the other or the peripheral – seems to be a necessary move of the avant-garde, in which the artist acts like an ethnographer, which was initially criticized by Hal Foster (1996). The artistic gesture of working with the others, in this manner, or in the name of someone else (e.g. the proletariat as it was originally specified in Benjamin's essay, see Benjamin 1998 [1966]), poses at least one serious threat. It compulsively sets up the artistic and the ethnographic domain high over the unconscious, peripheral other, and strives to affect/rebuild his or her consciousness and, at the same time, designs a model of participation and togetherness.

The scene is thus quite complex here. The image of an artist getting into the peripheral field, like an anthropologist, in Foster's vision, is full of either ethical or conceptual contradictions, and also full of methodological doubts. Also, the strategies of artistic work in such environments remain unsure, and there is a serious attempt to criticize and rebuild the model of acting and working with a certain group, a social environment, often already described as unprivileged or silent. Overall, this is the image quite similar to the doubts put on the vision of an anthropologist coming into the singled, disconnected field and giving access to the worlds of the (subaltern) others, which was much criticized within the field of anthropology (see Marcus 1995, 1997). Thus, to a significant degree, anthropology and the social sciences themselves have moved at the same time away from the position of 'conventional' observer of events, and a field. Anthropology and the social sciences absorb, with increasing intensity, the tools of action and engagement, and especially of art-related practices (Alexander 2005; Wright and Schneider 2006, 2010; Leavy 2009; Ssorin-Chaikov 2013; see also Grimshaw and Ravetz 2015), trying to build up in this way a working knowledge, a rising moment of Aristotle's 'practical philosophy', the *phronesis* (Carr 2006). This has led – to give an example – to a situation where the artist and the ethnographer started to work together in the new paradigm of the ethnographic scene, a chronotope for coming encounters, not merely recording a closed and ready-to-describe cultural experience, but starting to actively co-produce it.

The challenge is then both an artistic and an anthropological quest for a new form of acting in conditions of emerging social, economic and political tensions of the contemporary, and to get beyond the perspective of artist and ethnographer; something imagined, designed or, as it was put by Nicolas Bourriaud, 'being felt' about the coming, and yet unrecognized, social conditions (see Bourriaud 2002). Thus, first of all, the meeting of the other is no longer only a matter of initiating any 'qualified' or 'intimate' contact with people. It is rather a starting point for developing a new scene for coming ethnographic (or artistic) events, conditions, and fields of knowledge. This was

Figure 7.1 Acting/Beginning, photo by Zuzanna Naruszewicz, used with permission.

made explicit by Holmes and Marcus (2005, 2008) when they built a slightly different sense of ethnographic endeavour, in which the idea of the field of research started to be conceived as co-produced with the others, thus leaving behind Malinowski's vision of a dyad: a detached community and an anthropological visitor-insider. In this sense, the people they work with have been recognized as individuals capable of expanding the ethnographic field, anticipating the scene of formulating the knowledge, and deeply engaged in the epistemic process while creating the field. As Holmes and Marcus wrote, 'the point is to integrate fully our subjects' analytical acumen and insights to define the issues at stake in our project, as well as the means by which we explore them' (Holmes and Marcus 2008: 86). A continuation of this methodological move was, one could say, 'follow the artists' directive' (a paraphrase of George Marcus postulate; see Marcus 1995). But still, the situation is at the same time like Marcus and Myers (1995) made explicit: it is prevalently the art world that incorporates ethnographic work into their discourse. And it is also, as in Foster's image, the artist who intends to meet alterity and engage in an ethnography-like activity.

The Project 'Devices from Broniów and Ostałówek'

The local context is significant here. Massive unemployment first affected the villages of Broniów and Ostałówek and the nearby area during the 1990s and it continued until quite recently. Available work tends to be in the black market and based on junk contracts. This leads to constant work migration; men mostly go to Germany and Scandinavia, and women to Italy. At the same time, many farms, mostly small, have had stunted growth and become economically unviable. Most of the farming land in the area has gone fallow. Above all, the most important thing to us was that journalists, social scientists and public institutions had constantly presented these local people as a kind of ballast on the road to the moderniza- tion of Poland, like a systemic residue – that is, a social group ill- prepared for transformation (one of the Polish intellectuals, Janusz Majcherek, called them a 'brake on modernization') and social/civic competence. They were said to be incessantly making demands, being fatalistic, and, above all, narrow-minded, thus unable to think in terms of any form of innovation or creative activity (for more about the anthropological critique of this discourse, see Buchowski 2006).

While doing ethnographic research in these villages and then real- izing the ethnographic-artistic projects, we aimed to confront these types of representations – images of cultural and social lack – but also to reveal the unnoticed actions, skills and activities of inhabit- ants of both villages (Rakowski 2013). For example, this consisted of reconstructing the particular villagers' sociopolitical thought, reveal- ing local 'silent activists', and their unique imaginaries, but also, for instance, the widespread production of self-made machines, tractors, cars and various devices, even bricks. There was research on wide- spread topics: the art of informal building works; the aesthetics of home interiors and backyards; the circulation of handmade commod- ities; illegal jobs; conflicts and acting around local institutions; col- lecting herbs to live on; organizing community celebrations; leading village sports clubs and voluntary fire departments; and youngsters' self-made gyms. In the span of two years, over twenty project-events emerged, based on this knowledge. There was, for instance, an installation opened in the village day-room on local 'sociopolitical thinkers'; brides' parade performed together by a community artist and women rarely seen in the public space of the villages; making a mobile gallery of devotionals with comments made by their owners;

photographs of fantasies about abandoned places around the villages; and dozens of other actions.

Yet, from the beginning, the problem was that all the activities, both research- and action-based, could still unconsciously be seen as a form of revealing the silent agent, the unprivileged and the less powerful social actors; they could be even considered a preparation for 'mobilizing culture', 'improvement', all the way up to 'forcing' into shared action. This is frequently connected with the fact that such activities, conducted with good intentions, sometimes led not so much to a positive effect, but rather into a situation of 'double colonization' (see Gandhi 1998: 84–86), in which the participants (or 'recipients') of such projects are once again fitted into the roles of stereotypical or incomplete characters. How is it then possible to act through art projects in the face of this burden? Is still reaching for experiences that are someone else's – that is, of the other and the peripheral – not a necessary move of the avant-garde artist-ethnographer, as Hal Foster (1996) asked?

I will strive here to present that the most important point of proving that this is possible is the form of the meeting of various actors that took place in the villages. It was a collaboration of the people with the outsiders, the cultural workers coming from different traditions and using various methods of work: artists, ethnographers and community artists. Yet, while preparing the project we, the team, were thinking about building a dynamic, horizontal platform for producing the events. One could even say we were navigating towards a process that could in a sense be 'curated' together (something very much like the experiment of Intermediae in Madrid – an open, progressive cultural institution provided for artists, local people, activists and various other actors; see Fernández López 2015). It was then also an attempt to make room for 'mediating and catalysing' the cultural production, as well as to resign from any curatorial or epistemological authority (a kind of curatorial 'emptying'), which was very much in line with the idea of producing and sharing a certain learning process at the crossroads of the encountering groups and participants (see ibid.: 97–99). This may then be treated as another trial of constructing a dynamic form, a flow of collaboration or, to take into account the possible social tensions, of constructing a 'contact zone' (term used by Mary Louise Pratt referring to post-colonial spheres of contact; ibid.). As Olga Fernández López writes about the experiment of Intermediae, this is the particular process in which the 'observer' – the ethnographer, the activist, the artist – 'is to be affected and transformed by the Other, and his/her power dissolved' (ibid.: 100).

For this chapter, I will mainly concentrate on describing the project dedicated to the self-made devices, conducted by the team and the artist Łukasz Skąpski, who had worked before on documenting self-made vehicles in Poland, and who had been invited a few weeks before the beginning of the collaboration. Within the framework of this project, the world of village modification of machines and devices was explored. Constructing self-made machines and devices has quite a long history in Poland, and was related to the massive migration of people from villages to industrial areas in the period of socialism. Many of them started to learn and construct various devices and machines, especially tractors, by themselves (Skąpski 2009; Skuza 2009). The reason for this was that these objects simply functioned better than the ones produced in socialist factories, which were often of very poor quality, plus there was a huge deficit of technical commodities and technical spare parts. The devices were later constructed in many villages during the period of socio-political transformation and massive unemployment in order to reduce the costs of living, but also to give life to a local mode of creativity and invention, reaching far beyond the sole purpose of 'getting by' (Frąckowiak and Rakowski 2011).

In this particular project, we entered households to meet the people who made things such as ladders, welding machines, tractors (*SAMy*), cars (*buggies*), gym equipment made by youngsters, and lawn mowers fitted with engines from 'Frania' washing machines.

Figure 7.2 'Go-kart': A buggy made by youngsters. Photo by Zuzanna Naruszewicz, used with permission.

After some time, we came to notice them nearly everywhere: for example, I discovered that the three circular saws owned by a farmer from Ostałówek were made by his son from four other saws by rearranging their parts – sparkplugs, guides, and so on – so that the newly created tools would cut best. I also started noticing anew the young people's cars in the area. At night they have visible neon lights under their windshields and headlights. They have blue turn signals and painted brake pads. Several of us discovered how one of the residents, Wiesław Zielonka, who was a railway worker, a stonemason and a constructor, welded oil lamps taken from trains onto the gate of his property. His son also constructed some unusual devices for his scooter: its undercarriage is lit by blue lights, which react accordingly to various types of sound, including voices.

All of these epistemic sensibilities constitute an increasingly ethnographic knowledge, a kind of common interest and a certain ability to pay attention to any device or machine one comes across; many conversations and interviews focused on these objects and on their owners' skills or nuances of repairing and improving them. The artist Łukasz Skąpski documented this; he made films about these objects and their constructors. He conducted photo sessions using soft light with young, muscled people in their gyms, along with props and weights in their hands. Here I should stress that these recordings and documentations flowed from the ethnographic meetings and situations (mutual interest). It began with increasingly frequent experiences of encountering people on their properties and in their workshops. These meetings were precarious and uncertain, and developing relations was also difficult. The makers of the devices and alterations might see their creations as their own, worthy of personal pride, but when they interacted with artists and ethnographers they often saw that these creations were uncertain, and they became bashful about them, and a bit anxious. After all, these were unregistered, self-made machines and tractors that went against the government regulations and standardized techniques and technologies. They were also part of the world of silent and hidden dealing with quotidian needs and a parochial strategy for lowering the costs of living.

The junkyard guys came to understand better our interest in what they were doing after we had conversations with them and looked through Łukasz's album *Machines* (2009) together. We found a kind of shared interest in the technical nuances of tractors and cars, and then the gathered objects. On the other hand, we also began to see what they do differently: when they started to reveal their best dismounted engines (BMW 2000, Seat DOHC 16V) we saw that these were reserves of the cream of the crop. We began to talk shyly about our idea for a night exhibition of engines and devices. In this location, and up to that point, such events were unimaginable.

From that moment a convergence of sensibilities started to form, a delicate connection between 'us' (artists, ethnographers) and 'them' (owners of the machines). We not only paid attention to self-made devices, but we also began to think how to use them, thereby shifting them into a different context – we wanted to do something with the villagers, and everything revolved around their know-how, capabilities, and technical imaginations. Yet, we differed much from the artist: Łukasz Skąpski was doing his work following his own drives and motives, and his consequent idea of artwork. From the beginning he was quite critical towards the project, and he was very polemic towards the objectives of collaboration as they were presented and promoted by the group; the important context to note is that he was a member of the critical-artistic group 'Azorro', making absurd happenings and movies related to the world of art galleries and institutions. At first, some inhabitants were irritated and anxious by his presence, and also by the presence of the rest of the team. Only later on, when he started to work with a team of two or three ethnographers and community artists, did he finally develop very good relations with the owners of the devices. It was related to the fact that he was focused, as were other people from the villages, on the technical nuances, making rigorous documentation of the devices, and preparing professional information/specification. His work was concrete and product-oriented; he was engaged in producing films, making detailed photographs and gathering the necessary data about the self-made objects. What is important is that when he started to collaborate with the team and the villagers, he became particularly engaged in the project within a matter of days. He began to follow the brilliant technical knowledge of the youngsters about their cars and machines, appreciating their humour and tendency to set riddles for other people. He was touched by meeting an elderly and somewhat quiet and excluded man, who let him into his workshops to show and get to know about his simple but very ingenious devices (such as a moving, wooden ladder).

Several weeks later, towards the end of this project, people transported all these machines to the front of the village community centre, which led to an assembly and showcase. Skąpski gave the exhibits comprehensive descriptions, with specifications straight out of the world of institutionalized exhibitions. Yet, there was something more going on – everyone was looking at their own machines

Figure 7.3 'Cream of the Crop': The dismounted SEAT engine. Photo by Zuzanna Naruszewicz, used with permission.

and those of their neighbours as if anew. With every passing moment, someone discovered and announced that they had many other such devices – a trailer, a welder, a moving ladder – and they would carry or tow them along too, and present them. The machines needed to enter this 'best of' exhibition. What was accomplished was a kind of launching or actualization, something like the emergence of the new scene of the encounter. The process of presenting the self-made machines, together with the previous public documentation in films and photos, thus became the common effect of the work and research, opening up the eyes of all of the participants to something that had remained hidden until then.

Describing the Experimental: Cultural Cyclotron and the Problem of Acting in the Field

What is most characteristic about such actions? I would say that the boundary between the acts of ethnographic knowledge and action becomes semi-permeable: it works both ways. Ethnography becomes something that rather puts the local technical knowledge (imaginary) into play. Still, it is done right within the field site. The ethnographic knowledge here seems to stick to the artistic action. Skąpski enters the field together with the group and opens a kind of ethnographic imagination in his project: he begins to follow the particular creativity present among the owners of the devices and among the youngsters. Thus, over time, they become powerful agents, forming and transforming his ideas and his attitude to the people. What is more, his collaboration is twofold, as it also works the other way round: his actions create the conditions, initiate or foster the field, create the new environment of the ethnographic, as if the conceptual would have preceded the empirical, like in 'ethnographic conceptualism' (see Ssorin-Chaikow 2013). What he is doing is arranging, together with other actors, a new field scene; the ethnographers, the people find themselves suddenly in completely different surroundings – the world of self-made devices and machines brought out by the artist and by the idea of the exhibition. One could say that this is the fundamental shift from examining the accumulated past typically (in 'cultural forms'), to gaining knowledge about something that is, like in design anthropology (Otto and Smith 2013), more future-oriented. It is then linked to an act of mutual opening to future possibilities, 'refreshing' the world, something like practices of 'acting on the world' (ibid.: 11) that generate something like common, collaborative work in imagining, and improvising, right before our eyes. Here in this case these two mutually reinforcing spheres of activity – the accumulated past (the ethnographic) and the imagined future (action/ design anthropology) – take on a structure of a kind of 'cultural cyclotron', in which each one of them accelerates the circulation of particles of activity thus unveiling unrecognized imaginaries heading towards the possible, future meanings that thereby remain in the state of potentiality. The meanings and the acts achieved during the project on machines may then lead to the events, the social facts that can 'no longer [be] seen as the result of human action – as we may read from design anthropology – but as something that carries the potential of change in its very execution' (ibid.: 13).

In this way, collaboration in the form of common improvisation becomes an almost irresistible consequence of fieldwork, a form of encounter and ethnographic situation. But what does this actually mean? It means that from the beginning the research done in this way transforms itself into something collaborative and dynamic – fieldwork transforms into an encounter, participant observation into acting (performing), the object of study into an ethnographic situation (intervention and interaction). The common influence on the future is something that causes the action that, I believe, can be called common improvisation here, as it was described by Gatt and Ingold (2013: 145), stemming from both skilled flexibility and a kind of foresight. This common designing of the situation, the improvisation, with its elements of flexibility, 'lies not only in finding the grain of the world's becoming – the way it wants to go – but also in bending it to an evolving purpose'. And, they continue, 'it is not, then, a matter of going with the flow, for one can give it direction as well' (ibid.). An example of such a moment is when we talked to a young junkyard mechanic, Andrzej Chylicki, who squatted on his self-made car (buggy, or 'go-kart', as they call it) with a frame cobbled together from an old school radiator-heater.

Andrzej was retying the fuel line with the line for the handbrake (it had to be thinner now), and he wanted to fire up the vehicle to show it off to us, and have it ready for the planned display of the machines in the community centre square. He was doing what he had already been doing before we came, using his invented technical solution; but in our presence it took on a different meaning – he had improved something that was needed for his own use anew. On the one hand, the meaning of this modification ceased to be obvious, on the other, it was already a new experience, an experience in common. Everyone had their own way of reminiscing about their modified cars, about the Ford Taunus they had horsed around with in fields, or about the 'three hundred' cars that one guy, while still at school, had totally taken apart with his brother. The ethnographers and artists also came to view all this differently by entering the world that they knew existed, but it now existed for them newly. We saw not only the work of villagers as the spontaneous work of young people on machines, but also as something that we can co-create and set into a new, different context of the future. This leads to a transformation in the sense that we look at ourselves a little bit askance, without fully recognizing ourselves, but, simultaneously, discovering ourselves anew; 'I am born, so that you can be born', all the sides seem to say, if I may borrow Jerzy Grotowski's (1972) metaphor.

Still, one could ask a question here: does the incommensurability of roles, worlds from which we emerge, goals, motivations for the meetings, witness this course of action as something that is artificial and unreal for both sides? Was it a sustained role play? Of course, to a certain extent, that is how it was. We have all entered roles that are different from real life; all the partakers of the collaborative environment were acting inside the project goals and a kind of epistemic microcosm that arose (e.g. the common yet distorted field of attention). However, the point is that it is possible to change and alter its

Figure 7.4 'Repairing the Buggy': Andrzej Chylicki, the mechanic. Photo by Zuzanna Naruszewicz, used with permission.

meaning by calling this process a 'game' or 'pretending'. If we find in this action some elements of being someone else or playing a certain role, then the collaboration is made much more complicated. Victor Turner (1982) demonstrates this very clearly: every such interaction is still, above all, acting in the specific meaning of the word: both an activity and role playing. It is being together, in the sense of collaboration rather than co-participation, and here comes something that I would call a situation of ambiguous acting in the ethnographic realm. 'Acting', Turner writes, can be equally 'the essence of sincerity – the commitment of the self to a line of action for ethical motives, perhaps to achieve "personal truth", or it may be the essence of pretence – when one "plays a part" in order to conceal or dissimulate' (Turner 1982: 102).

Thus, what transpires in this project is a situation emerging out of roles and actions played by the collaborators, the co-designers of future events (Otto and Smith 2013; see also Binder and Foverskov 2010). This results in the encounter and surprises to the participants: a certain tension, present in nearly every interaction appears. Then also a certain new logic of the project appears and takes shape before our eyes; yet, that logic of the event, is not a logic of some alleged local setting of culture, nor a logic of the external project, built by the artists, something that they bring to the people. Instead it is more likely to be something that Erika Fischer-Lichte (2008) described (in the domain of performative arts) as the unpredictable birth of an entirely new situation – a new design of the future. This is the process in which energy begins to stir the action, beyond the will of the particular partaker; a kind of 'emergence of meaning' starts to run the situation. It is the very moment in which the previously established meaning of actions changes: a situation takes place that exceeds both the plans of the artists, ethnographers and the local modes of existence among the people. Thus, one could say, this is a certain form of gaining the ability 'to be yourself', which is very much the same as the capacity to change and to live 'a thousand lives', as it is in the Nigel Rapport's figure of Anyone, a figure of an individual armed with unrelenting rights and abilities to 'pass' the cultural forms of existence (Rapport 2010). When seen in this way, in the actions we are dealing with, creating the specific conditions and situations in which the appearance and take-off of certain unexpected mechanisms of collaborated realm are made possible.

(De)colonizing the Scene: Collaboration, Complicity, Deformation

Let us return to the beginning now. The projects 'Prologue' and 'Ethnography/Animation/Art' aimed at creating a slightly new perspective: this desired perspective would be capable of reversing and thus decolonizing the local, dominant Polish discourse. The Polish governmental and journalistic discourse itself was one of progress and cultural education that promotes creative cities, hubs of innovation, and entrepreneurial experimenting. It leaves behind village environments that require a so-called awakening and education to become a 'proper' creative culture. However, there is also a tension between the art world and the environments such as peripheral villages. Making art in such settings is particularly difficult, and vulnerable to any acts, causing the further petrification of the situation, or building an image of the detached site of otherness. In this sense the collaborative experiments are crucial here: they have the ability to reformulate the field and rebuild the larger scene of social/ethnographic knowledge. What precisely does the collaboration depend upon in this project? I would like to give some main flashpoints here.

The collaboration is made possible as there is an acknowledgment of a certain clash of different forms of knowledge and different energies. On the one hand, the artists and ethnographers brought with them ideas for action; on the other, the ideas only materialized there on the spot. At first, during the meetings with Łukasz Skąpski, we had visions of working with converted and tuned vehicles using a typically village aesthetic, driving them around town, a procession or parade with them participating on hastily built self-made floats. All of this underwent a complete revision later during our consecutive visits. Thus, there was a stream hidden below the project – it was not so much a process of mutual action, as a process of a shared, sometimes slow and difficult, building up of possible design of it. Action, installation, and the display of machines – and its final transformation – were based on testing what is imaginable and simultaneously possible in consecutive meetings, conversations and discussions. Thus, this transformation of the project is an effect of an internal process – the starting point where our relations with the inhabitants of both villages developed in the process of our actions. Frequently these were bonds of particular closeness and intimacy that came into being through living together, spending time together, and taking part in the lives of particular families.

However, is such an ethnographic entrance into the 'interior' of the community, or forming ties with people, the thing that really happened there? After the critique of the image of almost 'natural' intimacy achieved in the field, we are more likely to see this situation as simultaneously alien and intimate. We may see it in the very detailed way proposed by David Mosse (2006) as a potentially anti-social effect of ethnographic practice. He uses the Malinowski field–desk dichotomy here: on the one hand, there is engagement, intimacy, informality, and a certain closeness (field); on the other hand, there is also much distanced work on the project (desk), psychological detachment from the field scene, and the professional environment (institutions, roles, duties) of the ethnographer and the artist. Thus, initially, in the process of collaboration there is the researcher-actor, an envoy of the academy and institutions of culture, bringing together an artist and ethnographers who carry their own concepts of 'acting', 'development' or 'change'; but on the other hand, there is society itself, people and places with their problems, and often with their sense of marginalization. Linking these levels is something that is unavoidable; it is the axis of the ethical tension and the whole ambiguity inherent in an ethnographic-artistic project.

What I am going to propose here is to look at these situations differently, not so much with the help of criteria of 'natural' intimacy, which could be (and often is) achieved in the field, but using the

Figure 7.5 'Devices from Broniów and Ostałówek': An Exhibition (curated by Łukasz Skąpski). Photo by Zuzanna Naruszewicz, used with permission.

George Marcus (1997) concept of ethnographic interaction as complicity. However much collaboration carries within itself that accusation of mixing up proximity and professional distance, complicity permits those tensions to remain rather than to be transcended. It unearths them, gives them back their existence, and makes them present rather than hiding them from sight. Therefore, it acknowledges that there are different motivations for taking part in the artistic-animating events for all of the sides: artists, ethnographers working on the project, and the people on the spot. Marcus defines the word 'complicity' as meaning both 'a state of engagement' and 'cooperation in a crime', thereby acknowledging the whole ambivalence of the situation – a (de)colonization rather than the exact process of decolonization. In opposition to the familiar co-participation (meaning: a relation of proximity and intimacy) this perspective brings with it the necessity to accept the irremovable tension of the encounter and further collaboration; it maintains a lastingly present difference between the actors, pointing towards tensions that are more external – for example, systemic, and often extra-local, rooted in the institutional politics of engagement. Taking into account that the project was instigated by institutions of culture which were to foster new cultural activities (in the regional environments) in order to follow a certain idea of creativity-based development (see Liep 2001), this tension, and the existence of an external, framing policy was especially felt/present as a 'third actor' shaping the situation and the local endeavours.

In this case the process of designing and leading the project was a kind of constant transforming of the planned action and also the material effects of it. We have produced in collaboration the publications such as a DiGi-pack and a book with a CD (Rakowski 2013). The publication contains documentation of all the projects, more than twenty in total, but the project 'Devices from Broniów and Ostałówek' is particularly broadly described and documented in two large articles and dozens of photographs and films. There were also exhibitions focused on devices: the one in the Broniów square, but also another in the Ethnographic Museum in Cracow, an institution known for transforming its goals towards art-oriented exhibitions of ethnographic collections, and in the 'Kordegarda' art gallery governed by the Polish National Centre of Culture and the Ministry of Culture. In these cases, the experiences and the emerged knowledge on the devices were presented as visual records in various forms; yet their usage was discussed with the people who were asked to consent to their public use and distribution. There was, for instance, a self-made mower made by Wiesław Zielonka, the brilliant mason-master to many men in the villages, placed as the central point in all of our exhibitions. There were also films displayed in the exhibitions in separate posts and photographs of the devices and the documentation of meetings during the exhibition in the Broniów square.

People from both villages came to the exhibitions, the meetings, some of them even spontaneously serving as guides in the 'Kordegarda' gallery during the vernissage. The people were present in large numbers during the final presentation of the photos, films and documentation of the projects in the Broniów community space, and also at the launch of the book published a year later containing texts describing the whole work. The book and also printed photos were distributed in the villages; some of them were deposited in the community space only to disappear within a few days. The films and photos were displayed several times and watched together; some of the photos were included in the family albums and archives, including the directed ones, depicting youngsters in their gyms (made by Skąpski).

The youngsters' gyms also became a part of another project. Łukasz Skąpski, after talking to the boys, became the owner of the gym sets – the boys exchanged the self-made equipment for brand new exercises and body-building equipment sets that they had found and chosen on a web store (the artist covered the costs). Then several of the self-made gym sets were exhibited by Skąpski in galleries in Berlin, Szczecin and Katowice.[2] They were signed with the artist's name and exposed as 'quotes' showing the do-it-yourself artworks found during field research, and as artistic ready-mades, specialized art objects. In an interview with a curator, the artist admitted that he feels to be the author of the situation (Skąpski 2013); he claimed it was him who inserted the gym's equipment into modern art galleries and built the whole context. Some of those attending noticed, and pointed out that the artist had presented them as his own work, and that he had made himself out to be the one who had arranged the whole situation and prepared the exhibition. The youngsters from the villages, however, were not bothered about it; they did not follow the exhibitions or see their gym pieces as art products; it seems these entered a different world and a different circuit of reference. At the same time, the boys still use the body-building equipment that they obtained via the web store in their sheds and barns. In the following years, we saw them once or twice a year, and some of them admitted that they regretted the change, and missed their self-made equipment, which was much more useful and 'stronger'. They still own and store the collection of photos taken by the artist – we experienced some situations when they were proud of them. We have also been talking to Wiesław Zielonka and his family, watching together the films from the projects, late into the night; after a few months, once the exhibition had closed, he shyly asked for his mower to be returned. His son bought a new one, as he found out the mower had been borrowed for some months; yet Mr Zielonka still missed the self-made one, as it turned out to be much more efficient and, as he told us, more 'handy'.

The Emerging Field of Collaboration

We may notice that collaboration has certain temporal dynamics here. Working together, engaging in action (complicity) means going along with the villagers' desires, their ideas, their schedules, and especially with their practical needs. Therefore, I would say that we wanted the project not to be about any mechanical effect or distinct change in this community; it did not depend on a direction that was desired or preplanned. The collaboration was opened to the future on a few levels: it was about common construction of a new situation that revealed the ethnographic content anew – a certain environment has been produced, which would never have occurred in this form if it were not for the collaborative acts of paying attention to,

Figure 7.6 'A Self-made Gym': The Gallery (*'Fitness'*, Łukasz Skąpski, Galeria Zona Sztuki Aktualnej, courtesy of Zachęta Sztuki Współczesnej – Szczecin). Photo by Łukasz Skąpski, used with permission.

exhibiting and documenting the machines (and also other aspects of the village life, touched upon in the whole project). Then we shared the experience of the material and visual effects of the work, watched and commented on many times. The records of the meetings and the knowledge that arose around the devices, rediscovering them anew with every group, seemed to be the main result of the project. Still, the records were stored, commented upon and circulated in a different manner among the villagers, the ethnographer community, and the artist who exhibited the results in his own, specific way.

The testimonies of the process were thus built collaboratively, yet they carried the specific sense of tension and complicity. If we think of the possibility of sharing the archives and records of the ethnographic content as no longer closed and linked only to the interpreting anthropologist (Marcus 1998), then we may encounter a situation where people produce, transform and get together in contact with materials, but they do it in their own, different ways. For the artists, the records of knowledge became a deposit in their own archive, and material for making a unique and ready-to-exhibit product. For the ethnographers it became knowledge produced in an emergent, often unexpected way, transforming their interpretations. For the people from the villages, the records often brought about silent engagement or even excitement, and accidental revelations – for example, when one of us discovered that the sports field where the project was taking place had been restored by one of the local voluntary firemen, who had found a kind of installation, the decoration elements of a plough in a junkyard (coloured by Chylicki and his brother with the paints taken from the project), or when we discovered slogans inside the community centre, newly painted on the walls, that had been made using the technique acquired during the project. I would even claim that the most vivid stream of the project, the real 'collaborative force', as it was put by Anna Lisa Ramella (while commenting on this text), the hidden one, unpredictable and uncontrolled to a large extent, can be found primarily in the spontaneous actions undertaken by the people who followed the encounters and events of the project (and suddenly appeared).

The people from the villages followed the events and the materials in their own way and context, like the ethnographers and the artist did, but there was still a palpable sense of tension in this, a feeling of an outer 'governance' in the process of production of the records/ archives (see Stoler 2002). Even though the collaborative idea of dis-covering creativity and technical imagination was arranged over the projects in many ways in order to appreciate this sphere, the whole action was still linked to the realm of certain politics of creativity (Bilton 2007), and of being involved in larger structures (the project was a part of the Ministry of Culture's wider policy concerning 'normative' creativity). In this way, the production and storage of the records were in a sense placed under pressure from ministerial motives and drives for the project. Even if the idea of collaboration was underpinning the project when it began to be documented, the strong external motivations embedded in it became more and more visible. Thus, the records again caused the sense of complicity and interplay of different agents, bringing into the scene some pressures of larger structures and discourses. They elicit a certain field of ten-sions and requirements, and one could say that they formed certain 'grains' of archives (Stoler 2002) under the particular discourse and bureaucratic practice; yet I would say that these 'grains' were also immediately captured by the people, the artist and the ethnographers, and transformed and used by them with their different logics.

In this sense the collaboration caused a certain stir, a multi-way translation, therefore leading to real effects and action; it was some-thing that suddenly appeared like a *deus ex machina* lowered by lines right into the middle of the stage, to suddenly change the course of events. These effects have an underground character: they are a kind of accumulation, they take on their own dynamics slowly, very much in line with certain internal (biographic) turns, until they finally become visible, forming a precipitation of events. Going this way, we may see in these experiments how ethnography combined with artistic action reveal an implicit, tense and multidirectional field of the collaborative; what is to follow is the still-arising 'emergence of meaning' on all sides of this project.

Acknowledgements

This article is based on the research project *The Challenges of Creative Ethnography* granted by the Polish National Science Centre, no. 2012/05/D/HS2/03639. I am grateful to the editors of this volume and also Anna Lisa Ramella for their thoughtful and scrupulous comments made on the consecutive versions of the text. Writing this article was also possible thanks to very close and productive collaboration with the group Field Collective (I am also a member of this group), the artist Łukasz Skąpski and the people from the villages Broniów and Ostałówek. I would like to express my deep gratitude to all of them.

Tomasz Rakowski is Assistant Professor at the Institute of Ethnology and Cultural Anthropology, University of Warsaw, and Lecturer at the Institute of Polish Culture. His research interests include social art, phenomenological anthropology, postsocialist transformation, anthropology of poverty and bottom-up development. He is also a medical doctor, a specialist in Accident and Emergency medicine. Recently he published *Hunters, Gatherers, and Practitioners of Powerlessness: An Ethnography of the Degraded in Postsocialist Poland* (Berghahn Books, 2016). He is also the editor, with Helena Patzer, of *Pretextual Ethnographies: Challenging the Phenomenological Level of Anthropological Knowledge-Making* (Sean Kingston Publishing, 2018).

Notes

1. The title 'Prologue' is related to the fact that it was an invited project preceding the congress 'Shortcut Europe 2011', which was held in Warsaw

in October 2011, and aimed to set up 'good practices' of arranging democratic cultural production, based on partnership, in the peripheral terrains of Poland (see http://www.ciecie.org/en/prolog-opis-projektu/, last accessed 12 July 2017; Rakowski 2013).

2. See http://skapski.art.pl/en/projects/fitness/ (last accessed 4 September 2017).

References

Alexander, B.K. 2005. 'Performance Ethnography: The Reenacting and Inciting of Culture', in N.K. Denzin, Y.S. Lincoln (eds), *The Sage Handbook of Qualitative Research*. Thousand Oaks, CA: Sage Publications, pp. 411–442.

Benjamin, W. 1998 [1966] 'The Author as Producer'. In W. Benjamin, *Understanding Brecht*, London: Verso, pp. 86–103.

Bilton, C. 2007. 'The Politics of Creativity', in *Management and Creativity: From Creative Industries to Creative Management*. London: Blackwell Publishing, pp. 159–175.

Binder, T., and M. Foverskov. 2010. 'Design as Everyday Theater: Rethinking Co-design as Social Drama', in J. Halse, E. Brandte, B. Clark and T. Binder (eds), *Rehearsing the Future*, Copenhagen: The Danish Design School Press, pp. 204–205.

Bishop, C. 2012. *Artificial Hells: Participatory Art and the Politics of Spectatorship*. London: Verso.

Bourriaud, N. 2002. *Relational Aesthetics*. Paris: Presses du Reel.

Bruyne, P. de, and P. Gielen (eds). 2011. *Community Art: the Politics of Trespassing*. Amsterdam: Valiz.

Buchowski, M. 2006. 'The Specter of Orientalism in Europe: From Exotic Other to Stigmatized Brother'. *Anthropological Quarterly* 3(79): 463–82.

Calzadilla, F., and G.E. Marcus. 2006. 'Artists in the Field: Between Art and Anthropology', in A. Schneider and C. Wright (eds), *Contemporary Art and Anthropology*. Oxford: Berg, pp. 95–115.

Carr, W. 2006. 'Philosophy, Methodology, and Action Research'. *Journal of Philosophy of Education* 4(40): 421–35.

Crehan, K. 2011. *Community Art: An Anthropological Perspective*. Oxford: Berg.

Fernández López, O. 2015. 'What If an Institution Was Curated? Intermediae as an Institutional Hypothesis', in P. O'Neill and M. Wilson (eds), *Curating Research*. London: Open Additions / Amsterdam: De Appel Arts Centre, pp. 87–112.

Fischer-Lichte, E. 2008. *The Transformative Power of Performance: A New Aesthetics*. London: Routledge.

Foster H. 1996. *The Return of the Real: The Avant-garde at the End of the Century*. Chicago, IL: MIT Press.

Frąckowiak, M., and T. Rakowski. 2011. 'Beyond a Privilege: The Interview with Tomasz Rakowski about the Creativity of the Excluded', in M. Frąckowiak, L. Olszewski and M. Rosińska (eds), *Collaboratory: On Participatory Social Change*. Poznań: Wydawnictwo: Fundacja SPOT, pp. 201–202.

Gandhi, L. 1998. *Postcolonial Theory: A Critical Introduction*. New York: Columbia University Press.

Gatt, C., and T. Ingold. 2013. 'From Description to Correspondence: Anthropology in Real Time', in W. Gunn, T. Otto and R.C. Smith (eds), *Design Anthropology: Theory and Practice*. London: Bloomsbury, pp. 139–158.

Grimshaw, A., and A. Ravetz. 2015. 'The Ethnographic Turn – and After: A Critical Approach towards the Realignment of Art and Anthropology'. *Social Anthropology* 23(4): 418–34.

Grotowski, J. 1972. 'Święto'. *Odra* 6: 47–51.

Gunn, W., T. Otto and R.C. Smith (eds). 2013. *Design Anthropology: Theory and Practice*. London: Bloomsbury.

Holmes, D., and G. Marcus. 2005. 'Refunctioning Ethnography: The Challenge of an Anthropology of the Contemporary', in N.K. Denzin and Y.S. Lincoln (eds), *The Sage Handbook of Qualitative Research*. Thousand Oaks, CA: Sage Publications, pp. 1099–1113.

———. 2008. 'Collaboration Today and the Re-imagination of the Classic Fieldwork Encounter'. *Collaborative Anthropology* 1: 81–101.

Kester, G. 2011. *The One and the Many: Contemporary Collaborative Art in a Global Context*. Durham, NC: Duke University Press.

Leavy, P. 2009. *Method Meets Art: Arts-Based Research Practice*. New York: Guilford Press.

Liep, J. 2001. 'Introduction', in J. Lied (ed.), *Locating Cultural Creativity*. London: Pluto Press, pp. 1–13.

Marcus, G. 1995. 'Ethnography in/of the Word System: The Emergence of Multi-sited Ethnography'. *Annual Review of Anthropology* 24: 95–117.

———. 1997. 'The Uses of Complicity in the Changing Mise-en-Scène of Anthropological Fieldwork'. *Representations* 59: 85–108.

———. 1998. 'The Once and Future Ethnographic Archive'. *History of the Human Sciences* 11(4): 49–63.

Marcus G. and Myers F. 1995. 'The Traffic in Art and Culture: An Introduction' In G. Marcus and F. Meyers (eds.) *The Traffic in Culture: Refiguring Art and Anthropology*, Berkeley and Los Angeles, CA: University of California Press, pp. 1–54.

Mosse, D. 2006. 'Anti-social Anthropology? Objectivity, Objection, and the Ethnography of Public Policy and Professional Communities'. *Journal of the Royal Anthropological Institute* 12: 935–56.

Otto, T., and R.C. Smith. 2013. 'Design Anthropology: A Distinct Style of Knowing', in W. Gunn, T. Otto and R.C. Smith (eds), *Design Anthropology: Theory and Practice*. London: Bloomsbury, pp. 1–29.

Rakowski, T. (ed.). 2013. *Etnografia/animacja/sztuka: Nierozpoznane wymiary rozwoju kulturalnego*. Warsaw: Narodowe Centrum Kultury.

Rapport, N. 2010. 'Apprehending Anyone: The Non-indexical, Post-cultural and Cosmopolitan Human Actor'. *Journal of Royal Anthropological Institute* 1: 84–101.

Skąpski, Ł. 2009. *Machines: Homemade Tractors from Podhale*. Cracow: Fundacja Sztuk Wizualnych.

———. 2013. 'O urządzeniach z Broniowa i Ostałówka, Etnografia/ animacja/sztuka', in T. Rakowski (ed.), *Etnografia/animacja/sztuka: Nierozpoznane wymiary rozwoju kulturalnego*. Warsaw: Narodowe Centrum Kultury, pp. 220–235.

Skuza, Z. 2009. 'Nowe obszary zainteresowań na przykładzie kolekcji SAMów – ciągników chłopskiej produkcji'. *Etnografia Nowa* 1: 85–90.

Ssorin-Chaikov, N. 2013. 'Ethnographic Conceptualism: An Introduction'. *Laboratorium* 5(2): 5–18.

Stoler, A.L. 2002. 'Colonial Archives and the Arts of Governance'. *Archival Science* 2: 87–109.

Turner, V. 1979. 'Dramatic Ritual / Ritual Drama: Performative and Reflexive Anthropology'. *The Kenyon Review* 1(3): 80–93.

———. 1982. *From Ritual to Theatre: The Human Seriousness of Play*. New York: PAJ Publications.

Wright, C., and A. Schneider. 2006. *Contemporary Art and Anthropology*. Oxford: Berg Publishing.

———. 2010. *Between Art and Anthropology: Contemporary Ethnographic Practice*. Oxford: Berg Publishing.

Żmijewski, A. 2007. 'Stosowane sztuki społeczne' [Applied Social Arts]. *Krytyka Polityczna* 11–12: 14–24.

8

Making Fieldwork Public

Repurposing Ethnography as a Hosting Platform in Hackney Wick, London

Isaac Marrero-Guillamón

Unexpected Trajectories

After a long and convoluted bureaucratic process – sixteen months of paperwork and delays associated with the Spanish Ministry of Education's postdoctoral grant programme – I was able to officially start fieldwork in Hackney Wick (East London) on 5 April 2011. It was a rainy day; I cycled there from my home elsewhere in Hackney, and got lost trying to find See Studio, the then still unopened gallery where I was to observe artist Jim Woodall at work installing his piece 'Olympic State'. Wet, twenty minutes late and embarrassed, I finally found Jim and his team having breakfast in a cafe next door to the gallery. The mood was relaxed, and my being late not an issue.

I had met Jim the previous January, during a two-day conference co-organized by Birkbeck College and Gasworks Gallery, entitled 'Learning from Barcelona: Art, Real Estate and the Pre-Olympic City'. The conference was meant to mark the launch of the larger research project my postdoc was part of – a collaboration between artists and academics, which explored the relations between critical art, urban renewal and the Olympics – comparing the cases of Barcelona 1992 and London 2012.[1] Unfortunately, the required funding could not be secured, and after the conference the comparative angle was not pursued. My own project focused on the uses of art in the production of spaces of dissent in relation to the impact that the 2012 Games were having on East London. The original plan was to conduct a series of 'mini-ethnographies', following the work of selected artists and the social life of their projects. My intention was to explore the possibility of a symmetric attention to three distinct types of processes: the social organization of artistic labour, the artwork as a specific kind of object (or event), and the kind of relations that unfolded around its public life. When Jim Woodall presented his Olympic State project at the conference, I was clear I had found my first 'case study'.

He took us to a rooftop in Hackney Wick overlooking the Olympic site, where the previous November he had self-built a counter-surveillance hut and then lived in it for two weeks, keeping watch on the construction work taking place on the other side of the canal through several CCTV cameras and monitors. The electronic equipment had subsequently been removed, but the hut was still in good shape, in spite of the tough winter. It was easy to imagine the strangeness, solitude and slight paranoia of the performance. We discussed the project on the rooftop, and among other things Jim let us know that the hut was going to be exhibited at a nearby gallery the following spring. The transformation of the performance into an installation instantly caught my attention as an opportunity for fieldwork. When I told Jim about my research plans he quickly agreed that I could follow the process. In addition, he wanted me to collaborate in the curation and organization of a 24-hour event that he was planning as part of the exhibition, which would be an opportunity to open up the space and invite others working along similar themes to present their work. From my point of view, the translation of such a performative piece into a gallery object was particularly interesting, as it would allow me to explore the shifting relation between artworks, display context and publics – especially in relation to the project's political dimension. Besides, the idea of collaborating in organizing the 24-hour event was priceless as a platform for getting to know other artists quite possibly relevant to my research project. At this point, I had not only 'gained access' to the field, but become entangled in a multiplicity of roles that prefigured the very terms and conditions of my fieldwork to come.

I was not sure what to expect when I arrived in Hackney Wick that wet morning in April, three months after the rooftop visit, and ready for my first day of 'proper' ethnographic fieldwork. I had brought a notebook and a camera, and once we moved from the cafe to the gallery and they started reassembling the hut, I retreated to a corner and tried to stay out of the way. I took a few photographs, engaged in some conversation, felt the familiar discomfort of the ethnographer

Figure 8.1 Installation of Jim Woodall's 'Olympic State' at See Studio, Hackney Wick. Photo by Isaac Marrero-Guillamón.

at work in an unfamiliar territory – of not knowing what to do, what to say, when to ask a question, or when to take a picture. I was wary of offering my help – I assumed that, being an artistic project, special skills that I did not have would be required. After about two hours, however, it became apparent that that was not the case. Time was very tight, and even I could, for instance, carry wooden beams and panels and screw them together with a drill. Over the course of the afternoon, and for the next ten days, I became another 'intern' or 'assistant'.

This allowed me to get a first insight into the dynamics of the work and labour involved in the project, whose success depended on Woodall's ability to assemble a team that could do the job almost for free (the budget the gallery had agreed to was a fifth of his initial estimate, which resulted in no artist's fees, and money only for materials and expenses). He had advertised an internship opportunity at different art schools he had access to, as well as through his extensive social network, and had interviewed candidates. He had also asked friends for help. In total, I counted up to nine people who took part during the ten-day installation of Olympic State. This included reassembling the hut, setting up the gallery's lights, preparing the playback of the multi-camera feed footage, building frames, framing prints, writing the press release and promoting the show. Unable to pay a fair wage, but appreciative of the help received, Jim tried to give the assistants something in return. He would, for instance, forward job opportunities, facilitate contacts with service providers (such as printers), or offer a chance to work with him in paid jobs. All of the assistants, except me, were 'struggling' artists, or artists in the making. They told me that working with Jim was an opportunity to 'gain experience', 'make contacts', and 'get to know people'. In other words, the 'internship' implied an intangible investment in their own career.

The previous couple of days had been hectic and not without major setbacks, but things were mostly in place when people started entering the gallery shortly after 6 p.m. on 14 April 2011. The hut was an accurate reconstruction of the original (including the whisky bottles, the coffee pot, the sleeping bag), the two weeks of original footage were playing back in sync on the monitors inside, and a series of printed video stills hung framed on the walls.

During the installation, and more consistently once it was finished, Jim, Cristina Garrido and I met regularly to discuss, as co-curators, the organization of '24-hour Olympic State', to be held on 5–6 May. I was certainly surprised to be granted co-responsibility for the event (an odd juxtaposition with being, at the same time, an unskilled intern), but went along with it – at that point, I was more interested in the possibilities that such engagement could bring for further research than in the curation of the event in and of itself. The latter was designed as a 'marathon' of talks, screenings and performances that would bring together artists and practitioners whose work related to the main issues that Olympic State was tackling: the impact of the Olympic Games on East London in terms of increased surveillance, the privatization of public land, and the effacement of local history. We discussed the parameters we wanted to work with, located relevant artists and practitioners and issued invitations, organized a timetable and promoted the event. I discovered I was deemed especially useful in relation to writing tasks – a scarce skill in the context. And so I ended up leading the writing of most of the blurbs we sent around, as well as a longer, more conceptual introduction to the event that was included in the zine publication distributed on the night (see Marrero-Guillamón 2014 for a more detailed description of '24-hour Olympic State'). Again, we worked with almost no budget and relied instead on an extended economy of (deferred) reciprocity. I discovered that artists were generally happy to support each other's projects, be it through direct collaboration, the exchange of favours, or facilitating contacts and promotion. In doing this, a relational infrastructure of support was woven: associations were established,

Figure 8.2 Jim Woodall's '24-hour Olympic State' at See Studio. Photo by Isaac Marrero-Guillamón.

some links strengthened, and relations prolonged – including, to be sure, my own.

Variations of this process happened repeatedly during the following two years, a period in which my attempted mini-ethnographies resulted mostly in successive, unplanned collaborative entanglements: among others, a community newspaper (*The Wick*), a co-edited book (Powell and Marrero-Guillamón 2012), a co-curated exhibition ('Juxtaposition', with Daren Ellis at See Studio), a jointly authored contribution to an architecture exhibition ('Planning for Protest', with public works at the Lisbon 2013 Architecture Triennale), and several public discussions (e.g. on Olympic-related military urbanism, the New Localism Act, and the makeshift city). Below I return and expand on two such collaborations.

The point of this long preamble is to introduce with some detail the 'original sin' of my ethnographic endeavours in Hackney Wick: I had wanted to *follow* some artists' work, but I was invited to become a *collaborator*; I had imagined that fieldwork would be based on some kind of *distance* with the objects and subjects of study, but I instead *participated* in the production of the very things I was studying; I failed to keep up with essentials such as fieldnotes, and I wrote *for* the projects I wanted to study more often than *about* them.

I was troubled by these developments, and yet incapable of doing anything about it, as they were also hugely enabling in fostering new relations. For the most part, I experienced this process as an ethnographic failure, or 'derailment'. Yes, I had built good relations and rapport in the field through these collaborations, but I tended to see them as a form of methodological opportunism, something that was instrumental to developing the relations I needed for the higher duty of 'proper' ethnographic research (which I was failing to conduct). Moreover, to the extent that I seemed to be recognized in the field through these collaborations rather than in my capacity as a researcher, and had even initiated myself some of the artistic projects I was meant to analyse, at times I feared I was going native (an unfounded fear, it has to be said, since my appeal as a collaborator most likely had to do with the fact that I was *not* an artist). In short, I had approached fieldwork from an 'aesthetics of encounter', but ended up practising an 'aesthetics of collaboration' (Marcus 2010). Had I been, back then, familiar with the debates around experimental collaborations in ethnography, many a frustration could have been avoided.

Caveating my argument in such a cumbersome way is necessary for a very specific reason: I wish to make visible the fact that the conceptualization of collaboration I will attempt in this chapter is an analytic reconstruction, a retrospective epistemological artefact. I do not intend to present my experience as an enlightened form of fieldwork or a successful experiment; it was rather a mess, one that I am now, a posteriori, turning into a more or less coherent methodological device. I would like to retain this retrospective gesture as present as possible throughout the text, and in doing so avoid the risk of describing my fieldwork strategies as being the result of the agency and inventiveness of the researcher. This is certainly not the case in this instance where, as I will show below, I seem to have adopted the vernacular of the field.

On Collaboration

Given that my fieldwork ended up taking the form of successive collaborations with artists and cultural producers, it may be productive to frame the discussion in relation to recent debates in the anthropology of art, before relating those to wider issues around collaboration in anthropology at large. There is an extensive literature on the relationship between art and anthropology, examining the appropriations and mutual influence between the two (e.g. Coles 2001;

Schneider 2008; Schneider and Wright 2006, 2010), as well as, more recently, their different understanding of 'relations' and 'collaborations' (Marcus 2010; Schneider and Wright 2013; Sansi 2015). This body of work has been very useful in reclaiming the productiveness of the dialogue between these two disciplines, partly against earlier critiques such as Hal Foster's (1995) 'mutual envy' argument.

There has also been an interesting shift within these debates, which I would describe, following Marcus (2010), as a gradual distancing from the textualist concerns of the *Writing Culture* era. This is especially apparent in the volumes edited by Arnd Schneider and Chris Wright. Their first book (2006) identifies the realm of 'representation' as the locus for the experimental sensibility they want to foster through the dialogue between art and anthropology. It is because both disciplines are concerned with (representing) alterity that the exchange and contraband of ideas and strategies is not only possible, but enriching. In their subsequent volumes, however, they shift their focus to sensory approaches (2010) and collaborative work (2013). This change of emphasis is in itself an important intervention in the debate, as it recognizes a whole range of collaborations between art and anthropology that take place beyond representation, at the level of 'ways of working' (Hallam and Ingold 2007).

Roger Sansi (2015) has discussed the importance of the work of Alfred Gell for the anthropology of art along similar lines – as a way out of the overarching concern with the politics of representation, which had dominated the sub-discipline. For Gell (1999) looked at works of art as actors, rather than texts to be decoded; he was interested in what they *do*, not what they *stand for*. This perspective implies a displacement of the locus of analysis towards the forms of relationality that artworks foster, as well as their effects. As Sansi (2015) argues, this allows us to conceptualize (certain) art as 'non-representational' – that is, as performative and generative of social relations.

I shall pursue a similar line of argumentation here. The collaborations I engaged in during my fieldwork can be productively understood in relation to the performative at two levels. Firstly, in Hackney Wick, artistic projects often grew out of social relations, and at the same time prolonged them or triggered new ones. Group exhibitions, the exchange of useful contacts and opportunities, reciprocal invitations to present work at public events, or favours in the form of materials, expertise or labour provided an infrastructure of support that sustained artistic practice in a context of limited resources and generalized precarity. Through these exchanges, I would argue that artists created the conditions for (re)distributing their work and their personhood (their name, their reputation) – in other words, rather than merely producing objects (making things out of people), they used art to produce social relations (making people out of things) (Sansi 2015). Within this context, my ethnographic endeavours were an extension of this dynamic – I was 'entrapped' into a widespread 'way of working', and at the same time attempted to trap others into it (see Gell 1996). The collaborations I was part of were, in many ways, merely an adoption of a ubiquitous local vernacular.

Secondly, these collaborations adopted a performative orientation towards the production of public forums. These forums may be described as 'platforms' to 'make things public' – that is, an infrastructure of encounter and mediation in which certain groups or issues can be staged and a public enacted (McLagan and McKee 2012; Keenan and Weizman 2012). Different platforms will involve different modes of address and techniques of soliciting attention, interpellate distinct audiences, and enable particular claims to be made while foreclosing others. I find the notion useful to capture a performative context, or forum, in which certain claims and certain publics can be enacted and encounter each other. As McLagan and McKee argue, these platforms are not neutral spaces, they 'amplify, interpret, and publicly perform' (2012) the significance of materials that circulate within them.

What I am trying to describe here is therefore a performative turn in which ethnography is reimagined as a form of public intervention geared towards the co-production of public platforms. These forums would, in turn, contribute to extending the relational infrastructure that acts as its foundation – hence becoming the kernel for further collaborations and encounters with a public. Importantly, as already mentioned, in the case of my research in Hackney Wick this is but a version of a local practice and, in that sense, it amounts to a 'parasitic' or 'recursive' gesture (see the editors' introduction). One of the particularities of my fieldwork experience is that this recursive dynamic took place around the co-production of textual objects that may be described as 'more than texts'. As I describe below in more detail through two examples, these textual objects became at once spaces of collaboration (but not of co-writing), instances of fieldwork (rather than its culmination) and public platforms (rather than conceptual endeavours) – thereby exerting a number of displacements with regard to more established narratives of collaboration in ethnography.

For Holmes and Marcus (2008), for instance, the goal of collaborative ethnography is the production of 'epistemic partnerships'. In a nutshell, their argument is that (at least in the elite and expert contexts they are concerned with) subjects are already conducting ethnographic research (of sorts) and producing (para-)ethnographic knowledges, meaning there is no need for anthropologists to dupli-cate things – or worse, to try to add '"critique", moral injunction, or higher meaning to these accounts' (ibid.: 84). Instead, the ethnogra-pher would do well to *defer* to their subjects' modes of knowing:

> Ethnography advances today by deferring to, absorbing, and being altered by found reflexive subjects – by risking collaborative encounters of uncertain outcomes for the production of ethnographic knowledge in the forms that have been regulated by the disciplinary communities that propel anthropologists into fieldwork. (Holmes and Marcus 2008: 84)

The acknowledgement of a full-fledged epistemic counterpart (as opposed to a mere 'informant'), with a capacity to engage in concep-tual work analogous to that of the ethnographer, demands a radical renegotiation of the rules of engagement in ethnographic research:

> We have no interest in collaboration as a 'division of labor' among the investigators who control the design of a project, or as the basis for blend-ing academic expertise, or as a gesture to a canonical interdisciplinarity. The point is, again, to integrate fully our subjects' analytical acumen and insights to define the issues at stake in our projects, as well as the means by which we explore them. (Holmes and Marcus 2008: 86)

In its emphasis on 'epistemic' collaboration, Holmes and Marcus's proposal is surprisingly close to Joanne Rappaport's 'collaborative ethnography'. The latter, articulated in response to a very different context (the study of Colombian indigenous movements) and with radically different political goals (contributing to the emancipation of oppressed groups), nonetheless identifies 'theoretical innova-tion' and the 'coproduction of theory' as the 'crucial venue in which knowledge is created through collaboration' (Rappaport 2008: 2). Collaboration, Rappaport argues, 'converts the space of fieldwork from one of data collection to one of co-conceptualization' (ibid.: 5). The co-production of concepts, therefore, becomes the vehicle for the democratic reimagining of ethnographic research. To be sure, this is not the only vehicle, and Rappaport indeed discusses the collab-orative turn at all stages of the research process, including the setting of the questions, the methods, a two-way discussion of the emerging data, and forms of making public the results that speak to all parties' interests. In any case, both Holmes and Marcus and Rappaport coincide in identifying the production of conceptual and theoretical knowledge as the prime locus, as well as the final aim, of a collaborative refunctioning of ethnography.

In contrast, the kind of ethnographic collaboration I am attempting to conceptualize in this chapter, structured around the co-production of 'public platforms', had little, if any, theoretical ambition. Theorization was neither a shared disposition amongst participants, nor the aim of the collaborations that ended up taking shape. In fact, it is not unlikely that we collaborated with different motivations, and engaged in these public outings for equally different reasons (see Kelty et al. 2009). What these platforms had in common was an aspiration to act as 'hosting devices' – in other words, to enact a space of hospitality, of structured (and fragile) reciprocity between guests and hosts. I will now describe two examples of textual objects as platforms.

Platform No. 1: A Distributive Whole

One of the 'outputs' included in my postdoctoral funding application was an edited collection bringing together critical artistic work done in relation to the Olympics. In the summer of 2011, during fieldwork, I met artist Hilary Powell and discovered, to my surprise, that she was preparing a book along very similar lines. This realization led to us co-organizing a series of public debates around art and the Olympics, which would feed our respective projects. That collaboration went well, and soon afterwards (and in response to issues she was having with her publisher), we decided to merge our projects and work together on a single co-edited volume. Later in the process (and in response to further issues with the publishers resulting in our going independent) we hired Daren Ellis of See Studio as designer for the project. It was an intense ten-month collaboration involving, among other things, compiling and editing work by more than sixty contributors, changing publishing houses, raising funds, and getting actively involved in the design, production and distribution of the book. It also meant learning to work together, both at a conceptual level (sharing ideas and theories, developing analytical ways into the material) and at a practical one (finding suitable working patterns, for example, in the midst of other commitments). The resulting publication, *The Art of Dissent: Adventures in London's Olympic State* (Powell and Marrero-Guillamón 2012), is, to my mind, an interesting encounter of methods and procedures: Hilary's artistic poetics, Daren's bold design approach, and my academic perspective.

I want to focus on one seemingly secondary aspect of the process, the material dimension of the book (i.e. the book-as-object). *The Art of Dissent* was conceived from the outset as a hybrid between an art catalogue, an academic publication and an activist archive – it was indeed meant to operate in the space between academia, activism and the non-commercial art world. During the process of commissioning, locating and assembling content, we realized that putting the book together would mean negotiating notable disparities in the authors' expectations around the publishing relation. There were important differences regarding remuneration, for instance, between those who worked in the cultural sector and expected payment, and activists and those employed in academia, who would normally provide their material 'for free'. When it came to the editing process, these differences were no less sharp. Whereas for those in academia the review process is assumed to imply potential changes to one's argument and presentation, artistic projects were provided in a much more definite shape (including sometimes precise printing instructions). Hilary and I dealt with many of these issues during the process of editing and organizing the material thematically and conceptually, but it was at the design stage (understood as the development of a visual 'concept' and its translation into a layout, a page count, the selection of paper and binding type, etc.) that the sometimes diverging expectations around the contributions had to be confronted at a material level. A text's page allocation, the number of images included and how many we could afford to print in colour, the hierarchy between text and image within and between contributions ... these were all decisions that created possibilities for disagreements, which we resolved through (endless) conversation and iteration. Daren's final design, rather than the implementation of a template, was the material imprint of a trajectory of negotiations, collective decision-making and budgetary constraints.

Throughout the production process it became apparent that as an edited collection, *The Art of Dissent* had to be assembled in a way that the individuality of the participants was not diffused by the composition of a more powerful collective identity. A name may be all an artist/author has, and the openness to collaborate with us, which was tangible and widespread, was also based on the ability to retain one's individual singularity within the proposed alliance. The book, as an artefact, mostly through its design, had to achieve becoming what Deleuze (2006) calls a 'distributive whole' (as opposed to 'collective whole') – that is, a type of aggregate in which the identity of the parts is not lost to the resulting assemblage. The concern that some authors

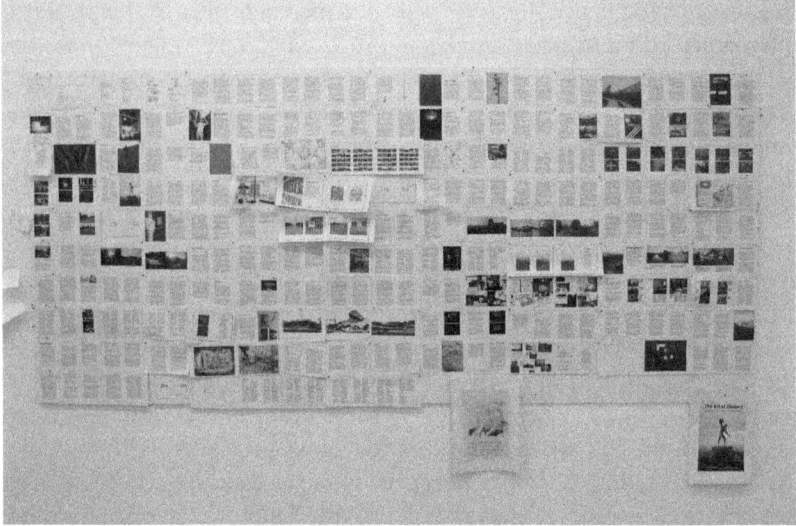

Figure 8.3 Draft design layout for *The Art of Dissent*. Photo by Isaac Marrero-Guillamón.

had over the way their work was presented, and what it was associated to, are quite easy to understand in relation to the construction of their public trajectory – a publication, after all, is a specific proposition of publicness.

In relation to this, I would like to discuss the question of how this aggregate book, as a material (textual) object released to the public, acted as a hosting platform. *The Art of Dissent* came out of a long trajectory of public discussions[2] about art and the Olympics in which Hilary had played a central role, and in many ways it returned and contributed to this milieu once it was published. The people, groups, institutions and spaces that had been part of this diffuse network constituted the relational backbone of the project – the source of many (if not most) of the works featured, and also its immediate audience. So once the book was finished we engaged in the organization of a series of public events, which recharted this geography of affinities. The book became quite literally a platform, a device for the enactment of public encounters, and a stage for groups and individuals to make their claims and connect with an audience.

I will give one example. We launched the book at the Chisenhale Gallery in East London. We invited three of the book's contributors (artists Alberto Duman and Laura Oldfield Ford, and sociologist Paul Watt), Anna Minton (a well-known journalist who had been publicly critical of the Olympics), and geographer Mike Raco, who introduced and chaired the event. Instead of presenting the book as such, we handed the stage over to our guest speakers, who discussed their own engagement with the Olympic-led transformation of East London and highlighted the issues they thought were pressing. Duman spoke of the commodification of public space by way of the rebranding of outdoors gyms as Adidas-sponsored sites. Ford read the latest piece of her ongoing project 'Savage Messiah', a dystopian drift around Westfield Shopping Centre, which summoned some of the ghosts of the old Lower Lea Valley. Watt spoke about the dispossession of the poor in Stratford, just on the fringe of the Olympic Park, as a result of Olympic-led regeneration. Minton and Raco provided more general comments about the governance of the Games and the neoliberalization of urban development.

The idea in putting together this panel was that the book should act as a platform for further discussions, rather than be seen as the culmination of a process. The approach seems to have worked, in that the book was never the centre of the debate, and many among those who attended (close to one hundred people – a heterogeneous amalgam of neighbours, artists, journalists, activists, academics, students, and so on) felt compelled to participate and share their own stories and ideas. In most of the events we organized during the summer of 2012

Figure 8.4 The public speaks at the launch of *The Art of Dissent* at Chisenhale Gallery, London, in June 2012. Photo by Dan Edelstyn, used with permission.

(at bookshops, cultural centres, universities, and film festivals) we adopted a similar strategy – the book acted as a hosting device which allowed contributors and others to raise issues of concern, present ideas, and make new connections.

Clearly, this process could only be sustained by the willingness of those involved to be associated with the book. This association seemed to produce a win-win situation, in which the lower-profile artists and authors that tended to feature more prominently in these events reached out to new venues and audiences, which in turn allowed us to prolong the social life of the book as a platform for public engagement (and to sell it, too). These collaborations around particular events created a solid relational infrastructure: the discussions that took place, the connections that were made, and the collaborations that were plotted became a myriad of virtual possibilities for future relations, some of which were indeed actualized.[3]

Participating in these events was a pivotal moment for the project; it was only then that I realized the capacity that the book-as-object had to act as a platform and produce new social relations. Until then, I had thought of the book mainly as a discursive artefact, one that tried to make certain connections and produce certain debates. But once it existed as a material textual object and became the vehicle for organizing public events, it quickly gained a social life of its own. Some of those 'debates' and 'connections' became tangible, others did not happen, and many unexpected ones unfolded.

Platform No. 2: Activating Subterranean Knowledges

Hackney Wick, up until the late 2000s, had been a not-so-well-known area of East London, characterized by a tangible sense of detachment from the rest of the city. It was isolated from its surroundings by a network of canals and dual carriageways, and presented a typically post-industrial gritty juxtaposition of small industries, empty plots, converted factories (transformed into lofts, affordable workspaces and unofficial live/work warehouses), and informal uses of public space (e.g. street markets, unsanctioned playgrounds, raves). When I started fieldwork in 2011 the area had more than seven hundred artist studios but still very few amenities. The construction of the Olympic Park on its doorstep, however, inevitably led to mainstream attention, and by 2013 a number of new businesses and venues had opened and several planning applications for high-density residential developments had been put forward.

This process coincided with the end of my two-year postdoc, and resulted in a slight change of direction in my research. Rather than the role of art in the production of spaces of dissent in relation to the Olympic transformation, the key issue became the ways in which residents and groups who were engaged in the area were trying to steer planning and development in a direction more favourable to their interests. It is in this context that I wish to discuss my collaboration with art/architecture collective public works.[4]

I met Andreas Lang from public works early during fieldwork, but it was not until after the Games that we started to work together in curating public events and publications. These collaborations were framed within their project R-Urban Wick,[5] part of a larger initiative led by the French collective *atelier d'architecture autogérée* (aaa). R-Urban is described as a participatory strategy for the development of 'practices and networks of local resilience', bringing together concerns with sustainability in a wide sense with the development of bottom-up strategies of 'commoning' (aaa 2016). In Hackney Wick, the main focus of the project has been on 'reuse', broadly understood as the repurposing of techniques, objects and materials towards new uses. Crucially, public works' method relies on identifying and supporting existing, yet largely unknown, practices and tactics.

A good example was a dossier we published as part of issue 3 of *The Wick* newspaper in 2013. The issue as a whole aspired to contribute to reimagining the future of the area by providing an alternative point of view to that of private developers, drawing from the rich landscape of alternative practices already existing in the area. public works' contribution presented, as a paradigmatic case of the 'culture of reuse' in the area, the Frontside Gardens skatepark. This successful space had been self-built by Andrew Willis (under the auspice of a London Legacy Development Corporation Interim Use Pilot Project grant) on a publicly owned empty plot; it used almost exclusively reused materials, and was completed with a negligible budget. public works, who had already supported the project in the construction phase by hosting the making of workshops, produced a detailed map for the newspaper showing where the materials had come from, how they had been sourced (e.g. donation, exchange), and the techniques used in the assemblage of the components (e.g. never using nails but rather screws, which are reusable). The map described a dense web of (mostly personal) relations that sustained the exchange of materials, ideas and knowledge. It spoke of a non-monetary economy, based on reciprocity, as well as a collective, 'makeshift' intelligence, which the

Figure 8.5 A tour of the makeshift spaces of Hackney Wick. Photo by Isaac Marrero-Guillamón.

dossier presented as a locally situated model for resisting the com-modification of urban space.

A year after publishing the map in *The Wick*, and with the support of a small grant from Goldsmiths College, we decided to collaborate again and revisit the notion of the 'makeshift' more systematically. We had discovered it was a concept we found useful when thinking about Hackney Wick, and wanted to test its capacity to generate a public debate about models of development for the area. Drawing from our previous experience, we opted for a multilayered event consisting of: a 'tour of the makeshift spaces of Hackney Wick'; a public discussion on the 'makeshift city' with practitioners, officials and researchers involved in the production, regularization or study of such spaces (both locally and beyond); and a zine publication bringing together written and visual responses to these two activities.

This particular collaboration is perhaps the most developed example of the kind of repurposing of ethnography I have tried to describe in this chapter. Here, we can observe a complete alignment between my (research) interests and those of my collaborators, and a clear intention to work through them in a public fashion. Our inter-vention consisted in, first of all, identifying relevant local practices for thinking about the makeshift (which we defined around three lines of tension: non-permanence, informality and precariousness); second,

making them more widely public as alternative models of urbanization; and third, supporting the argument by situating the issue locally
(providing a policy context) and beyond (discussing analogous experiences elsewhere). Crucially, we understood that the main vehicle for
this could not be the production of academic knowledge (accessible to
a few), but rather the actual occupation of public space – understood
in a wide sense, both as a physical space and a realm of public life
and opinion. Hence the emphasis on visiting certain spaces and
learning from them through direct experience, organizing the debate
in a relevant local venue (90 Main Yard, itself a makeshift project),
and disseminating the discussion further via a publication available
both in print and online. The publication, *Wick Zine no. 5*, precisely
adopted the form of a zine: a DIY, quickly produced publication that
did not aspire to longevity as much as to responding to immediate
concerns by achieving fast circulation and instigating discussion.[6] In
other words, we enacted three different platforms, which enabled
three different modes of address and debate.

The projects we visited in the tour included a temporary guerrilla
playground; an official 'public realm improvement' intervention,
which quoted the language of the makeshift (art/architecture collective muf's 'Street Interrupted'); Richard Brown's Affordable Wick
cabin, a 'roaming workspace' that had been operational in several
locations in the area; and a range of self-built and self-managed
spaces (live/work warehouses, the Yard theatre, Frontside Gardens
skatepark, Stour Space). Having seen and experienced these spaces
first-hand, the public debate attempted to expand the frame to
consider the opportunities and limitations afforded by the policy
context (locally, by the London Legacy Development Corporation's
Interim Use Programme, and more generally by the New Localism
agenda), and to discuss other relevant international initiatives such
as El Campo de Cebada (a community-run park in Madrid), past
experiences like Reclaim the Beach, and current projects elsewhere
in London such as The Field (in New Cross). This shifting of scales
was important in order to understand both the specificity of the
conditions in Hackney Wick, and the way in which some of the projects discussed resonated with processes of grass-roots urbanization
taking place elsewhere.

The zine publication – which featured a range of writers including students of mine – developed these resonances more thoroughly,
and framed the discussion around the makeshift in relation to two
diverging political projects: urban commoning and austerity urbanism. More specifically, we attempted to go beyond a critical reading

that argues that the makeshift is mostly a convenient strategy in the context of the rolling back of the state; that it substitutes public provision with engaged citizens, plays into the 'big society' ideology, and helps to underplay the consequences of state retrenchment. In this analysis, makeshift projects are 'cut-price locational boosters' that occupy interstitial spaces and prepare them for development, actively contributing to gentrification processes and the neoliberal city (see Tonkiss 2013).

We argued that, whilst all the above can be true to an extent, makeshift spaces are also islands of resistance against the increasing enclosure and privatization of public space; they produce urban commons, spaces that are neither public nor private, but shared, decommodified, removed from the logic of the market. We thought that these projects could constitute 'an infrastructure of common life that provides sites of autonomy, creativity and collectivity in the making and re-making of cities' (Tonkiss 2013: 322); experimental spaces where 'people come together to assemble alternative lifeworlds' (Vasudevan 2015: 332). From our perspective, the makeshift practices we had identified in Hackney Wick and elsewhere embodied an alternative to hegemonic forms of urbanization; they were a prototype for a city made from below, collectively, by non-experts – a machinic assemblage of lay knowledges, tools and subjects engaged in their own co-production.

Apart from its discursive qualities, the makeshift event relied on the combination of three distinct platforms – the tour, the debate and the zine – as the instruments that enacted, through hosting, the possibility of an encounter with a public. In this sense, the event was a collaborative ethnographic device in which what was at stake was not making anthropology public (*a la* Scheper-Hughes), but rather making fieldwork public – that is, turning ethnographic research into a public activity, an activity that openly partakes in its context (and its transformation) through the production of public forums.

Concluding Remarks

In hindsight, I would argue that collaborating with those I came to study translated into a series of productive shifts in the practice of ethnographic research. First, echoing Rappaport (2008), my own pre-established research goals became secondary to the priorities emerging out of the collaborations unfolding in the field. Letting go of these initial aims, and of my own reluctance to let go, became a necessary step towards embracing this becoming-collaborative and realigning my ethnographic practice to issues of contextual relevance. This 'deferral' did not on the whole take place at a conceptual level (cf. Holmes and Marcus 2008) but rather in the form of a recursive adoption of a particular way of doing extended in the field, namely hosting and co-producing public platforms.

It is worth noting, however briefly, how the notion of collaboration emerging from this gesture differs from the idea of 'allowing' participants to shape, even co-design 'our' research projects. Not only is the presumption of inequality, which underlies such formulations, radically abandoned (see Strohm 2012), but the very direction of the relationship is reversed, with the ethnographer attempting instead (parasitically, recursively) to produce a *version* of the 'ways of the field'. In this process, the very notion of a 'research project' (particularly as a bureaucratic unit of accountability) is transformed into – if not abandoned in favour of – a *trajectory* of participation in the field. Collaboration, in this sense, is an *effect*, not a presupposition or a vocation, of certain forms of ethnographic engagement (Corsín Jiménez and Estalella, 2017). In my case, this meant reimagining ethnography as a collaborative device for the production of public forums or platforms – a prolongation of an already existing impulse to make things public, to generate public opinion and to think collectively about matters of concern.

The strategy of deferral and the focus on collaborative public interventions had obvious effects, however, in terms of 'research outputs' (the main unit of evaluation of our work). I never wrote the monograph I was supposed to, for instance, and I have published less than I expected. Our shared commitment to a wider reach and a quicker temporality made those academic vehicles inappropriate for collaboration – and the time to do them 'on the side' on my own was simply absent. When these are not only the bearers of disciplinary reputation, but also the instruments for disciplining evaluation exercises (such as the UK's Research Excellence Framework, or REF), the consequences of such 'derailment' are not insignificant.

In any case, I am personally more interested in the epistemological dimension of the debate around alternative forms of knowledge production and distribution than in the question of their assimilation into hegemonic audit cultures (Strathern 2000). I would like to think that there is scope within the discipline to accept and value the embodied, practical and situated knowledge collectively developed through public platforms. Recent developments in the anthropology

198 ◆ *Isaac Marrero-Guillamón*

ogy (Grimshaw and Ravetz 2004) offer a model for a performative
reimagining of ethnography through collaboration, in which the
co-production of knowledge is decoupled from the production of
theory.

Neighbourhood tours, visual interventions on the street, public
discussions, exhibitions and workshops were some of the collaborative devices I participated in during my fieldwork. Through these
things, among others, local makeshift wisdom was made visible, the
industrial history of the area reinstated in public space, and artistic
methods used to highlight the contingency of 'the given' (see also
Marrero-Guillamón 2016). My argument is that the successful
reimagining of ethnography as a public activity that contributes,
through the production of platforms, to the social life of the contexts
within which it takes place will require a collective effort to find ways
of recognizing, assimilating and passing on the forms of knowledge
concomitant to these public forums.

Isaac Marrero-Guillamón (Goldsmiths, University of London) is a
lecturer in Anthropology. His work is concerned with the entanglements between politics and aesthetics and the ways in which activism and artistic practice may contribute to the production of new
conditions of possibility for collectives. He has explored this through
a range of visual and collaborative ethnographic methodologies,
focusing on urban renewal conflicts (in Barcelona and London) and
public art controversies (in Tindaya, Fuerteventura). He is the editor,
with Hilary Powell, of *The Art of Dissent: Adventures in London's
Olympic State* (Marshgate Press).

Notes

1. The project was entitled 'Looking at/for the Militant City: Political Space
   and Audiovisual Art in Two Olympic Cities – Barcelona and London',
   and was to be led by Mari Paz Balibrea. I retained the monicker 'the
   militant city' for my own postdoctoral research project.
2. These include the Olympic Artist Forum and the *Legacy Now* event series
   initiated by SPACE Studios in 2005; the *Salon de Refuse Olympique*
   convened by Hilary (2008–2010); and public works' *Friday Sessions*
   (2006–ongoing).

3. I, for one, engaged in a number of collaborations coming out of *The Art of Dissent*, including: exhibiting the work of a number of contributors in the 'Juxtaposition' exhibition at See Studio; publishing work by others in *The Wick* and being published by others (e.g. Uncertain States 2012 exhibition catalogue); inviting artists to speak at university and being invited to speak.
4. At the time of writing, public works is led by Andreas Lang and Torange Khonsari, and involves a shifting network of collaborators.
5. See http://r-urban-wick.net/ for an archive of all the activities that have taken place under the project.
6. The zine is available for download here: http://wickcuriosityshop.net/collection/r-urban-wick-zine_5.

References

atelier d'architecture autogérée (aaa). 'R-URBAN – Participative Strategy for Development, Practices and Networks of Local Resilience'. Available online at http://www.urbantactics.org/projets/r-urban/ (last accessed 16 February 2016).

Coles, A. (ed.). 2001. *Site-Specificity in Art: The Ethnographic Turn*. London: Black Dog Publishing Ltd.

Corsín Jiménez, A., and A. Estalella. 2017. 'Ethnography: A Prototype'. *Ethnos: Journal of Anthropology* 82(5): 846-866.

Deleuze, G. 2006. *The Fold: Leibniz and the Baroque*. London and New York: Continuum.

Foster, H. 1995. 'The Artist as Ethnographer?', in G.E. Marcus and F.R. Myers (eds), *The Traffic in Culture: Refiguring Art and Anthropology*. Berkeley, CA: University of California Press, pp. 203–309.

Gell, A. 1996. 'Vogel's Net Traps as Artworks and Artworks as Traps'. *Journal of Material Culture* 1(1): 15–38.

———. 1999. *The Art of Anthropology: Essays and Diagrams*. Edited by Eric Hirsch. Oxford: Berg.

Grimshaw, A., and A. Ravetz (eds). 2004. *Visualizing Anthropology*. Bristol: Intellect Books.

Hallam, E., and T. Ingold (eds). 2007. *Creativity and Cultural Improvisation*. Oxford: Berg.

Holmes, D.R., and G.E. Marcus. 2008. 'Collaboration Today and the Re-Imagination of the Classic Scene of Fieldwork Encounter'. *Collaborative Anthropologies* 1(1): 81–101.

Keenan, T., and E. Weizman. 2012. *Mengele's Skull: The Advent of a Forensic Aesthetics*. Berlin: Sternberg Press.

Kelty, C., et al. 2009. 'Collaboration, Coordination, and Composition: Fieldwork after the Internet', in J.D. Faubion and G.E. Marcus (eds),

Fieldwork Is Not What It Used to Be: Learning Anthropology's Method in a Time of Transition. Ithaca, NY: Cornell University Press, pp. 184–206.

Marcus, G.E. 2010. 'Contemporary Fieldwork Aesthetics in Art and Anthropology: Experiments in Collaboration and Intervention'. *Visual Anthropology* 23(4): 263–77.

Marrero-Guillamón, I. 2014. 'Together Apart: Hackney Wick, the Olympic Site and Relational Art'. *Architectural Research Quarterly* 18(4): 367–76.

———. 2016. 'The Politics and Aesthetics of Assembling: (Un)Building the Common in Hackney Wick, London', in A. Blok and I. Farías (eds), *Urban Cosmopolitics: Agencements, Assemblies, Atmospheres*. Oxford and New York: Routledge, pp. 125–46.

McLagan, M., and Y. McKee. 2012. 'Introduction', in M. McLagan and Y. McKee (eds), *Sensible Politics: The Visual Culture of Nongovernmental Activism*. Cambridge, MA: Zone Books, pp. 8–26.

Powell, H., and I. Marrero-Guillamón (eds). 2012. *The Art of Dissent: Adventures in London's Olympic State*. London: Marshgate Press.

Rappaport, J. 2008. 'Beyond Participant Observation: Collaborative Ethnography as Theoretical Innovation'. *Collaborative Anthropologies* 1(1): 1–31.

Sansi, R. 2015. *Art, Anthropology and the Gift*. London: Bloombury.

Schneider, A. 2008. 'Three Modes of Experimentation with Art and Ethnography'. *Journal of the Royal Anthropological Institute* 14(1): 171–94.

Schneider, A., and C. Wright (eds). 2006. *Contemporary Art and Anthropology*. Oxford: Berg.

——— (eds). 2010. *Between Art and Anthropology: Contemporary Ethnographic Practice*. Oxford and New York: Berg.

——— (eds). 2013. *Anthropology and Art Practice*. London: Bloomsbury Press.

Strathern, M. (ed.). 2000. *Audit Cultures: Anthropological Studies in Accountability, Ethics and the Academy*. London: Routledge.

Strohm, K. 2012. 'When Anthropology Meets Contemporary Art: Notes for a Politics of Collaboration'. *Collaborative Anthropologies* 5(1): 98–124.

Tonkiss, F. 2013. 'Austerity Urbanism and the Makeshift City'. *City* 17(3): 312–24.

Vasudevan, A. 2015. 'The Autonomous City: Towards a Critical Geography of Occupation'. *Progress in Human Geography* 39(3): 316–37.

Afterword

Refiguring Collaboration and Experimentation

Sarah Pink

Introduction

This book has brought two themes to the fore: experimentation and collaboration, introduced by the editors in the terms of 'experimental collaboration'. The research experiences discussed in the chapters of the volume, drawing often from recent PhD research, reveal a generation of academics who are clearly seeking a renewal of ethnographic practice. Their work has sought to acknowledge how ethnographic processes are constituted/shared/invented with others, and are indeed shaped and framed by the collaborative relationships through which they are played out. The accounts in this book also recognize the realities of the conventional ethnographic stance of 'being there' with people. They have emerged from the authors' recent experiences of engaging with others in a processual world in ways that shape not only researchers' relationships to participants in research but also shape the very fields of research. What was conventionally called 'the ethnographic field' is ongoingly made and remade through our active participation as ethnographers in collaboration with research participants, other stakeholders in research and future readers and viewers. It is clear that the ideas of ethnography being something that is fixed in (even multiple or moving) field sites, or of ethnographic knowing being produced in momentary encounters, are insufficient. Instead the temporalities and sites of the emergence of ethnographic knowing stretch beyond this; various collaborators may shape it – they are part of what I have elsewhere called the 'ethnographic place' (Pink 2015). That is place not as locality, but a theory of place as an ongoingly emergent and changing configuration of things and processes. What ethnographers and their different types of collaborators come to know and learn is emergent from the multiple and temporally distributed encounters that assemble into projects of research and intervention.

Much of this will sound rather familiar to the seasoned anthropologist, even if put in new ways. It would be tempting to simply claim that the work presented in this volume is likewise merely wrapping old questions in new concepts. Yet I believe there is a good answer to the question of what *is* new about this work, and there are implications for how the approaches and perspectives it argues for may carry a new generation of researchers into what I hope will be an increasingly prominent rendering of ethnographic and anthropological practice in the future. To pre-empt the answers to these questions, rather than asking the reader to wait until the end of this short afterword: I propose that what is new and different is that within this volume these calls for change are specifically coming through the enthusiasm of a new generation of recent PhD scholars; they are not the reflections of a senior fieldworker who, after years of participant observation, has started to generalize about ethnographic methodology. Instead they are directly from the coalface of new experiences of fieldwork; they draw on the specificity of early-career experiences that collectively call for a reconceptualization of what is possible and what is acceptable in ethnographic practice. The exciting prospect would be the possibility of carrying this forward to pervade the discipline more deeply: imagine a renewed mainstream anthropological practice that situated the discipline as one open to the kinds of collaborations with others that might indeed chip away at its critical core. Mainstream anthropology is well overdue for a stream of emphasis on work that goes beyond the conventional practice of ethnography. However, I would argue for going further than the emphasis on collaboration within the context of conventional fieldwork practice that is presented in the majority of the chapters of this book. I argue for what I have called a form of 'blended practice' – that is, ways of working that surpass the disciplinary conventions of practice and theory (in the case of the contributors to this volume, to the parameters of anthropology, sociology and science and technology studies). Such approaches instead work towards forms of research and intervention practice whereby, for instance ethnography, design and documentary practice become part of a shared process, and in doing so reshape each other (Pink and Akama 2015). Likewise, where Tomás Sánchez Criado and Adolfo Estalella argue for us to go beyond the model of the lone and heroic anthropologist, I would again go further. My call is for a move beyond the authoritative and sometimes jousting stance of the single author ethnographic essay. I elaborate on this further below.

Renewal

The wave of contemporary scholarship represented in this book seeks to depart from, rather than bow to, what has conventionally been the participant observation model of ethnographic practice, focused in the long-term fieldwork method. It is encouraging to witness the enthusiasm of this group of researchers to surpass such conventions, and to attempt to refigure their own long-term fieldwork methods through alternative metaphors and frameworks. It remains challenging for many anthropology PhD students to evade the convention of long-term fieldwork. Indeed, why would one wish to evade what may be the single opportunity in a whole career to develop in-depth insights and experiences produced through immersion in the particularity of everyday environments?

However, for the contributors to this volume, this also involves being active in and modifying those environments, as they show in their respective descriptions of how they managed to carve out roles for themselves in the worlds in which they participated. Their descriptions will most likely resonate with the experiences of many anthropologists who have, in the more distant as well as recent pasts, come to play roles in the context that conventional narratives of anthropology would have had it that they went to 'study'. For example, in my own long-term PhD research in Cordoba in southern Spain in 1991–94, I found myself photographing, writing newspaper and local journal articles, and speaking on local radio about the very topic I was seeking to research, and as such was participating in the constitution of the local histories and presents that I sought to understand (Pink 1997). For instance, on one occasion I won a prize for journalistic photography with a photograph of a woman bullfighter, precisely while researching the visual culture of the bullfight, including bullfight journalism relating to women performers. My experiences of making the very artefacts that I sought to comprehend were probably not particularly different from those of many anthropologists of my generation. However, at that time, while there was a strong focus on writing about the social and gendered elements of the fieldwork encounter, there was less said about the forms of making that were part of how fieldworkers weave their way through material, social and sensory worlds. The second aspect of the writings in this book, which also forms a continuity with earlier collaborative ethnographies, is where another step is needed: the tendency to write single-author accounts of collaborative works. If fieldwork is shaped and ways of knowing emerge from collaborative and experimental encounters, should authorship be invested in one single person? And where might shared authorship rest in different scenarios?

In some fields of anthropology, the idea that ethnographers might collaborate with participants in research has long since been established and has already involved a series of 'experimental' works in collaboration. This has, for a while, been particularly overt in visual anthropology, for instance through Jean Rouch's 'shared anthropology' (Rouch 1974). Collaboration is particularly significant in a subfield of visual anthropology to which I have had a long-term commitment, and have called 'applied visual anthropology'. Here, as the contributors to my book *Visual Interventions* (Pink 2007) show, collaboration has been fundamental to ways of working with participants in visual anthropology research and interventions, leading to co-filmmaking projects and the production of texts where ethnographic and other forms of practice become blended. Collectively the projects presented in *Visual Interventions* show how collaborative, shared research can both transform the lives of participants, and make forms of public pedagogy. Other fields with which my work overlaps, and in some work blends, also involve overt forms of collaboration, not only with participants but with other academic researchers, industry partners and other people and organizations external to the university. Such as developing blended approaches to ethnography and design (Pink, Akama and Fergusson 2017, Pink et al. 2015) and bringing together design and ethnography in ways that subdue neither to the other (Pink and Akama 2015, Akama, Pink and Sumartojo 2018).

I propose there is a need to re-appropriate the concepts of collaboration and of experimentation for a renewed anthropological/ ethnographic methodology. Such an anthropology departs from not only its observational past, but goes further to untie the identity of the discipline from the long-term fieldwork method which guards the boundaries of 'proper' practice. The chapters of this book are militating towards such a form of practice, but I would urge their authors to go further, and to experiment with doing ethnography in ways that go beyond reflecting on how their fieldwork practices were shaped by relationships and collaborations with participants.

Collaboration

While collaboration has long since been cited as something that we should strive for in research, it has infrequently been interrogated as a concept in anthropology. Indeed, collaboration often tends to be used as a descriptive term, rather than as a concept that can stand for a set of principles for ethnographic practice. In 2014, I co-organized a symposium on the topic of design and collaboration, and wrote the following, as part of my pre-symposium provocation, in the symposium catalogue:

> Collaboration is often seen as positive. There seems to be an implicit assumption that it is a good thing for us to do, and we have even framed this symposium with the hope that a collaborative impulse and potential will emerge as one of its outcomes. Collaboration in this understanding has a feel-good element, and successful collaboration [is] likely to be celebrated. However, it is interesting to note that collaboration has not always had such positive connotations, and dictionary definitions point out that it has also been associated with the less virtuous idea of collaboration with enemies. Indeed historically, and in some contexts, [being] a collaborator would mean being a traitor. (Pink 2014: 48–49)

There is something about this point that resonates with the wish to disrupt disciplinary conventions, which is part of any position that urges anthropologists or sociologists towards collaborations that will fundamentally alter the ways in which they engage with the core conventions, practices and discourses of their disciplines. In this sense, to collaborate means to step out of line, and could perhaps lead to accusations of being a traitor to one's discipline.

Building on this, my call is for an undisciplined anthropology that is nevertheless principled, ethical and collaborative. Such a practice is advocated in the manifesto of the Future Anthropologies Network (Salazar et al 2017, Chapter 1). By this I mean a form of practice that challenges the conventional critical boundaries of the discipline while keeping at its core the principles of researching *with* (Ingold 2008) and of the 'deep reflexivity' that can emerge from the relationship between filmmaker and participants in ethnographic film, which stands in contrast to the after-the-event reflexivity of ethnographic writing (MacDougall 1998), and that is inevitably critical. In such an anthropology experimentation, creative practice, intervention and future-making become precisely such principled forms of practice. They offer a route to being an anthropologist in the world beyond the discipline. As such they serve as a much-needed relief to those anthropological articles, books and conference papers that talk primarily to other anthropologists rather than looking outwards towards other disciplines, public audiences and more.

Such an undisciplined anthropology would treat collaboration as the inevitable core of its work. Again, drawing on earlier work in visual anthropology (Banks 2001; Pink 2013) we might refigure 'taking' a photograph or video as a collaborative encounter through which both participate in an activity of making, from which a photographic image is emergent. Once rethought in this way, and always conducted with the respect that such a model commands (that is, not using covert research methods and the like), it is possible to comprehend the situatedness of moments of collaboration with participants, and as such to understand 'research materials', like photographs, as emergent from a specific configuration of things and processes. Likewise, any of the research encounters described by the contributors to this volume might be understood as productive of emergent ways of knowing, and as such seen as part of a processual world. It would be difficult not to see such fieldwork as collaborative according to such a model. However, the forms of collaboration I would advocate entail going beyond collaboration with participants.

This involves thinking about collaboration theoretically. My own argument is that '[c]ollaboration is precisely about the relationality between persons and things; it is about process, agency, shared knowing, making and practice' (Pink 2014: 48). My proposal is to consider how to situate a renewed concept of collaboration within a processual theory of the world. This would conceptualize collaboration as not necessarily a thing in itself or something we can apply to a project of process. Neither is it a label that might be simply applied to define a particular type of ethnographic encounter *after* the event. Instead it might be considered to be an emergent quality of the relationships within the encounters that constitute the mixed temporalities of the ongoing event of ethnographic research. I do not develop this line of argument further here, because my point is not that this particular theoretical approach is 'the' one that 'we' should develop. Rather, if collaboration is at the core of our work then we need theories of collaboration through which to comprehend our methodological processes. In the context of this volume, where contributors have drawn on fields of theory including those of anthropology, sociology and science and technology studies, the implication is that in each case the theory engaged should be coherent and compatible with those also used to understand whatever is learned through that research process.

Experimentation

Like the idea of collaboration, the concept of the experiment has a confusing history in anthropology. As the discipline has twisted and turned from the efforts to make it into a convincing scientific scholarly endeavour in the second part of the twentieth century (see Mills 2005) towards the ensuing focus on intersubjectivity between researcher and participant, and reflexivity were established by the end of that century. Here covert research could be regarded both as unaligned with an anthropological approach and as productive of kinds of research knowledge that disregarded the relevance of participants' own voices. The anthropologist Kate Fox's experiments are a good example of a method that does not conform to conventional anthropological ethnography. Take, for example, the opening discussion in her book *Watching the English*:

> I am sitting in a pub near Paddington station, clutching a small brandy. It's only about half past eleven in the morning – a bit early for drinking, but the alcohol is part reward, part Dutch courage. Reward because I have just spent an exhausting morning accidentally-on-purpose bumping into people and counting the number who said 'Sorry'. Dutch courage because I am now about to return to the train station and spend a few hours committing a deadly sin: queue jumping.
>
> I really, *really* do not want to do this. I want to adopt my usual method of getting a unsuspecting research assistant to break sacred social rules while I watch the result from a safe distance ... (Fox 2004)

Yet these experiments are also far distant from the experimental approach advocated in this book. This is partly the reason why the notion of doing experiments in ethnography creates something of a jolt, and why it needs to be refigured and indeed reclaimed to fit with a contemporary understanding of ethnographic practice.

The experiment has interesting potential in ethnographic practice, and I suggest it will best realize this if it is refigured beyond being a way of describing collaborative activities undertaken within 'business as usual' fieldwork practice. Instead I believe that there could be multiple modes of experiment or experimental forms that ethnographers might develop within research processes. Such research processes might involve experiments with participants, or with research partners from other disciplines. They might involve non-conventional (for ethnography) forms of doing and authoring research, such as using the workshop as method. For example, in 2014 I developed a one-day workshop with a group of designers as part of an event at Western Sydney University in Australia, during which we collaborated to undertake research that in some cases extended out of the workshop context, bring together personal and theoretical narratives, and to design a prototype intervention. The outcome is an article authored by seven people, including a non-academic whose story was written into our shared publication – they were M. Catanzaro, K. Sandbach, A. Barnes, J. Mcneill, M. Gusheh, E. Scotece, C. Catanzaro and myself (Pink et al. 2015). Indeed, seeing workshops as a mode of encounter offers a striking contrast to conventional ethnographic research. At RMIT University with my colleague the designer Yoko Akama, we developed a series of experimental workshops during 2014 as part of our design+ethnography+futures (D+E+F) research programme. These are reported on in a series of publications (Pink and Akama 2015; Akama, Moline and Pink 2016; and Akama, Pink and Sumartojo 2018). In such workshops, participants have been complicit in the idea that we are developing an experiment, that we will learn together and that new ways of knowing will be emergent from this process. As we announce on the D+E+F website: 'We explore how the future orientation of combining [a] design + ethnography approach invites new forms of change-making, where uncertainty and the 'not-yet-made' is at the centre of inquiry. It brings [together] the improvisory, playful, imaginative, sensorial and somewhat contested edges of both fields to create an opening to experiment with what might emerge out of an assembly of ideas, people, feelings, things and processes'.[1]

In such work, experimental ethnography becomes a rather different practice, both from the experimental modes that Fox suggests, and from conventional long-term ethnography. Indeed, there comes a moment when the conventional defining features of ethnography are abandoned. The research event is compressed into a short period, and the tasks of the ethnographer are refigured to include working with people to make things, while also seeking to document and understand the processes that are at play. It is towards these more radical forms of experimentation that I would call the new generation of researchers. In making this point I am not suggesting that they should copy this method. Instead my proposal is that new ethnographic forms are possible; ones that go beyond seeing experimentation as merely happening when ethnographers make things, processes and ways of knowing and being with participants, within a long-term participant observation process. Rather, we should ask how intentionally formed experimental environments might reflect but also change ethnographic conventions.

There are a number of other ways in which 'experimental collaborations' might be carried out. In the chapters of this volume, the collaborations that were seen as being experimental were often developed in the context of learning from and working with other types of experts. This resonates to some degree with the examples of my collaborations with designers outlined above. Other models for collaboration include the formation of expert teams who can together carry out research that would not otherwise be possible. For instance, when I undertake research into worker safety in the construction industry this is always in collaboration with experts in that field as well as with ethnographers who can dedicate time to doing in-depth fieldwork (e.g. Pink et al. 2017); to undertake a project about domestic life and technologies in Indonesia, I worked with an anthropologist who had expertise and language skills in this area, and an Indonesian documentary filmmaker, so the first public output of our work was not a written article but a co-directed film (Pink and Astari 2015); and to write about knowing across ethnography, architecture and acoustics I have done so with an architect, a designer and an acoustic engineer. There is good reason for pitching these ways of working as experimental collaborations, rather than seeing ethnography as providing a service to more technical or design-focused disciplines. Indeed, I would see all of these works, at least in their first iterations, as experiments into how such disciplines can work in collaboration.

It is in such ways that the argument for refiguring the concept of the experiment as part of ethnographic practice might be played out – that is, by using principled, overt, ethical and collaborative experimentation as a means through which to practice ethnography in *new* ways.

Conclusion

It is my assessment that anthropological ethnography is beginning a new critical revisionist wave. This book forms part of that. Indeed, it is not only concepts such as experimentation and collaboration that need to be reclaimed by a contemporary generation of anthropological ethnographers. As I have argued elsewhere, concepts of 'intervention' (Green and Pink 2014) and digital materiality (Pink, Ardevol and Lanzeni 2016) can also be redefined to understand the roles we can play in making, changing and understanding the kinds of contemporary environments in which ethnographic practice is played out.

Whether or not this wave of change will shift the conventions that form the basis of mainstream anthropological theory and practice is yet to be seen. In fact there is a strong argument for respecting the maintenance of the core long-term fieldwork method as a *rite de passage* into the discipline (after all, most of the contributors to this book have accomplished it). Moreover, the role of the mainstream anthropologists as a 'community of critics' (Strathern 2006) who keep the discipline on its own track through internal debates, remains important for theory building, comment and critique.

Simultaneously, at the edge of anthropology there are exciting things happening, including an increasing enthusiasm for calling our work collaborative and experimental, as well as call for future anthropologies (Pink and Salazar 2017). It is here where ethnographic practice, as it becomes blended, compromised and blurred, can play an active role in collaboratively reshaping the world.

Sarah Pink (RMIT) is a distinguished professor in Design and Media Ethnography at the School of Media and Communication, RMIT, Australia. Her work currently focuses on emerging technologies and digital futures across research projects that combine theoretical and methodological scholarship with applied practice. Her work is often developed through interdisciplinary collaborations across design, engineering and arts disciplines. Her recent publications include *Anthropologies and Futures* (2017), *Theoretical Scholarship and Applied Practice* (2017) and *Making Homes* (2017), and her websites include www.energyanddigitalliving.com and www.laundrylives.com.

Note

1. http://d-e-futures.com/about/, last accessed 11 November 2015.

References

Akama, Y., S. Pink and S. Sumartojo. 2018. *Uncertainty and Possibility: New Approaches to Future Making in Design Anthropology*. London: Bloomsbury.

Akama, Y., K. Moline and S. Pink (2016). 'Design+Ethnography+Futures: Knowing through Uncertainty', in L. Hjorth et al. (eds), *The Routledge Companion to Digital Ethnography*. Oxford: Routledge.

Banks, M. 2001. *Visual Methods in Social Research*. London: Sage.

Fox, K. 2004. *Watching the English: The Hidden Rules of English Behaviour*. London: Hodder and Stoughton.

Green, L., and S. Pink. 2014. 'Using Digital Interventions to Engage in the Everyday'. *Media International Australia, Incorporating Culture & Policy* 153: 73–77.

Ingold, T. 2008. 'Anthropology is Not Ethnography'. *Proceedings of the British Academy*, volume 154.

MacDougall, D. 1998. *Transcultural Cinema*. Princeton, NJ: Princeton University Press.

———. 2005. *The Corporeal Image: Film, Ethnography, and the Senses*. Princeton, NJ: Princeton University Press.

Mills, D. 2005. 'Dinner at Claridges?: Anthropology and the "Captains of Industry", 1947–1955', in S. Pink (ed.), *Applications of Anthropology: Professional Anthropology in the Twenty-First Century*. New York: Berghahn Books, pp. 55–70.

Pink, S. 1997. *Women and Bullfighting: Gender, Sex and the Consumption of Tradition*. Oxford: Berg.

———. (ed.). 2007. *Visual Interventions: Applied Visual Anthropology*. New York: Berghahn Books.

———. 2013. *Doing Visual Ethnography*. Revised and expanded 3rd edition. London: Sage.

———. 2014. 'Collaboration and its Contentions', in *Collaboration: Organising for Design Impact and Value*, programme for the Transdisciplinary Design Research Symposium, 7–9 April at ELISAVA, Barcelona School of Design and Engineering, pp. 48–50.

———. 2015. *Doing Sensory Ethnography*. Second edition. London: Sage.

Pink, S., and Y. Akama. 2015. *Un/Certainty*. iBook, available to download from http://d-e-futures.com/.

Pink, S., Y. Akama and A. Fergusson. 2017. 'Researching Future as an Alterity of the Present', in J. Salazar et al. (eds), *Anthropologies and Futures: Researching Emerging and Uncertain Worlds*. London: Bloomsbury, pp.133–150.

Pink, S., E. Ardevol and D. Lanzeni. 2016. 'Digital Materiality: Configuring a Field of Anthropology/Design?', in S. Pink, E. Ardevol and D. Lanzeni (eds), *Digital Materialities: Anthropology and Design*. Oxford: Bloomsbury, pp. 1–26.

Pink, S., and N. Astari (Directors). 2015. *Laundry Lives: Everyday Life and Environmental Sustainability in Indonesia* (film).

Pink, S., et al. 2015. 'Making and Sharing the Commons in Riverlands Sydney: Reimagining "the West" through a Dialogue between Design, Ethnography and Theory'. *Global Media Journal* 9(2). Available online at http://www.hca.westernsydney.edu.au/gmjau/?p=1939 (last accessed 18 October 2017).

Pink, S., A. Dainty and J. Morgan (2017) 'Making Theory, Making Interventions: Doing Applied Scholarship at the In-between' in V. Fors, T. O'Dell and S. Pink (eds), *Theoretical Scholarship and Applied Practice*. New York: Berghahn Books, pp. 97–119.

Pink, S. and J.F. Salazar. 2017. 'Anthropologies and Futures: Setting the Agenda' in J. Salazar, S. Pink, A. Irving and J. Sjoberg (eds), *Future Anthropologies*. Oxford: Bloomsbury, pp. 3–22.

Rouch, J. (1974) 2003. 'The Camera and Man', in S. Feld (ed.), *Cine-Ethnography*. London: University of Minnesota Press, pp. 29–46.

Salazar, J.F., S. Pink, A. Irving and J. Sjoberg (eds). 2017. *Anthropologies and Futures: Techniques for Researching an Uncertain World*. London: Bloomsbury.

Strathern, M. 2006. 'A Community of Critics? Thoughts on New Knowledge'. *Journal of the Royal Anthropological Institute* 12: 191–209.

Index

EASA Series

Published in Association with the European Association of Social Anthropologists (EASA)

Series Editor: Aleksandar Bošković, University of Belgrade

Social anthropology in Europe is growing, and the variety of work being done is expanding. This series is intended to present the best of the work produced by members of the EASA, both in monographs and in edited collections. The studies in this series describe societies, processes, and institutions around the world and are intended for both scholarly and student readership.

.

CPSIA information can be obtained
at www.ICGtesting.com
Printed in the USA
JSHW031427130921
18569JS00004B/63

9 781800 730151